Co

About the author

Adam Boduch has been involved with large-scale JavaScript development for nearly 10 years. Before moving to the frontend, he worked on several large-scale cloud computing products using Python and Linux. No stranger to complexity, Adam has practical experience with real-world software systems and the scaling challenges they pose. He is the author of several JavaScript books, including *React and React Native*, by Packt Publishing and is passionate about innovative user experiences and high performance.

About the reviewers

Michel Engelen started off as a web designer and soon began to realize that frontend development is the course he wants to take. So, he started self-learning for the skills he would need for that. Nearly 8 years later, he is now a full-fledged JavaScript React/Redux developer and software architect with one additional year of experience in DevOps as well.

Jonatan Ezequiel Salas is a highly skilled developer and a passionate entrepreneur. He is the founder and CTO of BlackBox Vision, a software agency focusing mainly on high-quality products and user experience, and also working at Ingenia as a Software Architect. He is currently focusing on growing his company, and has been working with some major firms from Argentina. In his spare time, he loves contributing to open source software related to DevOps, Kubernetes, JavaScript, Node.js, and React. Find him on GitHub, Medium, or Twitter.

I would like to thank my family, my girlfriend, and my friends for their never-ending support. Without them, I could have never reached where I am today. I am also thankful to Packt Publishing and their amazing books. I'd especially like to thank the author of the book, as well as Pragati Shukla for giving me the opportunity to review this book.

Olivier Tassinari is a curious and persevering person who has always loved solving problems. His passion for building things started at a very young age, and he began to launch websites 10 years ago while studying math, physics, and computer science. He is a big fan of open source. He has been working on Material-UI since its inception.

I would like to thank all Material-UI's contributors for their devotion to the project.

Packt is searching for authors like you

If you're interested in becoming an author for Packt, please visit `authors.packtpub.com` and apply today. We have worked with thousands of developers and tech professionals, just like you, to help them share their insight with the global tech community. You can make a general application, apply for a specific hot topic that we are recruiting an author for, or submit your own idea.

React Material-UI Cookbook

Build captivating user experiences using React and Material-UI

Adam Boduch

BIRMINGHAM - MUMBAI

React Material-UI Cookbook

Content Development Editor: Pranay Fereira
Technical Editor: Aishwarya More
Copy Editor: Safis Editing
Project Coordinator: Pragati Shukla
Proofreader: Safis Editing
Indexer: Pratik Shirodkar
Graphics: Alishon Mendonsa
Production Coordinator: Jisha Chirayil

First published: March 2019

Production reference: 1290319

Published by Packt Publishing Ltd.
Livery Place
35 Livery Street
Birmingham
B3 2PB, UK.

ISBN 978-1-78961-522-7

www.packtpub.com

For anyone whose lives have been touched by autism. Never give up.

– Adam Boduch

mapt.io

Mapt is an online digital library that gives you full access to over 5,000 books and videos, as well as industry leading tools to help you plan your personal development and advance your career. For more information, please visit our website.

Why subscribe?

- Spend less time learning and more time coding with practical eBooks and Videos from over 4,000 industry professionals

- Improve your learning with Skill Plans built especially for you

- Get a free eBook or video every month

- Mapt is fully searchable

- Copy and paste, print, and bookmark content

Packt.com

Did you know that Packt offers eBook versions of every book published, with PDF and ePub files available? You can upgrade to the eBook version at www.packt.com and as a print book customer, you are entitled to a discount on the eBook copy. Get in touch with us at customercare@packtpub.com for more details.

At www.packt.com, you can also read a collection of free technical articles, sign up for a range of free newsletters, and receive exclusive discounts and offers on Packt books and eBooks.

Table of Contents

Preface

Material-UI is the world's most popular React UI framework. It should come as no surprise that Material-UI skills are a valuable asset to have. There are countless projects in the open source space and in the commercial space that rely on this framework. So, what makes Material-UI so popular?

First and foremost, Material-UI does an excellent job of bringing together two of the best frontend technologies out there. In a nutshell, Material-UI exposes Google's Material Design as components in Facebook's React. Many developers know enough React to build something that works. Many designers know enough about Material Design to design an experience that looks incredible. Material-UI is the bridge between these two worlds, simplifying the task of shipping production applications that delight customers.

At a high level, this sales pitch is enough to intrigue developers at every level and of every specialization. What keeps developers engaged with Material-UI is the breadth of functionality and the depth of resources available to help you tackle any scenario. My hope is that this book serves as a valuable contribution to those resources.

Who this book is for

This book is for any developer who thinks that Material-UI could potentially help them produce a better user experience for their application. From seasoned professionals to the junior developers of the world, this book has something to teach you about Material-UI.

No Material Design knowledge is assumed. To get the most out of this book, you should have at least a working knowledge of React and modern JavaScript. While this book isn't meant to teach you React, I do try to explain the React-specific mechanism at work in cases where it might help illuminate the example as a whole.

What this book covers

Chapter 1, *Grids – Placing Components on the Page*, uses the grid system to place components on the page.

Chapter 2, *App Bars – The Top Level of Every Page*, adds App Bars to the top of your UI.

Chapter 3, *Drawers – A Place for Navigation Controls*, uses drawers as a place to display your main navigation.

Chapter 4, *Tabs – Group Content into Tab Sections*, organizes your content into tabs.

Chapter 5, *Expansion Panels – Group Content into Panel Sections*, organizes your content into panels.

Chapter 6, *Lists – Display Simple Collection Data*, renders lists of items that the user can read and interact with.

Chapter 7, *Tables – Display Complex Collection Data*, shows in-depth details about a data collection.

Chapter 8, *Cards – Display Detailed Information*, uses cards to display details about a specific entity/thing/object.

Chapter 9, *Snackbars – Temporary Messages*, notifies the user about what's going on in your application.

Chapter 10, *Buttons – Initiating Actions*, explains how pressing buttons is the most common way for users to do something.

Chapter 11, *Text – Collecting Text Input*, allows users to input information.

Chapter 12, *Autocomplete and Chips – Text Input Suggestions for Multiple Items*, gives the user choices to select from as they type.

Chapter 13, *Selection – Make Selections from Choices*, allows the user to select from a predefined set of options.

Chapter 14, *Pickers – Selecting Dates and Times*, chooses date and time values using easy-to-read formats.

Chapter 15, *Dialogs – Modal Screens for User Interactions*, displays modal screens to collect input or show information.

Chapter 16, *Menus – Display Actions that Pop Out*, saves space on the screen by putting actions in menus.

Chapter 17, *Typography – Control Font Look and Feel*, controls the font of your UI in a systematic way.

Chapter 18, *Icons – Enhance Icons to Match Your Look and Feel*, customizes Material-UI icons and adds new ones.

Chapter 19, *Themes – Centralize the Look and Feel of Your App*, uses themes to change the look and feel of components.

Chapter 20, *Styles – Applying Styles to Components*, uses one of many styling solutions to design your UI.

To get the most out of this book

1. Make sure you understand the fundamentals of React. The tutorial is a good starting point: https://reactjs.org/tutorial/tutorial.html.
2. Clone the repository for this book: https://github.com/PacktPublishing/Material-UI-Cookbook.
3. Install the package by changing into the Material-UI-Cookbook directory and running npm install.
4. Start Storybook by running npm run storybook. You can now navigate through each of the examples as you read through the book. Some examples have property editor controls in the Storybook UI, but feel free to tweak the code as you learn!

Download the example code files

You can download the example code files for this book from your account at www.packt.com. If you purchased this book elsewhere, you can visit www.packt.com/support and register to have the files emailed directly to you.

You can download the code files by following these steps:

1. Log in or register at www.packt.com.
2. Select the **SUPPORT** tab.
3. Click on **Code Downloads & Errata**.
4. Enter the name of the book in the **Search** box and follow the onscreen instructions.

Once the file is downloaded, please make sure that you unzip or extract the folder using the latest version of:

- WinRAR/7-Zip for Windows
- Zipeg/iZip/UnRarX for Mac
- 7-Zip/PeaZip for Linux

The code bundle for the book is also hosted on GitHub at `https://github.com/PacktPublishing/React-Material-UI-Cookbook`. In case there's an update to the code, it will be updated on the existing GitHub repository.

We also have other code bundles from our rich catalog of books and videos available at `https://github.com/PacktPublishing/`. Check them out!

Download the color images

We also provide a PDF file that has color images of the screenshots/diagrams used in this book. You can download it here: `https://www.packtpub.com/sites/default/files/downloads/9781789615227_ColorImages.pdf`.

Conventions used

There are a number of text conventions used throughout this book.

`CodeInText`: Indicates code words in text, database table names, folder names, filenames, file extensions, pathnames, dummy URLs, user input, and Twitter handles. Here is an example: "Mount the downloaded `WebStorm-10*.dmg` disk image file as another disk in your system."

A block of code is set as follows:

```
const styles = theme => ({
  root: {
    flexGrow: 1
  },
```

Bold: Indicates a new term, an important word, or words that you see on screen. For example, words in menus or dialog boxes appear in the text like this. Here is an example: "Select **System info** from the **Administration** panel."

Warnings or important notes appear like this.

Tips and tricks appear like this.

Sections

In this book, you will find several headings that appear frequently (*Getting ready, How to do it..., How it works..., There's more...,* and *See also*).

To give clear instructions on how to complete a recipe, use these sections as follows:

Getting ready

This section tells you what to expect in the recipe and describes how to set up any software or any preliminary settings required for the recipe.

How to do it...

This section contains the steps required to follow the recipe.

How it works...

This section usually consists of a detailed explanation of what happened in the previous section.

There's more...

This section consists of additional information about the recipe in order to make you more knowledgeable about the recipe.

See also

This section provides helpful links to other useful information for the recipe.

Get in touch

Feedback from our readers is always welcome.

General feedback: If you have questions about any aspect of this book, mention the book title in the subject of your message and email us at `customercare@packtpub.com`.

Errata: Although we have taken every care to ensure the accuracy of our content, mistakes do happen. If you have found a mistake in this book, we would be grateful if you would report this to us. Please visit www.packt.com/submit-errata, selecting your book, clicking on the Errata Submission Form link, and entering the details.

Piracy: If you come across any illegal copies of our works in any form on the internet, we would be grateful if you would provide us with the location address or website name. Please contact us at copyright@packt.com with a link to the material.

If you are interested in becoming an author: If there is a topic that you have expertise in, and you are interested in either writing or contributing to a book, please visit authors.packtpub.com.

Reviews

Please leave a review. Once you have read and used this book, why not leave a review on the site that you purchased it from? Potential readers can then see and use your unbiased opinion to make purchase decisions, we at Packt can understand what you think about our products, and our authors can see your feedback on their book. Thank you!

For more information about Packt, please visit packt.com.

Grids - Placing Components on the Page

1

In this chapter, we'll cover the following recipes:

- Understanding breakpoints
- Filling space
- Abstracting containers and items
- Fixed column layout
- Column direction

Introduction

Material-UI grids are used to control the layout of screens in your app. Rather then implement your own styles to manage the layout of your Material-UI components, you can leverage the Grid component. Behind the scenes, it uses CSS flexbox properties to handle flexible layouts.

Applying breakpoints

A **breakpoint** is used by Material-UI to determine at what point to break the flow of content on the screen and continue it on the next line. Understanding how to apply breakpoints with Grid components is fundamental to implementing layouts in Material-UI applications.

How to do it...

Let's say that you have four elements that you want to lay out on the screen so that they're evenly spaced and occupy all available horizontal space. The code for this is as follows:

```
import React from 'react';
import { withStyles } from '@material-ui/core/styles';
import Paper from '@material-ui/core/Paper';
import Grid from '@material-ui/core/Grid';

const styles = theme => ({
  root: {
    flexGrow: 1
  },
  paper: {
    padding: theme.spacing(2),
    textAlign: 'center',
    color: theme.palette.text.secondary
  }
});

const UnderstandingBreakpoints = withStyles(styles)(({ classes }) => (
  <div className={classes.root}>
    <Grid container spacing={4}>
      <Grid item xs={12} sm={6} md={3}>
        <Paper className={classes.paper}>xs=12 sm=6 md=3</Paper>
      </Grid>
      <Grid item xs={12} sm={6} md={3}>
        <Paper className={classes.paper}>xs=12 sm=6 md=3</Paper>
      </Grid>
      <Grid item xs={12} sm={6} md={3}>
        <Paper className={classes.paper}>xs=12 sm=6 md=3</Paper>
      </Grid>
      <Grid item xs={12} sm={6} md={3}>
        <Paper className={classes.paper}>xs=12 sm=6 md=3</Paper>
      </Grid>
    </Grid>
  </div>
));

export default UnderstandingBreakpoints;
```

This renders four `Paper` components. The labels indicate the values used for the xs, sm, and md properties. Here's what the result looks like:

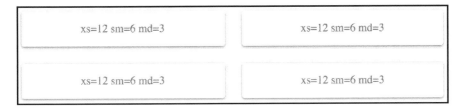

How it works...

Each of the breakpoint properties that you can pass to `Grid` components correspond to screen widths, as follows:

- xs >= 0px
- sm >= 600px
- md >= 960px
- lg >= 1280px
- xl >= 1920px

The screen shown previously had a pixel width of 725, which means that the `Grid` components used the sm breakpoint. The value passed to this property was 6. This can be a number from 1 to 12 and defines how many items will fit into the grid. This can be confusing, so it's helpful to think of these numbers in terms of percentages. For example, 6 would be 50% and, as the preceding screenshot shows, the `Grid` items take up 50% of the width.

For example, let's say that you want the width of each `Grid` item to take up 75% of the screen width when the small breakpoint is active. You could set the sm value to 9 (9/12 = 0.75), as follows:

```
<div className={classes.root}>
  <Grid container spacing={4}>
    <Grid item xs={12} sm={9} md={3}>
      <Paper className={classes.paper}>xs=12 sm=9 md=3</Paper>
    </Grid>
    <Grid item xs={12} sm={9} md={3}>
      <Paper className={classes.paper}>xs=12 sm=9 md=3</Paper>
    </Grid>
    <Grid item xs={12} sm={9} md={3}>
```

```
        <Paper className={classes.paper}>xs=12 sm=9 md=3</Paper>
      </Grid>
      <Grid item xs={12} sm={9} md={3}>
        <Paper className={classes.paper}>xs=12 sm=9 md=3</Paper>
      </Grid>
    </Grid>
  </div>
```

Here's the result when the screen width is still at 725 pixels:

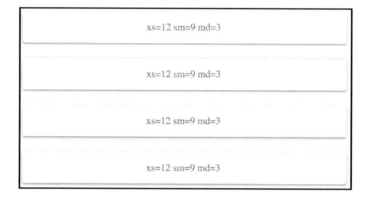

This combination of screen width and breakpoint value isn't optimal – there's a lot of wasted space to the right. By experimenting, you could make the sm value greater so that there's less wasted space, or you could make the value smaller so that more items fit on the row. For example, 6 looked better because exactly 2 items fit on the screen.

Let's take the screen width down to 575 pixels. This will activate the xs breakpoint with a value of 12 (100%):

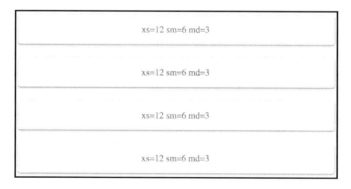

This layout works on smaller screens, because it doesn't try to fit too many grid items on one row.

There's more...

You can use the `auto` value for every breakpoint value if you're unsure of which value to use:

```
<div className={classes.root}>
  <Grid container spacing={4}>
    <Grid item xs="auto" sm="auto" md="auto">
      <Paper className={classes.paper}>
        xs=auto sm=auto md=auto
      </Paper>
    </Grid>
    <Grid item xs="auto" sm="auto" md="auto">
      <Paper className={classes.paper}>
        xs=auto sm=auto md=auto
      </Paper>
    </Grid>
    <Grid item xs="auto" sm="auto" md="auto">
      <Paper className={classes.paper}>
        xs=auto sm=auto md=auto
      </Paper>
    </Grid>
    <Grid item xs="auto" sm="auto" md="auto">
      <Paper className={classes.paper}>
        xs=auto sm=auto md=auto
      </Paper>
    </Grid>
  </Grid>
</div>
```

This will try to fit as many items as possible on each row. As the screen size changes, items are rearranged so that they fit on the screen accordingly. Here's what this looks like at a screen width of 725 pixels:

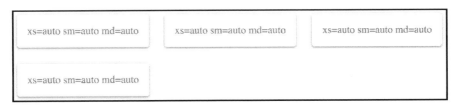

I would recommend replacing `auto` with a value from 1–12 at some point. The `auto` value is good enough that you can get started on other things without worrying too much about layout, but it's far from perfect for your production app. At least by setting up `auto` this way, you have all of your `Grid` components and breakpoint properties in place. You just need to play with the numbers until everything looks good.

See also

- Grid API documentation: https://material-ui.com/api/grid/
- Grid demos: https://material-ui.com/layout/grid/
- Breakpoint documentation: https://material-ui.com/layout/breakpoints/

Filling space

With some layouts, it is impossible to have your grid items occupy the entire width of the screen. Using the `justify` property, you can control how grid items fill the available space in the row.

How to do it...

Let's say that you have four `Paper` components to render in a grid. Inside each of these `Paper` components, you have three `Chip` components, which are **nested grid items**.

Here's what the code looks like:

```
import React from 'react';

import { withStyles } from '@material-ui/core/styles';
import Paper from '@material-ui/core/Paper';
import Grid from '@material-ui/core/Grid';
import Chip from '@material-ui/core/Chip';

const styles = theme => ({
  root: {
    flexGrow: 1
  },
  paper: {
    padding: theme.spacing(2),
    textAlign: 'center',
```

```
        color: theme.palette.text.secondary
    }
});

const FillingSpace = withStyles(styles)(({ classes, justify }) => (
  <div className={classes.root}>
    <Grid container spacing={4}>
      <Grid item xs={12} sm={6} md={3}>
        <Paper className={classes.paper}>
          <Grid container justify={justify}>
            <Grid item>
              <Chip label="xs=12" />
            </Grid>
            <Grid item>
              <Chip label="sm=6" />
            </Grid>
            <Grid item>
              <Chip label="md=3" />
            </Grid>
          </Grid>
        </Paper>
      </Grid>
      <Grid item xs={12} sm={6} md={3}>
        <Paper className={classes.paper}>
          <Grid container justify={justify}>
            <Grid item>
              <Chip label="xs=12" />
            </Grid>
            <Grid item>
              <Chip label="sm=6" />
            </Grid>
            <Grid item>
              <Chip label="md=3" />
            </Grid>
          </Grid>
        </Paper>
      </Grid>
      <Grid item xs={12} sm={6} md={3}>
        <Paper className={classes.paper}>
          <Grid container justify={justify}>
            <Grid item>
              <Chip label="xs=12" />
            </Grid>
            <Grid item>
              <Chip label="sm=6" />
            </Grid>
            <Grid item>
              <Chip label="md=3" />
```

```
          </Grid>
        </Grid>
      </Paper>
    </Grid>
    <Grid item xs={12} sm={6} md={3}>
      <Paper className={classes.paper}>
        <Grid container justify={justify}>
          <Grid item>
            <Chip label="xs=12" />
          </Grid>
          <Grid item>
            <Chip label="sm=6" />
          </Grid>
          <Grid item>
            <Chip label="md=3" />
          </Grid>
        </Grid>
      </Paper>
    </Grid>
  </Grid>
</div>
));

export default FillingSpace;
```

The justify property is specified on container Grid components. In this example, it's the container that contains the Chip components as items. Each container is using the flex-start value, which will align the Grid items at the start of the container. The result is as follows:

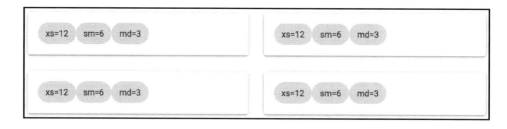

How it works...

The flex-start value of the justify property aligns all of the Grid items at the start of the container. In this case, the three Chip components in each of the four containers are all crammed to the left of the row. None of the space to the left of the items is filled. Instead of changing the breakpoint property values of these items, which results in changed widths, you can change the justify property value to tell the Grid container how to fill empty spaces.

For example, you could use the center value to align Grid items in the center of the container as follows:

```
<div className={classes.root}>
  <Grid container spacing={4}>
    <Grid item xs={12} sm={6} md={3}>
      <Paper className={classes.paper}>
        <Grid container justify="center">
          <Grid item>
            <Chip label="xs=12" />
          </Grid>
          <Grid item>
            <Chip label="sm=6" />
          </Grid>
          <Grid item>
            <Chip label="md=3" />
          </Grid>
        </Grid>
      </Paper>
    </Grid>
    <Grid item xs={12} sm={6} md={3}>
      <Paper className={classes.paper}>
        <Grid container justify="center">
          <Grid item>
            <Chip label="xs=12" />
          </Grid>
          <Grid item>
            <Chip label=" sm=6" />
          </Grid>
          <Grid item>
            <Chip label="md=3" />
          </Grid>
        </Grid>
      </Paper>
    </Grid>
    <Grid item xs={12} sm={6} md={3}>
      <Paper className={classes.paper}>
```

```
      <Grid container justify="center">
        <Grid item>
          <Chip label="xs=12" />
        </Grid>
        <Grid item>
          <Chip label="sm=6" />
        </Grid>
        <Grid item>
          <Chip label="md=3" />
        </Grid>
      </Grid>
    </Paper>
  </Grid>
  <Grid item xs={12} sm={6} md={3}>
    <Paper className={classes.paper}>
      <Grid container justify="center">
        <Grid item>
          <Chip label="xs=12" />
        </Grid>
        <Grid item>
          <Chip label="sm=6" />
        </Grid>
        <Grid item>
          <Chip label="md=3" />
        </Grid>
      </Grid>
    </Paper>
  </Grid>
</Grid>
</div>
```

The following screenshot shows what this change to the justify property value results in:

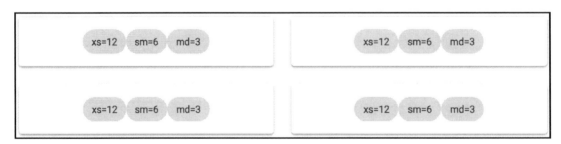

This does a good job of evenly distributing the empty space to the left and right of the `Grid` items. But the items still feel crowded because there's no space in between them. Here's what it looks like if you use the `space-around` value of the `justify` property:

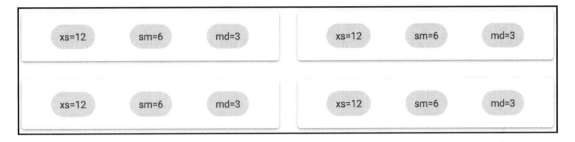

This value does the best job of filling all the available space in the `Grid container`, without having to change the width of the `Grid` items.

There's more...

A variation on the `space-around` value is the `space-between` value. The two are similar in that they're effective at filling all of the space in the row. Here's what the example in the preceding section looks like using `space-between`:

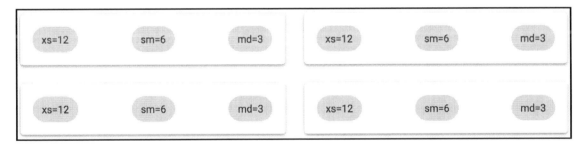

All of the excess space in the row goes in between the `Grid` items instead of around them. In other words, use this value when you want to make sure that there's no empty space to the left and right of each row.

See also

- `Grid` **demos:** `https://material-ui.com/layout/grid/`
- `Grid` API **documentation:** `https://material-ui.com/api/grid/`

Abstracting containers and items

You have lots of screens in your app, each with lots of `Grid` components, used to create complex layouts. Trying to read source code that has a ton of `<Grid>` elements in it can be daunting. Especially when a `Grid` component is used for both containers and for items.

How to do it...

The `container` or the `item` property of `Grid` components determines the role of the element. You can create two components that use these properties and create an element name that's easier to read when you have lots of layout components:

```
import React from 'react';

import { withStyles } from '@material-ui/core/styles';
import Paper from '@material-ui/core/Paper';
import Grid from '@material-ui/core/Grid';

const styles = theme => ({
  root: {
    flexGrow: 1
  },
  paper: {
    padding: theme.spacing(2),
    textAlign: 'center',
    color: theme.palette.text.secondary
  }
});

const Container = props => <Grid container {...props} />;
const Item = props => <Grid item {...props} />;

const AbstractingContainersAndItems = withStyles(styles)(
  ({ classes }) => (
    <div className={classes.root}>
      <Container spacing={4}>
        <Item xs={12} sm={6} md={3}>
          <Paper className={classes.paper}>xs=12 sm=6 md=3</Paper>
        </Item>
        <Item xs={12} sm={6} md={3}>
          <Paper className={classes.paper}>xs=12 sm=6 md=3</Paper>
        </Item>
        <Item xs={12} sm={6} md={3}>
          <Paper className={classes.paper}>xs=12 sm=6 md=3</Paper>
        </Item>
```

```
        <Item xs={12} sm={6} md={3}>
          <Paper className={classes.paper}>xs=12 sm=6 md=3</Paper>
        </Item>
      </Container>
    </div>
  )
);

export default AbstractingContainersAndItems;
```

Here's what the resulting layout looks like:

xs=12 sm=6 md=3	xs=12 sm=6 md=3
xs=12 sm=6 md=3	xs=12 sm=6 md=3

How it works...

Let's take a closer look at the `Container` and `Item` components:

```
const Container = props => <Grid container {...props} />;
const Item = props => <Grid item {...props} />;
```

The `Container` component renders a `Grid` component with the `container` property set to true, and the `Item` component does the same, except with the `item` property set to true. Each component passes any additional properties to the `Grid` component, such as `xs` and `sm` breakpoints.

When you have lots of `Grid` containers and items that make up your layout, being able to see the difference between `<Container>` and `<Item>` elements makes your code that much easier to read. Contrast this with having `<Grid>` elements everywhere.

There's more...

If you find that you're using the same breakpoints over and over in your layouts, you can include them in in your higher-order `Item` component. Let's rewrite the example so that, in addition to the `Item` property, the `xs`, `sm`, and `md` properties are included as well:

```
const Container = props => <Grid container {...props} />;
const Item = props => <Grid item xs={12} sm={6} md={3} {...props} />;

const AbstractingContainersAndItems = withStyles(styles)(
  ({ classes }) => (
    <div className={classes.root}>
      <Container spacing={4}>
        <Item>
          <Paper className={classes.paper}>xs=12 sm=6 md=3</Paper>
        </Item>
        <Item>
          <Paper className={classes.paper}>xs=12 sm=6 md=3</Paper>
        </Item>
        <Item>
          <Paper className={classes.paper}>xs=12 sm=6 md=3</Paper>
        </Item>
        <Item>
          <Paper className={classes.paper}>xs=12 sm=6 md=3</Paper>
        </Item>
      </Container>
    </div>
  )
);
```

Now, instead of four instances of `<Item xs={12} sm={6} md={3}>`, you have four instances of `<Item>`. Component abstractions are a great tool for removing excess syntax from your **JavaScript XML (JSX)** markup.

Any time you need to override any of the breakpoint properties that you've set in the `Item` component, you just need to pass the property to `Item`. For example, if you have a specific case where you need `md` to be 6, you can just write `<Item md={6}>`. This works because, in the `Item` component, `{...props}` is passed after the default values, meaning that they override any properties with the same name.

See also

- Grid **demos:** `https://material-ui.com/layout/grid/`
- Grid API **documentation:** `https://material-ui.com/api/grid/`

Fixed column layout

When you use `Grid` components to build your layout, they often result in changes to your layout, depending on your breakpoint settings and the width of the screen. For example, if the user makes the browser window smaller, your layout might change from two columns to three. There might be times, however, when you would prefer a fixed number of columns, and that the width of each column changes in response to the screen size.

How to do it...

Let's say that you have eight `Paper` components that you want to render, but you also want to make sure that there are no more than four columns. Use the following code to do this:

```
import React from 'react';

import { withStyles } from '@material-ui/core/styles';
import Paper from '@material-ui/core/Paper';
import Grid from '@material-ui/core/Grid';

const styles = theme => ({
  root: {
    flexGrow: 1
  },
  paper: {
    padding: theme.spacing(2),
    textAlign: 'center',
    color: theme.palette.text.secondary
  }
});

const FixedColumnLayout = withStyles(styles)(({ classes, width }) => (
  <div className={classes.root}>
    <Grid container spacing={4}>
      <Grid item xs={width}>
        <Paper className={classes.paper}>xs={width}</Paper>
      </Grid>
      <Grid item xs={width}>
```

```
      <Paper className={classes.paper}>xs={width}</Paper>
    </Grid>
    <Grid item xs={width}>
      <Paper className={classes.paper}>xs={width}</Paper>
    </Grid>
    <Grid item xs={width}>
      <Paper className={classes.paper}>xs={width}</Paper>
    </Grid>
    <Grid item xs={width}>
      <Paper className={classes.paper}>xs={width}</Paper>
    </Grid>
    <Grid item xs={width}>
      <Paper className={classes.paper}>xs={width}</Paper>
    </Grid>
    <Grid item xs={width}>
      <Paper className={classes.paper}>xs={width}</Paper>
    </Grid>
    <Grid item xs={width}>
      <Paper className={classes.paper}>xs={width}</Paper>
    </Grid>
    </Grid>
  </div>
));

export default FixedColumnLayout;
```

Here's what the result looks like with a pixel width of 725:

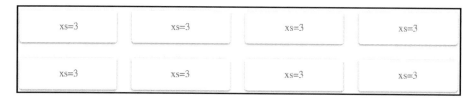

Here's what the result looks like with a pixel width of 350:

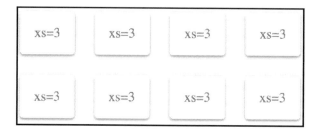

How it works...

If you want a fixed number of columns, you should only specify the xs breakpoint property. In this example, 3 is 25% of the screen width – or 4 columns. This will never change because xs is the smallest breakpoint there is. Anything larger is applied to xs as well, unless you specify a larger breakpoint.

Let's say that you want two columns. You can set the xs value to 6 as follows:

```
<div className={classes.root}>
  <Grid container spacing={4}>
    <Grid item xs={6}>
      <Paper className={classes.paper}>xs=6</Paper>
    </Grid>
    <Grid item xs={6}>
      <Paper className={classes.paper}>xs=6</Paper>
    </Grid>
    <Grid item xs={6}>
      <Paper className={classes.paper}>xs=6</Paper>
    </Grid>
    <Grid item xs={6}>
      <Paper className={classes.paper}>xs=6</Paper>
    </Grid>
    <Grid item xs={6}>
      <Paper className={classes.paper}>xs=6</Paper>
    </Grid>
    <Grid item xs={6}>
      <Paper className={classes.paper}>xs=6</Paper>
    </Grid>
    <Grid item xs={6}>
      <Paper className={classes.paper}>xs=6</Paper>
    </Grid>
    <Grid item xs={6}>
      <Paper className={classes.paper}>xs=6</Paper>
    </Grid>
  </Grid>
</div>
```

Here's what the result looks like at a pixel screen width of 960:

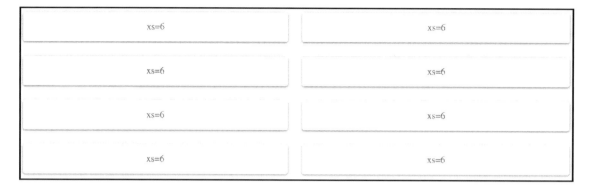

Because you've set the xs value to 6 (50%), these Grid items will only ever use two columns. The items themselves will change their width to accommodate the screen width, rather than changing the number of items per row.

There's more...

You can combine different widths in a fixed way. For example, you could have header and footer Grid items that use a full-width layout, while the Grid items in between use two columns:

```
<div className={classes.root}>
  <Grid container spacing={4}>
    <Grid item xs={12}>
      <Paper className={classes.paper}>xs=12</Paper>
    </Grid>
    <Grid item xs={6}>
      <Paper className={classes.paper}>xs=6</Paper>
    </Grid>
    <Grid item xs={6}>
      <Paper className={classes.paper}>xs=6</Paper>
    </Grid>
    <Grid item xs={6}>
      <Paper className={classes.paper}>xs=6</Paper>
    </Grid>
    <Grid item xs={6}>
      <Paper className={classes.paper}>xs=6</Paper>
    </Grid>
    <Grid item xs={6}>
      <Paper className={classes.paper}>xs=6</Paper>
    </Grid>
```

```
    <Grid item xs={6}>
      <Paper className={classes.paper}>xs=6</Paper>
    </Grid>
    <Grid item xs={12}>
      <Paper className={classes.paper}>xs=12</Paper>
    </Grid>
  </Grid>
</div>
```

The first and last `Grid` components have an `xs` value of 12 (100%), while the other `Grid` items have `xs` values of 6 (50%) for a two-column layout. Here's what the result looks like at a pixel width of 725:

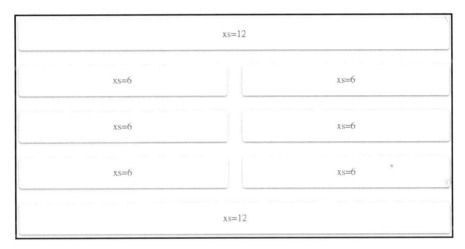

See also

- `Grid` **demos:** https://material-ui.com/layout/grid/
- `Grid` **API documentation:** https://material-ui.com/api/grid/

Changing column direction

When using a fixed number of columns for your layout, content flows from left to right. The first grid item goes in the first column, the second item in the second column, and so on. There could be times when you need better control over which grid items go into which columns.

How to do it...

Let's say that you have a four-column layout, but you want the first and second items to go in the first column, the third and fourth items in the second, and so on. This involves using nested `Grid` containers, and changing the `direction` property, as follows:

```
import React from 'react';

import { withStyles } from '@material-ui/core/styles';
import Paper from '@material-ui/core/Paper';
import Grid from '@material-ui/core/Grid';
import Hidden from '@material-ui/core/Hidden';
import Typography from '@material-ui/core/Typography';

const styles = theme => ({
  root: {
    flexGrow: 1
  },
  paper: {
    padding: theme.spacing(2),
    textAlign: 'center',
    color: theme.palette.text.secondary
  }
});

const ColumnDirection = withStyles(styles)(({ classes }) => (
  <div className={classes.root}>
    <Grid container justify="space-around" spacing={4}>
      <Grid item xs={3}>
        <Grid container direction="column" spacing={2}>
          <Grid item>
            <Paper className={classes.paper}>
              <Typography>One</Typography>
            </Paper>
          </Grid>
          <Grid item>
            <Paper className={classes.paper}>
              <Typography>Two</Typography>
            </Paper>
          </Grid>
        </Grid>
      </Grid>
      <Grid item xs={3}>
        <Grid container direction="column" spacing={2}>
          <Grid item>
            <Paper className={classes.paper}>
              <Typography>Three</Typography>
```

```
          </Paper>
        </Grid>
        <Grid item>
          <Paper className={classes.paper}>
            <Typography>Four</Typography>
          </Paper>
        </Grid>
      </Grid>
    </Grid>
    <Grid item xs={3}>
      <Grid container direction="column" spacing={2}>
        <Grid item>
          <Paper className={classes.paper}>
            <Typography>Five</Typography>
          </Paper>
        </Grid>
        <Grid item>
          <Paper className={classes.paper}>
            <Typography>Six</Typography>
          </Paper>
        </Grid>
      </Grid>
    </Grid>
    <Grid item xs={3}>
      <Grid container direction="column" spacing={2}>
        <Grid item>
          <Paper className={classes.paper}>
            <Typography>Seven</Typography>
          </Paper>
        </Grid>
        <Grid item>
          <Paper className={classes.paper}>
            <Typography>Eight</Typography>
          </Paper>
        </Grid>
      </Grid>
    </Grid>
  </Grid>
  </div>
));

export default ColumnDirection;
```

Here's what the result looks like at a pixel width of 725:

One	Three	Five	Seven
Two	Four	Six	Eight

Instead of values flowing from left to right, you have complete control over which column the item is placed in.

You might have noticed that the font looks different, compared to other examples in this chapter. This is because of the `Typography` component used to style the text and apply Material-UI theme styles. Most Material-UI components that display text don't require you to use `Typography`, but `Paper` does.

How it works...

There's a lot going on with this example, so let's start by taking a look at just the first item in the `Grid` code:

```
<Grid item xs={3}>
  <Grid container direction="column" spacing={2}>
    <Grid item>
      <Paper className={classes.paper}>
        <Typography>One</Typography>
      </Paper>
    </Grid>
    <Grid item>
      <Paper className={classes.paper}>
        <Typography>Two</Typography>
      </Paper>
    </Grid>
  </Grid>
</Grid>
```

The `Grid` item is using an `xs` value of 4, to create the four-column layout. Essentially, these items are columns. Next, you have a nested `Grid container`. This `container` has a `direction` property value of `column`. This is where you can place the `Grid` items that belong in this `column`, and they'll flow from top to bottom, instead of from left to right. Each column in this grid follows this pattern.

There's more...

There might be times when hiding the rightmost column makes more sense than trying to accommodate it with the screen width. You can use the `Hidden` component for this. It's already imported in the example, as follows:

```
import Hidden from '@material-ui/core/Hidden';
```

To use it, you wrap the last `column` with it. For example, here's what the last `column` looks like now:

```
<Grid item xs={3}>
  <Grid container direction="column" spacing={2}>
    <Grid item>
      <Paper className={classes.paper}>
        <Typography>Seven</Typography>
      </Paper>
    </Grid>
    <Grid item>
      <Paper className={classes.paper}>
        <Typography>Eight</Typography>
      </Paper>
    </Grid>
  </Grid>
</Grid>
```

If you want to hide this `column` at a certain breakpoint, you can wrap the `column` with `Hidden`, like this:

```
<Hidden smDown>
  <Grid item xs={3}>
    <Grid container direction="column" spacing={2}>
      <Grid item>
        <Paper className={classes.paper}>
          <Typography>Seven</Typography>
        </Paper>
      </Grid>
      <Grid item>
        <Paper className={classes.paper}>
          <Typography>Eight</Typography>
        </Paper>
      </Grid>
    </Grid>
  </Grid>
</Hidden>
```

The smDown property tells the Hidden component to hide its children when the sm breakpoint or lower is reached. Here's what the result looks like at a pixel width of 1000:

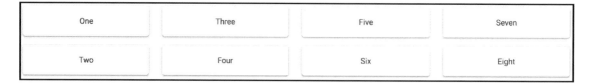

The last column is displayed because the sm breakpoint is smaller than the screen size. Here's the result at a pixel screen width of 550, without the last column displayed:

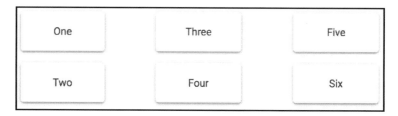

See also

- Grid demos: https://material-ui.com/layout/grid/
- Grid API documentation: https://material-ui.com/api/grid/
- Hidden API documentation: https://material-ui.com/api/hidden/

App Bars - The Top Level of Every Page

2

In this chapter, you'll learn about the following recipes:

- Fixed position
- Hide on scroll
- Toolbar abstraction
- With navigation

Introduction

App Bars are the anchor point of any Material-UI application. They provide context and are usually always visible as the user navigates around the application.

Fixed position

You probably want your `AppBar` component to stay visible at all times. By using `fixed` positioning, `AppBar` components remain visible even as the user scrolls down the page.

How to do it...

You can use the `fixed` value of the `position` property. Here's how you do it:

```
import React from 'react';

import { withStyles } from '@material-ui/core/styles';
import AppBar from '@material-ui/core/AppBar';
import Toolbar from '@material-ui/core/Toolbar';
```

```
import Typography from '@material-ui/core/Typography';
import Button from '@material-ui/core/Button';
import IconButton from '@material-ui/core/IconButton';
import MenuIcon from '@material-ui/icons/Menu';

const styles = theme => ({
  root: {
    flexGrow: 1
  },
  flex: {
    flex: 1
  },
  menuButton: {
    marginLeft: -12,
    marginRight: 20
  }
});

const FixedPosition = withStyles(styles)(({ classes }) => (
  <div className={classes.root}>
    <AppBar position="fixed">
      <Toolbar>
        <IconButton
          className={classes.menuButton}
          color="inherit"
          aria-label="Menu"
        >
          <MenuIcon />
        </IconButton>
        <Typography
          variant="title"
          color="inherit"
          className={classes.flex}
        >
          Title
        </Typography>
        <Button color="inherit">Login</Button>
      </Toolbar>
    </AppBar>
    <ul>
      {new Array(500).fill(null).map((v, i) => (
        <li key={i}>{i}</li>
      ))}
    </ul>
  </div>
));

export default FixedPosition;
```

Here's what the resulting `AppBar` component looks like:

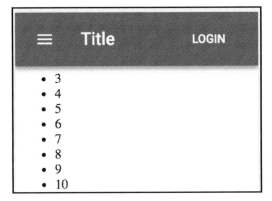

How it works...

If you scroll down, you'll see how the `AppBar` component stays *fixed*, and the content scrolls behind it. Here's what it looks like if you scroll to the bottom of the page in this example:

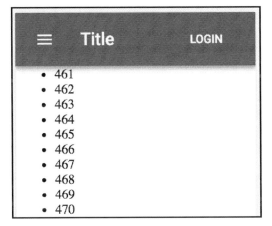

The `position` property defaults to `fixed`. However, explicitly setting this property can help readers better understand your code.

There's more...

When the screen in this example first loads, some of the content is hidden behind the `AppBar` component. This is because the position is fixed and it has a higher `z-index` value than the regular content. This is expected, so that when you scroll, the regular content goes behind the `AppBar` component. The solution is to add a top margin to your content. The problem is that you don't necessarily know the height of the `AppBar`.

You could just set a value that looks good. A better solution is to use the `toolbar mixin` styles. You can access this `mixin` object by making `styles` a function that returns an object. Then, you'll have access to the theme argument, which has a `toolbar mixin` object.

Here's what `styles` should be changed to:

```
const styles = theme => ({
  root: {
    flexGrow: 1
  },
  flex: {
    flex: 1
  },
  menuButton: {
    marginLeft: -12,
    marginRight: 20
  },
  toolbarMargin: theme.mixins.toolbar
});
```

The new style that's added is `toolbarMargin`. Notice that this is using the value from `theme.mixins.toolbar`, which is why you're using a function now – so that you can access `theme`. Here's what the `theme.mixins.toolbar` value looks like:

```
{
  "minHeight": 56,
  "@media (min-width:0px) and (orientation: landscape)": {
    "minHeight": 48
  },
  "@media (min-width:600px)": {
    "minHeight": 64
  }
}
```

The last step is to add a `<div>` element to the content underneath the `AppBar` component where this new `toolbarMargin` style can be applied:

```
<div className={classes.root}>
  <AppBar position="fixed">
    <Toolbar>
      <IconButton
        className={classes.menuButton}
        color="inherit"
        aria-label="Menu"
      >
        <MenuIcon />
      </IconButton>
      <Typography
        variant="title"
        color="inherit"
        className={classes.flex}
      >
        Title
      </Typography>
      <Button color="inherit">Login</Button>
    </Toolbar>
  </AppBar>
  <div className={classes.toolbarMargin} />
  <ul>
    {new Array(500).fill(null).map((v, i) => <li key={i}>{i}</li>)}
  </ul>
</div>
```

Now, the beginning of the content is no longer hidden by the `AppBar` component when the screen first loads:

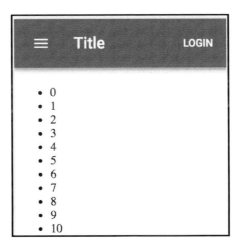

See also

- Guide to CSS positioning: `https://developer.mozilla.org/en-US/docs/Learn/CSS/CSS_layout/Positioning`
- `AppBar` demos: `https://material-ui.com/demos/app-bar/`
- `AppBar` API documentation: `https://material-ui.com/api/app-bar/`
- `Toolbar` API documentation: `https://material-ui.com/api/toolbar/`

Hide on scroll

If you have a lot of content on your screen that requires the user to scroll vertically, the App Bar could be a distraction. One solution is to hide the `AppBar` component while the user is scrolling down.

How to do it...

To hide the `AppBar` component while the user is scrolling down, you have to know when the user is scrolling. This requires listening to the `scroll` event on the `window` object. You can implement a component that listens to this event and hides the `AppBar` component while scrolling. Here's how it's done:

```
import React, { Component } from 'react';
import { withStyles } from '@material-ui/core/styles';
import AppBar from '@material-ui/core/AppBar';
import Toolbar from '@material-ui/core/Toolbar';
import Typography from '@material-ui/core/Typography';
import Button from '@material-ui/core/Button';
import IconButton from '@material-ui/core/IconButton';
import MenuIcon from '@material-ui/icons/Menu';
import Fade from '@material-ui/core/Fade';

const styles = theme => ({
  root: {
    flexGrow: 1
  },
  flex: {
    flex: 1
  },
  menuButton: {
    marginLeft: -12,
    marginRight: 20
```

```
  },
  toolbarMargin: theme.mixins.toolbar
});

const ScrolledAppBar = withStyles(styles)(
  class extends Component {
    state = {
      scrolling: false,
      scrollTop: 0
    };

    onScroll = e => {
      this.setState(state => ({
        scrollTop: e.target.documentElement.scrollTop,
        scrolling:
          e.target.documentElement.scrollTop > state.scrollTop
      }));
    };

    shouldComponentUpdate(props, state) {
      return this.state.scrolling !== state.scrolling;
    }

    componentDidMount() {
      window.addEventListener('scroll', this.onScroll);
    }

    componentWillUnmount() {
      window.removeEventListener('scroll', this.onScroll);
    }

    render() {
      const { classes } = this.props;

      return (
        <Fade in={!this.state.scrolling}>
          <AppBar>
            <Toolbar>
              <IconButton
                className={classes.menuButton}
                color="inherit"
                aria-label="Menu"
              >
                <MenuIcon />
              </IconButton>
              <Typography
                variant="h6"
                color="inherit"
```

```
                            className={classes.flex}
                        >
                            My Title
                        </Typography>
                        <Button color="inherit">Login</Button>
                    </Toolbar>
                </AppBar>
            </Fade>
        );
    }
  }
);

const AppBarWithButtons = withStyles(styles)(
  ({ classes, title, buttonText }) => (
    <div className={classes.root}>
      <ScrolledAppBar />
      <div className={classes.toolbarMargin} />
      <ul>
        {new Array(500).fill(null).map((v, i) => (
          <li key={i}>{i}</li>
        ))}
      </ul>
    </div>
  )
);

export default AppBarWithButtons;
```

When you first load the screen, the toolbar and content appear as usual:

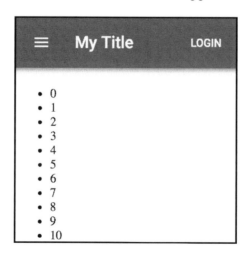

When you scroll down, the `AppBar` component disappears, allowing more space for the content to be viewed. Here's what the screen looks like when you scroll to the very bottom:

- 456
- 457
- 458
- 459
- 460

The `AppBar` component will reappear as soon as you start scrolling back up.

How it works...

Let's take a look at the `state` method and the `onScroll()` method of the `ScrolledAppBar` component:

```
state = {
  scrolling: false,
  scrollTop: 0
};

onScroll = e => {
  this.setState(state => ({
    scrollTop: e.target.documentElement.scrollTop,
    scrolling:
      e.target.documentElement.scrollTop > state.scrollTop
  }));
};

componentDidMount() {
  window.addEventListener('scroll', this.onScroll);
}

componentWillUnmount() {
  window.removeEventListener('scroll', this.onScroll);
}
```

When the component mounts, the `onScroll()` method is added as a listener to the `scroll` event on the `window` object. The `scrolling` state is a Boolean value that hides the `AppBar` component when true. The `scrollTop` state is the position of the previous scroll event. The `onScroll()` method figures out whether the user is scrolling by checking if the new scroll position is greater than the last scroll position.

Next, let's take a look at the `Fade` component that's used to hide the `AppBar` component when scrolling, as follows:

```
<Fade in={!this.state.scrolling}>
  <AppBar>
    <Toolbar>
      <IconButton
        className={classes.menuButton}
        color="inherit"
        aria-label="Menu"
      >
        <MenuIcon />
      </IconButton>
      <Typography
        variant="title"
        color="inherit"
        className={classes.flex}
      >
        My Title
      </Typography>
      <Button color="inherit">Login</Button>
    </Toolbar>
  </AppBar>
</Fade>
```

The `in` property tells the `Fade` component to fade its children, `in`, when the value is true. In this example, the condition is true when the `scrolling` state is false.

There's more...

Instead of fading the `AppBar` component in and out when the user scrolls, you can use a different effect. For example, the following code block demonstrates what it would look like if you wanted to use the `Grow` effect:

```
<Grow in={!this.state.scrolling}>
  <AppBar>
    <Toolbar>
      <IconButton
        className={classes.menuButton}
        color="inherit"
        aria-label="Menu"
      >
        <MenuIcon />
      </IconButton>
      <Typography
```

```
      variant="title"
      color="inherit"
      className={classes.flex}
  >
    My Title
  </Typography>
  <Button color="inherit">Login</Button>
</Toolbar>
</AppBar>
</Grow>
```

See also

- `Fade` **API documentation:** `https://material-ui.com/api/fade/`
- `Grow` **API documentation:** `https://material-ui.com/api/grow/`
- `Slide` **API documentation:** `https://material-ui.com/api/slide/`

Toolbar abstraction

Toolbar code can get verbose if you have to render toolbars in several places. To address this, you can create your own `Toolbar` component that encapsulates the content patterns of toolbars, making it easier to render `AppBar` components in several places.

How to do it...

Let's assume that your app renders `AppBar` components on several screens. Each `AppBar` component also renders `Menu` and `title` to the left, as well as `Button` to the right. Here's how you can implement your own `AppBar` component so that it's easier to use on several screens:

```
import React, { Fragment, Component } from 'react';

import { withStyles } from '@material-ui/core/styles';
import AppBar from '@material-ui/core/AppBar';
import Toolbar from '@material-ui/core/Toolbar';
import Typography from '@material-ui/core/Typography';
import Button from '@material-ui/core/Button';
import IconButton from '@material-ui/core/IconButton';
import MenuIcon from '@material-ui/icons/Menu';
import Menu from '@material-ui/core/Menu';
```

```
import MenuItem from '@material-ui/core/MenuItem';

const styles = theme => ({
  root: {
    flexGrow: 1
  },
  flex: {
    flex: 1
  },
  menuButton: {
    marginLeft: -12,
    marginRight: 20
  },
  toolbarMargin: theme.mixins.toolbar
});

const MyToolbar = withStyles(styles)(
  class extends Component {
    static defaultProps = {
      MenuItems: ({ closeMenu }) => (
        <Fragment>
          <MenuItem onClick={closeMenu}>Profile</MenuItem>
          <MenuItem onClick={closeMenu}>My account</MenuItem>
          <MenuItem onClick={closeMenu}>Logout</MenuItem>
        </Fragment>
      ),
      RightButton: () => <Button color="inherit">Login</Button>
    };

    state = { anchor: null };

    closeMenu = () => this.setState({ anchor: null });

    render() {
      const { classes, title, MenuItems, RightButton } = this.props;

      return (
        <Fragment>
          <AppBar>
            <Toolbar>
              <IconButton
                className={classes.menuButton}
                color="inherit"
                aria-label="Menu"
                onClick={e =>
                  this.setState({ anchor: e.currentTarget })
                }
              >
```

```
                    <MenuIcon />
                  </IconButton>
                  <Menu
                    anchorEl={this.state.anchor}
                    open={Boolean(this.state.anchor)}
                    onClose={this.closeMenu}
                  >
                    <MenuItems closeMenu={this.closeMenu} />
                  </Menu>
                  <Typography
                    variant="title"
                    color="inherit"
                    className={classes.flex}
                  >
                    {title}
                  </Typography>
                  <RightButton />
                </Toolbar>
              </AppBar>
              <div className={classes.toolbarMargin} />
            </Fragment>
          );
        }
      }
    );

    const ToolbarAbstraction = withStyles(styles)(
      ({ classes, ...props }) => (
        <div className={classes.root}>
          <MyToolbar {...props} />
        </div>
      )
    );

    export default ToolbarAbstraction;
```

Here's what the resulting toolbar looks like:

And here's what the menu looks like when the user clicks on the menu button beside the title:

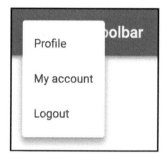

How it works...

Let's start by looking at the `render()` method of the `MyToolbar` component, as follows:

```
render() {
  const { classes, title, MenuItems, RightButton } = this.props;

  return (
    <Fragment>
      <AppBar>
        <Toolbar>
          <IconButton
            className={classes.menuButton}
            color="inherit"
            aria-label="Menu"
            onClick={e =>
              this.setState({ anchor: e.currentTarget })
            }
          >
            <MenuIcon />
          </IconButton>
          <Menu
            anchorEl={this.state.anchor}
            open={Boolean(this.state.anchor)}
            onClose={this.closeMenu}
          >
            <MenuItems closeMenu={this.closeMenu} />
          </Menu>
          <Typography
            variant="title"
            color="inherit"
            className={classes.flex}
```

```
                >
                  {title}
                </Typography>
                <RightButton />
              </Toolbar>
            </AppBar>
            <div className={classes.toolbarMargin} />
          </Fragment>
       );
    }
```

This is where the AppBar component and the Toolbar components from Material-UI are rendered. A Fragment component is used because two elements are returned: the AppBar component and the <div> element that sets the top margin for the page content. Within the toolbar, you have the following:

- The menu button that displays the menu when clicked
- The menu itself
- The title
- The right-side button

From the MyToolbar properties, there are two components that render() uses: MenuItems and RightButton. In addition to the title prop, these are the parts of the AppBar component that you want to customize. The approach here is to define default values for these properties so that the AppBar component can be rendered:

```
static defaultProps = {
  MenuItems: ({ closeMenu }) => (
    <Fragment>
      <MenuItem onClick={closeMenu}>Profile</MenuItem>
      <MenuItem onClick={closeMenu}>My account</MenuItem>
      <MenuItem onClick={closeMenu}>Logout</MenuItem>
    </Fragment>
  ),
  RightButton: () => <Button color="inherit">Login</Button>
};
```

You can pass custom values to these properties when you render MyToolbar. The defaults used here could be the values used for the home screen, for example.

You don't actually have to provide default values for these properties. But if you do, for the home screen, say, then it's easier for other developers to look at your code and understand how it works.

There's more...

Let's try setting some custom menu items and right-side buttons, using the `MenuItems` and `RightButton` properties respectively:

```
const ToolbarAbstraction = withStyles(styles)(
  ({ classes, ...props }) => (
    <div className={classes.root}>
      <MyToolbar
        MenuItems={({ closeMenu }) => (
          <Fragment>
            <MenuItem onClick={closeMenu}>Page 1</MenuItem>
            <MenuItem onClick={closeMenu}>Page 2</MenuItem>
            <MenuItem onClick={closeMenu}>Page 3</MenuItem>
          </Fragment>
        )}
        RightButton={() => (
          <Button color="secondary" variant="contained">
            Logout
          </Button>
        )}
        {...props}
      />
    </div>
  )
);
```

Here is what the toolbar looks like when rendered:

Here is what the menu looks like with the custom menu options:

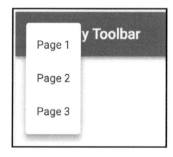

The values that you're passing to `MenuItems` and `RightButton` are functions that return React elements. These functions are actually functional components that you're creating on the fly.

See also

- `AppBar` **demos:** `https://material-ui.com/demos/app-bar/`
- `AppBar` **API documentation:** `https://material-ui.com/api/app-bar/`
- `Toolbar` **API documentation:** `https://material-ui.com/api/toolbar/`

With navigation

Material-UI apps are typically made up of several pages that are linked together using a router, such as `react-router`. Each page renders an App Bar that has information specific to that page. This is one example of when the abstraction that you created in the *Toolbar abstraction* recipe comes in handy.

How to do it...

Let's say that you're building an app that has three pages. On each page, you want to render an App Bar with the `title` prop of the page. Furthermore, the menu in the App Bar should contain links to the three pages. Here's how to do it:

```
import React, { Fragment, Component } from 'react';
import {
  BrowserRouter as Router,
  Route,
  Link
} from 'react-router-dom';

import { withStyles } from '@material-ui/core/styles';
import AppBar from '@material-ui/core/AppBar';
import Toolbar from '@material-ui/core/Toolbar';
import Typography from '@material-ui/core/Typography';
import Button from '@material-ui/core/Button';
import IconButton from '@material-ui/core/IconButton';
import MenuIcon from '@material-ui/icons/Menu';
import Menu from '@material-ui/core/Menu';
import MenuItem from '@material-ui/core/MenuItem';
```

```
const styles = theme => ({
  root: {
    flexGrow: 1
  },
  flex: {
    flex: 1
  },
  menuButton: {
    marginLeft: -12,
    marginRight: 20
  },
  toolbarMargin: theme.mixins.toolbar
});

const MyToolbar = withStyles(styles)(
  class extends Component {
    static defaultProps = {
      MenuItems: () => (
        <Fragment>
          <MenuItem component={Link} to="/">
            Home
          </MenuItem>
          <MenuItem component={Link} to="/page2">
            Page 2
          </MenuItem>
          <MenuItem component={Link} to="/page3">
            Page 3
          </MenuItem>
        </Fragment>
      ),
      RightButton: () => <Button color="inherit">Login</Button>
    };

    state = { anchor: null };

    closeMenu = () => this.setState({ anchor: null });

    render() {
      const { classes, title, MenuItems, RightButton } = this.props;

      return (
        <Fragment>
          <AppBar>
            <Toolbar>
              <IconButton
                className={classes.menuButton}
                color="inherit"
                aria-label="Menu"
```

```
          onClick={e =>
            this.setState({ anchor: e.currentTarget })
          }
        >
          <MenuIcon />
        </IconButton>
        <Menu
          anchorEl={this.state.anchor}
          open={Boolean(this.state.anchor)}
          onClose={this.closeMenu}
        >
          <MenuItems />
        </Menu>
        <Typography
          variant="title"
          color="inherit"
          className={classes.flex}
        >
          {title}
        </Typography>
        <RightButton />
      </Toolbar>
    </AppBar>
    <div className={classes.toolbarMargin} />
  </Fragment>
);
    }
  }
);

const WithNavigation = withStyles(styles)(({ classes }) => (
  <div className={classes.root}>
    <Route
      exact
      path="/"
      render={() => (
        <Fragment>
          <MyToolbar title="Home" />
          <Typography>Home</Typography>
        </Fragment>
      )}
    />
    <Route
      exact
      path="/page2"
      render={() => (
        <Fragment>
          <MyToolbar title="Page 2" />
```

```
          <Typography>Page 2</Typography>
        </Fragment>
      )}
    />
    <Route
      exact
      path="/page3"
      render={() => (
        <Fragment>
          <MyToolbar title="Page 3" />
          <Typography>Page 3</Typography>
        </Fragment>
      )}
    />
  </div>
));

export default WithNavigation;
```

Here's what you'll see when you first load the app:

Here's what the menu in the App Bar looks like when it's opened:

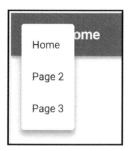

Try clicking on **Page 2;** here's what you should see:

The title of the App Bar has changed to reflect the title of the page, and the content of the page has also changed.

How it works...

Let's start by taking a look at the Routes component that define the pages in your app, as follows:

```
const WithNavigation = withStyles(styles)(({ classes }) => (
  <div className={classes.root}>
    <Route
      exact
      path="/"
      render={() => (
        <Fragment>
          <MyToolbar title="Home" />
          <Typography>Home</Typography>
        </Fragment>
      )}
    />
    <Route
      exact
      path="/page2"
      render={() => (
        <Fragment>
          <MyToolbar title="Page 2" />
          <Typography>Page 2</Typography>
        </Fragment>
      )}
    />
    <Route
      exact
      path="/page3"
      render={() => (
        <Fragment>
          <MyToolbar title="Page 3" />
          <Typography>Page 3</Typography>
        </Fragment>
      )}
    />
  </div>
));
```

Each `Route` component (from the `react-router` package) corresponds to a page in your app. They have a `path` property that matches the path in the browser address bar. When there's a match, this Routes component' content is rendered. For example, when the path is `/page3`, the content for the `Route` component where `path="/page3"` is rendered.

Each `Route` component also defines a `render()` function. This is called when its `path` is matched and the returned content is rendered. The Routes component in your app each render `MyToolbar` with a different value for the `title` prop.

Next, let's take a look at the menu items that make up the `MenuItems` default property value, as follows:

```
static defaultProps = {
  MenuItems: () => (
    <Fragment>
      <MenuItem component={Link} to="/">
        Home
      </MenuItem>
      <MenuItem component={Link} to="/page2">
        Page 2
      </MenuItem>
      <MenuItem component={Link} to="/page3">
        Page 3
      </MenuItem>
    </Fragment>
  ),
  RightButton: () => <Button color="inherit">Login</Button>
};
```

Each of these `MenuItems` properties is a link that points to each of the Routes component declared by your app. The `MenuItem` component accepts a `component` property that is used to render the link. In this example, you're passing it the `Link` component from the `react-router-dom` package. The `MenuItem` component will forward any additional properties to the `Link` component, which means that you can can pass the `to` property to the `MenuItem` component and it's as though you're passing it to the `Link` component.

There's more...

Most of the time, the screens that make up your app will follow the same pattern. Rather than have repetitive code in the `render` property of your routes, you can create a higher-order function that accepts arguments for the unique parts of the screen and returns a new component that can be used by the `render` prop.

In this example, the only two pieces of data that are unique to each screen are the title and the content text. Here's a generic function that builds a new functional component that can be used with every `Route` component in the app:

```
const screen = (title, content) => () => (
  <Fragment>
    <MyToolbar title={title} />
    <Typography>{content}</Typography>
  </Fragment>
);
```

To use this function, call it in the `render` property, such as in the following code block:

```
export default withStyles(styles)(({ classes }) => (
  <div className={classes.root}>
    <Route exact path="/" render={screen('Home', 'Home')} />
    <Route exact path="/page2" render={screen('Page 2', 'Page 2')} />
    <Route exact path="/page3" render={screen('Page 3', 'Page 3')} />
  </div>
));
```

Now you have a clear separation of the static `screen` structure that stays the same for every screen in the app, and the pieces that are unique to each screen that passed as arguments to the `screen()` function.

See also

- React Router documentation: `https://reacttraining.com/react-router/`
- AppBar demos: `https://material-ui.com/demos/app-bar/`
- AppBar API documentation: `https://material-ui.com/api/app-bar/`

3
Drawers - A Place for Navigation Controls

In this chapter, you'll learn about the following recipes:

- Drawer types
- Drawer item state
- Drawer item navigation
- Drawer sections
- AppBar interaction

Introduction

Material-UI uses drawers to present the user with the main navigation of the app. The `Drawer` component acts like a physical drawer that can move out of view when it is not being used.

Drawer types

There are three types of `Drawer` components that you'll use in your app, as follows:

- **Temporary**: A transient drawer that closes when an action is taken.
- **Persistent**: A drawer that can be opened and stays open until explicitly closed.
- **Permanent**: A drawer that is always visible.

How to do it...

Let's say that you want to support different types of drawers in your app. You can control the Drawer component type using the variant property. Here's the code:

```
import React, { useState } from 'react';

import Drawer from '@material-ui/core/Drawer';
import Grid from '@material-ui/core/Grid';
import Button from '@material-ui/core/Button';
import List from '@material-ui/core/List';
import ListItem from '@material-ui/core/ListItem';
import ListItemIcon from '@material-ui/core/ListItemIcon';
import ListItemText from '@material-ui/core/ListItemText';

export default function DrawerTypes({ classes, variant }) {
  const [open, setOpen] = useState(false);

  return (
    <Grid container justify="space-between">
      <Grid item>
        <Drawer
          variant={variant}
          open={open}
          onClose={() => setOpen(false)}
        >
          <List>
            <ListItem
              button
              onClick={() => setOpen(false)}
            >
              <ListItemText>Home</ListItemText>
            </ListItem>
            <ListItem
              button
              onClick={() => setOpen(false)}
            >
              <ListItemText>Page 2</ListItemText>
            </ListItem>
            <ListItem
              button
              onClick={() => setOpen(false)}
            >
              <ListItemText>Page 3</ListItemText>
            </ListItem>
          </List>
        </Drawer>
      </Grid>
```

```
      <Grid item>
        <Button onClick={() => setOpen(!open)}>
          {open ? 'Hide' : 'Show'} Drawer
        </Button>
      </Grid>
    </Grid>
  );
}
```

The `variant` property defaults to `temporary`. When you first load this screen, you'll only see the button to toggle the drawer display:

When you click on this button, you'll see a temporary drawer:

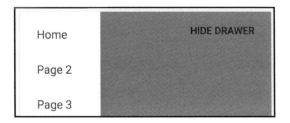

How it works...

Before you start changing the `variant` property, let's walk through the code in this example, starting with the `Drawer` markup, as follows:

```
<Drawer
  variant={variant}
  open={open}
  onClose={() => setOpen(false)}
>
  <List>
    <ListItem
      button
      onClick={() => setOpen(false)}
    >
      <ListItemText>Home</ListItemText>
    </ListItem>
    <ListItem
```

```
    button
    onClick={() => setOpen(false)}
  >
    <ListItemText>Page 2</ListItemText>
  </ListItem>
  <ListItem
    button
    onClick={() => setOpen(false)}
  >
    <ListItemText>Page 3</ListItemText>
  </ListItem>
  </List>
</Drawer>
```

The Drawer component takes an open property, which displays the drawer when true. The variant property determines the type of drawer to render. The screenshot shown previously is a temporary drawer, the default variant value. The Drawer component has List as its child, where each of the items displayed in the drawer are rendered.

Next, let's take a look at the Button component that toggles the display of the Drawer component:

```
<Button onClick={() => setOpen(!open)}>
  {open ? 'Hide' : 'Show'} Drawer
</Button>
```

When this button is clicked, the open state of your component is toggled. Likewise, the text of the button is toggled depending on the value of the open state.

Now let's try changing the value of the variant property to permanent. Here's what the drawer looks like when rendered:

A permanent drawer, as the name suggests, is always visible and is always in the same place on the screen. If you click on the **SHOW DRAWER** button, the open state of your component is toggled to true. You'll see the text of the button change, but since the Drawer component is using the permanent variant, the open property has no effect:

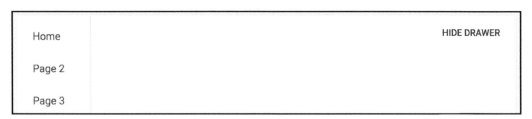

Next, let's try the persistent variant. Persistent drawers are similar to permanent drawers in that they stay visible on the screen while the user interacts with the app, and they're similar to temporary drawers in that they can be hidden by changing the open property.

Let's change the variant property to persistent. When the screen first loads, the drawer isn't visible because the open state of your component is false. Try clicking on the **SHOW DRAWER** button. The drawer is displayed, and it looks like the permanent drawer. If you click the **HIDE DRAWER** button, the open state of your component is toggled to false and the drawer is hidden.

Persistent drawers should be used when you want the user to be able to control the visibility of the drawer. For example, with temporary drawers the user can close the drawer by clicking on the overlay or by hitting the *Esc* key. Permanent drawers are useful when you want to use the left-hand navigation as an integral part of the page layout—they are always visible and other items are laid out around them.

There's more...

When you click on any of the items in the drawer, the event handlers set the open state of your component to false. This might not be what you want and could potentially confuse your users. For example, if you're using a persistent drawer, your app probably has a button outside of the drawer that controls the visibility of the drawer. If the user clicks on a drawer item, they're probably not expecting the drawer to close.

To address this issue, your event handlers can take into consideration a variant of the
`Drawer` component:

```
<List>
  <ListItem
    button
    onClick={() => setOpen(variant !== 'temporary')}
  >
    <ListItemText>Home</ListItemText>
  </ListItem>
  <ListItem
    button
    onClick={() => setOpen(variant !== 'temporary')}
  >
    <ListItemText>Page 2</ListItemText>
  </ListItem>
  <ListItem
    button
    onClick={() => setOpen(variant !== 'temporary')}
  >
    <ListItemText>Page 3</ListItemText>
  </ListItem>
</List>
```

Now, when you click on any of these items, the `open` state is only changed to `false` if the
`variant` property is `temporary`.

See also

- `Drawer` demos: `https://material-ui.com/demos/drawers/`
- `Drawer` API documentation: `https://material-ui.com/api/drawer/`

Drawer item state

The items that are rendered in `Drawer` components are rarely static. Instead, the drawer
items are rendered based on the state of your component, allowing for more control over
how items are displayed.

How to do it...

Let's say that you have a component that renders drawer navigation using the `Drawer` component. Instead of writing the `items` state directly in the component markup, you want to have the `items` state stored in the state of the component. For example, in response to permission checks on the user, items might be disabled or completely hidden.

Here's an example that uses an array of `item` objects from the component state:

```
import React, { useState } from 'react';

import Drawer from '@material-ui/core/Drawer';
import Grid from '@material-ui/core/Grid';
import Button from '@material-ui/core/Button';
import List from '@material-ui/core/List';
import ListItem from '@material-ui/core/ListItem';
import ListItemIcon from '@material-ui/core/ListItemIcon';
import ListItemText from '@material-ui/core/ListItemText';
import Typography from '@material-ui/core/Typography';

import HomeIcon from '@material-ui/icons/Home';
import WebIcon from '@material-ui/icons/Web';

export default function DrawerItemState() {
  const [open, setOpen] = useState(false);
  const [content, setContent] = useState('Home');
  const [items] = useState([
    { label: 'Home', Icon: HomeIcon },
    { label: 'Page 2', Icon: WebIcon },
    { label: 'Page 3', Icon: WebIcon, disabled: true },
    { label: 'Page 4', Icon: WebIcon },
    { label: 'Page 5', Icon: WebIcon, hidden: true }
  ]);

  const onClick = content => () => {
    setOpen(false);
    setContent(content);
  };

  return (
    <Grid container justify="space-between">
      <Grid item>
        <Typography>{content}</Typography>
      </Grid>
      <Grid item>
        <Drawer open={open} onClose={() => setOpen(false)}>
          <List>
```

```
        {items
          .filter(({ hidden }) => !hidden)
          .map(({ label, disabled, Icon }, i) => (
            <ListItem
              button
              key={i}
              disabled={disabled}
              onClick={onClick(label)}
            >
              <ListItemIcon>
                <Icon />
              </ListItemIcon>
              <ListItemText>{label}</ListItemText>
            </ListItem>
          ))}
        </List>
      </Drawer>
    </Grid>

    <Grid item>
      <Button onClick={() => setOpen(!open)}>
        {open ? 'Hide' : 'Show'} Drawer
      </Button>
    </Grid>
  </Grid>
);
}
```

This is what the drawer looks like when you click on the **SHOW DRAWER** button:

If you select one of these items, the drawer will close and the content of the screen will be updated; for example, after clicking on **Page 2**, you should see something similar to the following screenshot:

How it works...

Let's start by looking at the state of your component:

```
const [open, setOpen] = useState(false);
const [content, setContent] = useState('Home');
const [items] = useState([
  { label: 'Home', Icon: HomeIcon },
  { label: 'Page 2', Icon: WebIcon },
  { label: 'Page 3', Icon: WebIcon, disabled: true },
  { label: 'Page 4', Icon: WebIcon },
  { label: 'Page 5', Icon: WebIcon, hidden: true }
]);
```

The `open` state controls the visibility of the `Drawer` component, and the `content` state is the text that's displayed on the screen depending on which drawer item is clicked on. The `items` state is an array of objects that is used to render the drawer items. Every object has a `label` property and an `Icon` property that are used to render the item text and icon respectively.

> The `Icon` property is capitalized in order to maintain the React convention of capitalizing components. This makes it easier to differentiate React components from other data when reading the code.

The `disabled` property is used to render the item as disabled; for example, **Page 3** is marked as disabled by setting this property to `true`:

This could be due to permission restrictions for the user on this particular page, or some other reason. Because this is controlled through the component state instead of rendered statically, you could update the `disabled` state for any menu item at any time using any mechanism that you like, such as an API call. The `hidden` property uses the same principle, except when this value is `true`, the item isn't rendered at all. In this example, **Page 5** isn't rendered because it's marked as hidden.

Next, let's look at how the `List` items are rendered based on the `items` state, as follows:

```
<List>
  {items
    .filter(({ hidden }) => !hidden)
    .map(({ label, disabled, Icon }, i) => (
      <ListItem
        button
        key={i}
        disabled={disabled}
        onClick={onClick(label)}
      >
        <ListItemIcon>
          <Icon />
        </ListItemIcon>
        <ListItemText>{label}</ListItemText>
      </ListItem>
    ))}
</List>
```

First, the `items` array is filtered to remove `hidden` items. Then, `map()` is used to render each `ListItem` component. The `disabled` property is passed to `ListItem` and it will be visibly disabled when rendered. The `Icon` component also comes from the list item state. The `onClick()` event handler hides the drawer and updates the `content` label.

 The `onClick()` handler isn't executed when disabled list items are clicked on.

There's more...

You might want to separate the rendering of list items into its own component. This way, you can use the list items in other places. For example, you might want to use the same rendering logic to render a list of buttons elsewhere in your app. Here's an example of how you can extract the `ListItems` component into its own component:

```
const ListItems = ({ items, onClick }) =>
  items
    .filter(({ hidden }) => !hidden)
    .map(({ label, disabled, Icon }, i) => (
      <ListItem
        button
        key={i}
        disabled={disabled}
```

```
          onClick={onClick(label)}
        >
          <ListItemIcon>
            <Icon />
          </ListItemIcon>
          <ListItemText>{label}</ListItemText>
        </ListItem>
      ));
```

The `ListItems` component will return an array of `ListItem` components. It takes the `items` state to render as an array property. It also takes an `onClick()` function property. This is a higher-order function that takes the `label` component to display as an argument and returns a new function that will update the content when the item is clicked on.

Here's what the new JSX markup looks like, updated to use the new `ListItems` component:

```
<Grid container justify="space-between">
  <Grid item>
    <Typography>{content}</Typography>
  </Grid>
  <Grid item>
    <Drawer open={open} onClose={() => setOpen(false)}>
      <List>
        <ListItems items={items} onClick={onClick} />
      </List>
    </Drawer>
  </Grid>

  <Grid item>
    <Button onClick={() => setOpen(!open)}>
      {open ? 'Hide' : 'Show'} Drawer
    </Button>
  </Grid>
</Grid>
```

There is no more list item rendering code in this component. Instead, `ListItems` is rendered as the child of `List`. You pass it the items to render and the `onClick()` handler. You now have a generic `ListItems` component that can be used anywhere that you show lists in your app. It will consistently handle the `Icon`, `disabled`, and display logic wherever it is used.

See also

- Drawer demos: https://material-ui.com/demos/drawers/
- Drawer API documentation: https://material-ui.com/api/drawer/

Drawer item navigation

If your Material-UI app uses a router such as react-router to navigate from page to page, you'll probably want links as your Drawer items. To do so, you have to integrate components from the react-router-dom package.

How to do it...

Let's say that your app is composed of three pages. To navigate from page to page, you want to provide your users with links in the Drawer component. Here's what the code looks like:

```
import React, { useState } from 'react';
import { Route, Link } from 'react-router-dom';

import { withStyles } from '@material-ui/core/styles';
import Drawer from '@material-ui/core/Drawer';
import Grid from '@material-ui/core/Grid';
import Button from '@material-ui/core/Button';
import List from '@material-ui/core/List';
import ListItem from '@material-ui/core/ListItem';
import ListItemIcon from '@material-ui/core/ListItemIcon';
import ListItemText from '@material-ui/core/ListItemText';
import Typography from '@material-ui/core/Typography';

import HomeIcon from '@material-ui/icons/Home';
import WebIcon from '@material-ui/icons/Web';

const styles = theme => ({
  alignContent: {
    alignSelf: 'center'
  }
});

function DrawerItemNavigation({ classes }) {
  const [open, setOpen] = useState(false);
```

```
return (
  <Grid container justify="space-between">
    <Grid item className={classes.alignContent}>
      <Route
        exact
        path="/"
        render={() => <Typography>Home</Typography>}
      />
      <Route
        exact
        path="/page2"
        render={() => <Typography>Page 2</Typography>}
      />
      <Route
        exact
        path="/page3"
        render={() => <Typography>Page 3</Typography>}
      />
    </Grid>
    <Grid item>
      <Drawer
        className={classes.drawerWidth}
        open={open}
        onClose={() => setOpen(false)}
      >
        <List>
          <ListItem
            component={Link}
            to="/"
            onClick={() => setOpen(false)}
          >
            <ListItemIcon>
              <HomeIcon />
            </ListItemIcon>
            <ListItemText>Home</ListItemText>
          </ListItem>
          <ListItem
            component={Link}
            to="/page2"
            onClick={() => setOpen(false)}
          >
            <ListItemIcon>
              <WebIcon />
            </ListItemIcon>
            <ListItemText>Page 2</ListItemText>
          </ListItem>
          <ListItem
            component={Link}
```

```
                         to="/page3"
                         onClick={() => setOpen(false)}
                    >
                         <ListItemIcon>
                            <WebIcon />
                         </ListItemIcon>
                         <ListItemText>Page 3</ListItemText>
                      </ListItem>
                  </List>
              </Drawer>
          </Grid>
          <Grid item>
             <Button onClick={() => setOpen(!open)}>
                {open ? 'Hide' : 'Show'} Drawer
             </Button>
          </Grid>
        </Grid>
      );
    }

    export default withStyles(styles)(DrawerItemNavigation);
```

When you first load the screen, you'll see the **SHOW DRAWER** button and the home screen content:

Here's what the drawer looks like when it's opened:

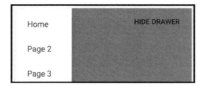

If you click on **Page 2**, which points to /page2, the drawer should close and you should be taken to the second page. Here's what it looks like:

You should see something similar if you click on **Page 3** or on **Home**. The content on the left side of the screen is updated.

How it works...

Let's start by looking at the Route components that render content based on the active the Route components:

```
<Grid item className={classes.alignContent}>
  <Route
    exact
    path="/"
    render={() => <Typography>Home</Typography>}
  />
  <Route
    exact
    path="/page2"
    render={() => <Typography>Page 2</Typography>}
  />
  <Route
    exact
    path="/page3"
    render={() => <Typography>Page 3</Typography>}
  />
</Grid>
```

There's a Route component used for each path in your app. The render() function returns the content that should be rendered within this Grid item when the path property matches the current URL.

Next, let's look at one of the ListItem components within the Drawer component, as follows:

```
<ListItem
  component={Link}
  to="/"
  onClick={() => setOpen(false)}
>
  <ListItemIcon>
    <HomeIcon />
  </ListItemIcon>
  <ListItemText>Home</ListItemText>
</ListItem>
```

By default, the `ListItem` component will render a `div` element. It accepts a `button` property that when true, will render a `button` element. You don't want either of these. Instead, you want the list items to be links that `react-router` will process. The `component` property accepts a custom component to use; in this example, you want to use the `Link` component from the `react-router-dom` package. This will render the appropriate link while maintaining the proper styles.

The properties that you pass to `ListItem` are also passed to your custom component, which, in this case, is `Link`. This means that the required `to` property is passed to `Link`, pointing the link to `/`. Likewise, the `onClick` handler is also passed to the `Link` component, which is important because you want to close the temporary drawer whenever a link is clicked.

There's more...

When the items in your drawer are links, you probably want a visual indication for the active link. The challenge is that you want to style the active link using Material-UI theme styles. Here's what the modified example looks like:

```
import React, { useState } from 'react';
import clsx from 'clsx';
import { Switch, Route, Link, NavLink } from 'react-router-dom';

import { withStyles } from '@material-ui/core/styles';
import Drawer from '@material-ui/core/Drawer';
import Grid from '@material-ui/core/Grid';
import Button from '@material-ui/core/Button';
import List from '@material-ui/core/List';
import ListItem from '@material-ui/core/ListItem';
import ListItemIcon from '@material-ui/core/ListItemIcon';
import ListItemText from '@material-ui/core/ListItemText';
import Typography from '@material-ui/core/Typography';

import HomeIcon from '@material-ui/icons/Home';
import WebIcon from '@material-ui/icons/Web';

const styles = theme => ({
  alignContent: {
    alignSelf: 'center'
  },
  activeListItem: {
    color: theme.palette.primary.main
  }
});
```

```
const NavListItem = withStyles(styles)(
  ({ classes, Icon, text, active, ...other }) => (
    <ListItem component={NavLink} {...other}>
      <ListItemIcon
        classes={{
          root: clsx({ [classes.activeListItem]: active })
        }}
      >
        <Icon />
      </ListItemIcon>
      <ListItemText
        classes={{
          primary: clsx({
            [classes.activeListItem]: active
          })
        }}
      >
        {text}
      </ListItemText>
    </ListItem>
  )
);

const NavItem = props => (
  <Switch>
    <Route
      exact
      path={props.to}
      render={() => <NavListItem active={true} {...props} />}
    />
    <Route path="/" render={() => <NavListItem {...props} />} />
  </Switch>
);

function DrawerItemNavigation({ classes }) {
  const [open, setOpen] = useState(false);

  return (
    <Grid container justify="space-between">
      <Grid item className={classes.alignContent}>
        <Route
          exact
          path="/"
          render={() => <Typography>Home</Typography>}
        />
        <Route
          exact
          path="/page2"
```

```
          render={() => <Typography>Page 2</Typography>}
        />
        <Route
          exact
          path="/page3"
          render={() => <Typography>Page 3</Typography>}
        />
      </Grid>
      <Grid item>
        <Drawer
          className={classes.drawerWidth}
          open={open}
          onClose={() => setOpen(false)}
        >
          <List>
            <NavItem
              to="/"
              text="Home"
              Icon={HomeIcon}
              onClick={() => setOpen(false)}
            />
            <NavItem
              to="/page2"
              text="Page 2"
              Icon={WebIcon}
              onClick={() => setOpen(false)}
            />
            <NavItem
              to="/page3"
              text="Page 3"
              Icon={WebIcon}
              onClick={() => setOpen(false)}
            />
          </List>
        </Drawer>
      </Grid>
      <Grid item>
        <Button onClick={() => setOpen(!open)}>
          {open ? 'Hide' : 'Show'} Drawer
        </Button>
      </Grid>
    </Grid>
  );
}

export default withStyles(styles)(DrawerItemNavigation);
```

Now, when the screen first loads and you open the drawer, it should look similar to the following screenshot:

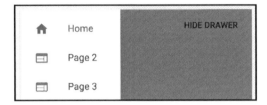

Since the **Home** link is active, it's styled using the primary color from the Material-UI theme. If you click on the **Page 2** link and then open the drawer again, it should look similar to the following screenshot:

Let's take a look at the two new components that you've added, starting with `NavItem`:

```
const NavItem = props => (
  <Switch>
    <Route
      exact
      path={props.to}
      render={() => <NavListItem active={true} {...props} />}
    />
    <Route path="/" render={() => <NavListItem {...props} />} />
  </Switch>
);
```

This component is used to determine whether or not the item is active, based on the current URL. It uses the `Switch` component from `react-router-dom`. Instead of just rendering `Route` components, `Switch` will only render the first route whose path matches the current URL. The first `Route` component in `NavItem` is the specific path (as it uses the `exact` property). If this `Route` component matches, it renders a `NavListItem` component with the `active` property set to true. Because it's in a `Switch` component, the second `Route` component will not be rendered.

If, on the other hand, the first `Route` component doesn't match, the second `Route` component will always match. This will render a `NavListItem` component without the `active` property. Now, let's take a look at the `NavListItem` component, as follows:

```
const NavListItem = withStyles(styles)(
  ({ classes, Icon, text, active, ...other }) => (
    <ListItem component={NavLink} {...other}>
      <ListItemIcon
        classes={{
          root: clsx({ [classes.activeListItem]: active })
        }}
      >
        <Icon />
      </ListItemIcon>
      <ListItemText
        classes={{
          primary: clsx({
            [classes.activeListItem]: active
          })
        }}
      >
        {text}
      </ListItemText>
    </ListItem>
  )
);
```

The `NavListItem` component is now responsible for rendering the `ListItem` components in the `Drawer` component. It takes a `text` property and an `Icon` property to render the label and the icon respectively, just like before your enhancements. The `active` property is used to determine the class that gets applied to the `ListItemIcon` and `ListItemText` components. The `activeListItem` CSS class is applied to both of these components if `active` is true. This is how you're able to style the `active` item based on the Material-UI theme.

> The `clsx()` function is used extensively by Material-UI–this isn't an extra dependency. It allows you to dynamically change the class of an element without introducing custom logic into your markup. For example, the `clsx({ [classes.activeListItem]: active })` syntax will only apply the `activeListItem` class if `active` is true. The alternative will involve introducing more logic into your component.

Lastly, let's take a look at the `activeListItem` class, as follows:

```
const styles = theme => ({
  alignContent: {
    alignSelf: 'center'
  },
  activeListItem: {
    color: theme.palette.primary.main
  }
});
```

The `activeListItem` class sets the color CSS property by using the `theme.palette.primary.main` value. This means that if the theme changes, your active link in the drawer will be styled accordingly.

See also

- React Router documentation: `https://reacttraining.com/react-router/`
- `Drawer` demos: `https://material-ui.com/demos/drawers/`
- `Drawer` API documentation: `https://material-ui.com/api/drawer/`

Drawer sections

When you have lots of items in your `Drawer`, you might want to divide your drawer into sections. When you have lots of drawer items and no sections, you end up having to put section names into the items themselves, which leads to messy and awkward drawer item labels.

How to do it...

Let's say that you're working on an app that has screens for managing different aspects of the CPU, memory, storage, and network. Instead of having a flat list of drawer items, you could display drawer items in their relevant sections, making it easier to navigate. Here's the code to do it:

```
import React, { useState } from 'react';

import { withStyles } from '@material-ui/core/styles';
import Drawer from '@material-ui/core/Drawer';
import Grid from '@material-ui/core/Grid';
```

```
import Button from '@material-ui/core/Button';
import List from '@material-ui/core/List';
import ListItem from '@material-ui/core/ListItem';
import ListItemIcon from '@material-ui/core/ListItemIcon';
import ListItemText from '@material-ui/core/ListItemText';
import ListSubheader from '@material-ui/core/ListSubheader';
import Typography from '@material-ui/core/Typography';

import AddIcon from '@material-ui/icons/Add';
import RemoveIcon from '@material-ui/icons/Remove';
import ShowChartIcon from '@material-ui/icons/ShowChart';

const styles = theme => ({
  alignContent: {
    alignSelf: 'center'
  }
});

const ListItems = ({ items, onClick }) =>
  items
    .filter(({ hidden }) => !hidden)
    .map(({ label, disabled, Icon }, i) => (
      <ListItem
        button
        key={i}
        disabled={disabled}
        onClick={onClick(label)}
      >
        <ListItemIcon>
          <Icon />
        </ListItemIcon>
        <ListItemText>{label}</ListItemText>
      </ListItem>
    ));

const DrawerSections = withStyles(styles)(({ classes }) => {
  const [open, setOpen] = useState(false);
  const [content, setContent] = useState('Home');
  const [items] = useState({
    cpu: [
      { label: 'Add CPU', Icon: AddIcon },
      { label: 'Remove CPU', Icon: RemoveIcon },
      { label: 'Usage', Icon: ShowChartIcon }
    ],
    memory: [
      { label: 'Add Memory', Icon: AddIcon },
      { label: 'Usage', Icon: ShowChartIcon }
    ],
```

```
    storage: [
      { label: 'Add Storage', Icon: AddIcon },
      { label: 'Usage', Icon: ShowChartIcon }
    ],
    network: [
      { label: 'Add Network', Icon: AddIcon, disabled: true },
      { label: 'Usage', Icon: ShowChartIcon }
    ]
  });

  const onClick = content => () => {
    setOpen(false);
    setContent(content);
  };

  return (
    <Grid container justify="space-between">
      <Grid item className={classes.alignContent}>
        <Typography>{content}</Typography>
      </Grid>
      <Grid item>
        <Drawer open={open} onClose={() => setOpen(false)}>
          <List>
            <ListSubheader>CPU</ListSubheader>
            <ListItems items={items.cpu} onClick={onClick} />
            <ListSubheader>Memory</ListSubheader>
            <ListItems items={items.memory} onClick={onClick} />
            <ListSubheader>Storage</ListSubheader>
            <ListItems items={items.storage} onClick={onClick} />
            <ListSubheader>Network</ListSubheader>
            <ListItems items={items.network} onClick={onClick} />
          </List>
        </Drawer>
      </Grid>

      <Grid item>
        <Button onClick={() => setOpen(!open)}>
          {open ? 'Hide' : 'Show'} Drawer
        </Button>
      </Grid>
    </Grid>
  );
});

export default DrawerSections;
```

When you click on the **SHOW DRAWER** button, your drawer should look like this:

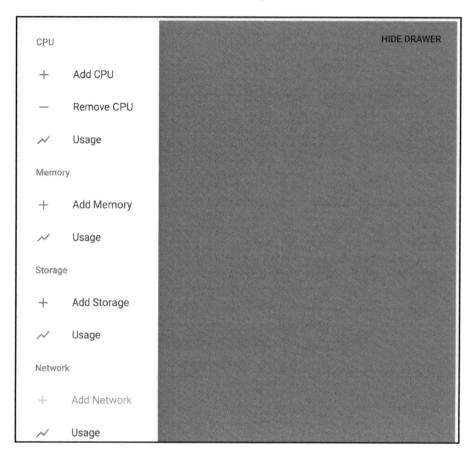

There are lots of add and usage items in this drawer. The sections make the items easier for your users to scan.

How it works...

Let's start by taking a look at the state of your component, as follows:

```
const [open, setOpen] = useState(false);
const [content, setContent] = useState('Home');
const [items] = useState({
  cpu: [
    { label: 'Add CPU', Icon: AddIcon },
    { label: 'Remove CPU', Icon: RemoveIcon },
```

```
      { label: 'Usage', Icon: ShowChartIcon }
    ],
    memory: [
      { label: 'Add Memory', Icon: AddIcon },
      { label: 'Usage', Icon: ShowChartIcon }
    ],
    storage: [
      { label: 'Add Storage', Icon: AddIcon },
      { label: 'Usage', Icon: ShowChartIcon }
    ],
    network: [
      { label: 'Add Network', Icon: AddIcon, disabled: true },
      { label: 'Usage', Icon: ShowChartIcon }
    ]
});
```

Instead of the items state being a flat array of items, it's now an object with arrays grouped by category. These are the drawer sections that you want to render. Next, let's look at the List markup for rendering the items state and the section headers:

```
<List>
  <ListSubheader>CPU</ListSubheader>
  <ListItems items={items.cpu} onClick={onClick} />
  <ListSubheader>Memory</ListSubheader>
  <ListItems items={items.memory} onClick={onClick} />
  <ListSubheader>Storage</ListSubheader>
  <ListItems items={items.storage} onClick={onClick} />
  <ListSubheader>Network</ListSubheader>
  <ListItems items={items.network} onClick={onClick} />
</List>
```

The ListSubheader component is used when you need a label above the list items. For example, underneath the **Storage** header, you have the ListItems component that renders items from the items.storage state.

There's more...

When you have a lot of drawer items and sections, you can still overwhelm your users with the amount of information to parse. One solution is to have collapsible sections. For this, you can add a Button component to the ListSubheader component so that it's clickable.

Here's what the code looks like:

```
<ListSubheader>
  <Button
    disableRipple
    classes={{ root: classes.listSubheader }}
    onClick={toggleSection('cpu')}
  >
    CPU
  </Button>
</ListSubheader>
```

The ripple effect that would normally happen when you click on a button is disabled here because you want the header text to still look like header text. This also requires a little bit of CSS customization in the `listSubheader` class:

```
const styles = theme => ({
  alignContent: {
    alignSelf: 'center'
  },
  listSubheader: {
    padding: 0,
    minWidth: 0,
    color: 'inherit',
    '&:hover': {
      background: 'inherit'
    }
  }
});
```

When the section header button is clicked, it toggles the state of the section, which in turn, toggles the visibility of the section items. Here's the `toggleSection()` function:

```
const toggleSection = name => () => {
  setSections({ ...sections, [name]: !sections[name] });
};
```

This is a higher-order function that returns a new function as the `onClick` handler for the button. The `name` argument is the name of the section state to toggle.

Here's the new state that was added to support toggling sections:

```
const [sections, setSections] = useState({
  cpu: true,
  memory: false,
  storage: false,
  network: false
});
```

When the screen first loads, the **CPU** section will be the only section with visible items since it's the only state that's true. Next, let's look at how the ListItems are actually collapsed when their corresponding section state is false:

```
const ListItems = ({ items, visible, onClick }) => (
  <Collapse in={visible}>
    {items
      .filter(({ hidden }) => !hidden)
      .map(({ label, disabled, Icon }, i) => (
        <ListItem
          button
          key={i}
          disabled={disabled}
          onClick={onClick(label)}
        >
          <ListItemIcon>
            <Icon />
          </ListItemIcon>
          <ListItemText>{label}</ListItemText>
        </ListItem>
      ))}
  </Collapse>
);
```

The ListItems component now accepts a visible property. This is used by the Collapse component, which will hide its children using a collapsing animation when hiding components. Finally, here's how the new ListItems component is used:

```
<ListItems
  visible={sections.cpu}
  items={items.cpu}
  onClick={onClick}
/>
```

When the screen first loads, and you click on the **SHOW DRAWER** button, you should see something similar to this:

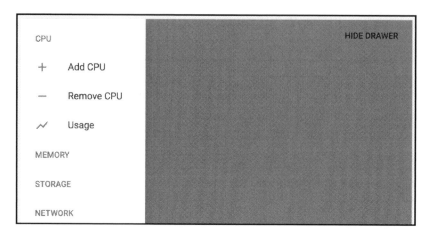

There's way less information for the user to parse now. They can click on the section headers to see the list items, and they can click again to collapse the section; for example, they could collapse the **CPU** section and expand the **MEMORY** section:

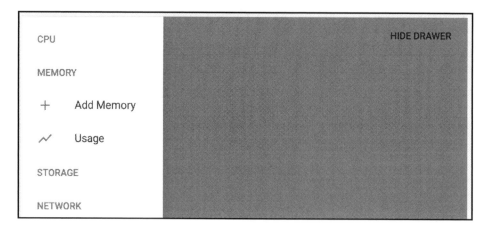

See also

- Drawer demos: https://material-ui.com/demos/drawers/
- Drawer API documentation: https://material-ui.com/api/drawer/

AppBar interaction

A common place to put a button that toggles the visibility of `Drawer` components is the `AppBar` component at the top of every page in your app. Furthermore, by selecting items in a drawer, the title of the `AppBar` component needs to change to reflect this selection. `Drawer` and `AppBar` components often need to interact with one another.

How to do it...

Let's say that you have a `Drawer` component with a few items in it. You also have an `AppBar` component with a menu button and a title. The menu button should toggle the visibility of the drawer, and clicking on a drawer item should update the title in the `AppBar`. Here's the code to do it:

```
import React, { useState, Fragment } from 'react';

import { withStyles } from '@material-ui/core/styles';
import AppBar from '@material-ui/core/AppBar';
import Toolbar from '@material-ui/core/Toolbar';
import Typography from '@material-ui/core/Typography';
import Button from '@material-ui/core/Button';
import Drawer from '@material-ui/core/Drawer';
import List from '@material-ui/core/List';
import ListItem from '@material-ui/core/ListItem';
import ListItemIcon from '@material-ui/core/ListItemIcon';
import ListItemText from '@material-ui/core/ListItemText';
import IconButton from '@material-ui/core/IconButton';
import MenuIcon from '@material-ui/icons/Menu';

const styles = theme => ({
  root: {
    flexGrow: 1
  },
  flex: {
    flex: 1
  },
  menuButton: {
    marginLeft: -12,
    marginRight: 20
  },
  toolbarMargin: theme.mixins.toolbar
});

const MyToolbar = withStyles(styles)(
```

```
    ({ classes, title, onMenuClick }) => (
      <Fragment>
        <AppBar>
          <Toolbar>
            <IconButton
              className={classes.menuButton}
              color="inherit"
              aria-label="Menu"
              onClick={onMenuClick}
            >
              <MenuIcon />
            </IconButton>
            <Typography
              variant="title"
              color="inherit"
              className={classes.flex}
            >
              {title}
            </Typography>
          </Toolbar>
        </AppBar>
        <div className={classes.toolbarMargin} />
      </Fragment>
    )
);

const MyDrawer = withStyles(styles)(
  ({ classes, variant, open, onClose, setTitle }) => (
    <Drawer variant={variant} open={open} onClose={onClose}>
      <List>
        <ListItem
          button
          onClick={() => {
            setTitle('Home');
            onClose();
          }}
        >
          <ListItemText>Home</ListItemText>
        </ListItem>
        <ListItem
          button
          onClick={() => {
            setTitle('Page 2');
            onClose();
          }}
        >
          <ListItemText>Page 2</ListItemText>
        </ListItem>
```

```
          <ListItem
            button
            onClick={() => {
              setTitle('Page 3');
              onClose();
            }}
          >
            <ListItemText>Page 3</ListItemText>
          </ListItem>
        </List>
      </Drawer>
    )
  );

  function AppBarInteraction({ classes }) {
    const [drawer, setDrawer] = useState(false);
    const [title, setTitle] = useState('Home');

    const toggleDrawer = () => {
      setDrawer(!drawer);
    };

    return (
      <div className={classes.root}>
        <MyToolbar title={title} onMenuClick={toggleDrawer} />
        <MyDrawer
          open={drawer}
          onClose={toggleDrawer}
          setTitle={setTitle}
        />
      </div>
    );
  }

  export default withStyles(styles)(AppBarInteraction);
```

Here's what the screen looks like when it first loads:

When you click on the menu icon button to the left of the title, you'll see the drawer:

If you click on the **Page 2** item, the drawer will close and the title of the AppBar will change:

How it works...

This example defines three components, as follows:

- The MyToolbar component
- The MyDrawer component
- The main app component

Let's walk through each of these individually, starting with MyToolbar:

```
const MyToolbar = withStyles(styles)(
  ({ classes, title, onMenuClick }) => (
    <Fragment>
      <AppBar>
        <Toolbar>
          <IconButton
            className={classes.menuButton}
            color="inherit"
            aria-label="Menu"
            onClick={onMenuClick}
          >
            <MenuIcon />
          </IconButton>
          <Typography
            variant="title"
            color="inherit"
            className={classes.flex}
          >
```

```
                {title}
              </Typography>
            </Toolbar>
          </AppBar>
          <div className={classes.toolbarMargin} />
        </Fragment>
    )
  );
```

The MyToolbar component renders an AppBar component that accepts a title property and a onMenuClick() property. Both of these properties are used to interact with the MyDrawer component. The title property changes when a drawer item selection is made. The onMenuClick() function changes state in your main app component, causing the drawer to display. Next, let's take a look at MyDrawer:

```
const MyDrawer = withStyles(styles)(
  ({ classes, variant, open, onClose, setTitle }) => (
    <Drawer variant={variant} open={open} onClose={onClose}>
      <List>
        <ListItem
          button
          onClick={() => {
            setTitle('Home');
            onClose();
          }}
        >
          <ListItemText>Home</ListItemText>
        </ListItem>
        <ListItem
          button
          onClick={() => {
            setTitle('Page 2');
            onClose();
          }}
        >
          <ListItemText>Page 2</ListItemText>
        </ListItem>
        <ListItem
          button
          onClick={() => {
            setTitle('Page 3');
            onClose();
          }}
        >
          <ListItemText>Page 3</ListItemText>
        </ListItem>
      </List>
```

```
      </Drawer>
    )
  );
```

The `MyDrawer` component is functional like `MyToolbar`. It accepts properties instead of maintaining its own state. For example, the `open` property is how the visibility of the drawer is controlled. The `onClose()` and `setTitle()` properties are functions that are called when drawer items are clicked on.

Finally, let's look at the app component where all of the state lives:

```
function AppBarInteraction({ classes }) {
  const [drawer, setDrawer] = useState(false);
  const [title, setTitle] = useState('Home');

  const toggleDrawer = () => {
    setDrawer(!drawer);
  };

  return (
    <div className={classes.root}>
      <MyToolbar title={title} onMenuClick={toggleDrawer} />
      <MyDrawer
        open={drawer}
        onClose={toggleDrawer}
        setTitle={setTitle}
      />
    </div>
  );
}
```

The `title` state is passed to the `MyDrawer` component, along with the `toggleDrawer()` function. The `MyDrawer` component is passed the drawer state to control visibility, the `toggleDrawer()` function to change visibility, and the `setTitle()` function to update the title in `MyToolbar`.

There's more...

What if you want the flexibility of having a persistent drawer that can be toggled using the same menu button in the App bar? Let's add a `variant` property to the `AppBarInteraction` component that is passed to `MyDrawer`. This can be changed from `temporary` to `persistent` and the menu button will still work as expected.

Here's what a persistent drawer looks like when you click on the menu button:

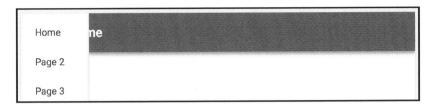

The drawer overlaps the App bar. Another problem is that if you click on any of the drawer items, the drawer is closed, which isn't ideal for a persistent drawer. Let's fix both of these issues.

First, let's address the `z-index` issue that's causing the drawer to appear on top of the App bar. You can create a CSS class that looks like this:

```
aboveDrawer: {
  zIndex: theme.zIndex.drawer + 1
}
```

You can apply this class to the `AppBar` component in `MyToolbar`, as follows:

```
<AppBar className={classes.aboveDrawer}>
```

Now when you open the drawer, it appears underneath the `AppBar`, as expected:

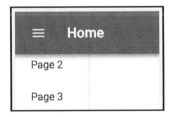

Now you just have to fix the margin. When the drawer uses the `persistent` variant, you can add the `toolbarMargin` class to a `<div>` element as the first element in the `Drawer` component:

```
<div
  className={clsx({
    [classes.toolbarMargin]: variant === 'persistent'
  })}
/>
```

With the help of the `clsx()` function, the `toolbarMargin` class is only added when needed – that is, when the drawer is persistent. Here's what it looks like now:

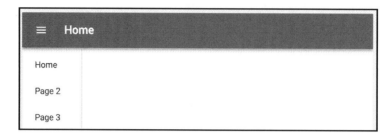

Lastly, let's fix the issue where the drawer closes when a drawer item is clicked on. In the main app component, you can add a new method that looks like the following code block:

```
const onItemClick = title => () => {
  setTitle(title);
  setDrawer(variant === 'temporary' ? false : drawer);
};
```

The `onItemClick()` function takes care of setting the text in the App bar, as well as closing the drawer if it's temporary. To use this new function, you can replace the `setTitle` property in `MyDrawer` with an `onItemClick` property. You can then use it in your list items, as follows:

```
<List>
  <ListItem button onClick={onItemClick('Home')}>
    <ListItemText>Home</ListItemText>
  </ListItem>
  <ListItem button onClick={onItemClick('Page 2')}>
    <ListItemText>Page 2</ListItemText>
  </ListItem>
  <ListItem button onClick={onItemClick('Page 3')}>
    <ListItemText>Page 3</ListItemText>
  </ListItem>
</List>
```

Now when you click on items in the drawer when it's persistent, the drawer will stay open. The only way to close it is by clicking on the menu button beside the title in the App bar.

See also

- Drawer **demos:** https://material-ui.com/demos/drawers/
- AppBar **demos:** https://material-ui.com/demos/app-bar/
- Drawer **API documentation:** https://material-ui.com/api/drawer/
- AppBar **API documentation:** https://material-ui.com/api/app-bar/

4
Tabs - Grouping Content into Tab Sections

In this chapter, you'll learn about the following recipes:

- AppBar integration
- Tab alignment
- Rendering tabs based on state
- Abstracting tab content
- Tab navigation with routes

Introduction

The `Tabs` Material-UI component is used to organize content on your screen. The tabs are organized in a horizontal fashion and they should feel natural for your users. You can use tabs any time your screen has lots of content that could be split into different category sections.

AppBar integration

`AppBar` components can be used with the `Tabs` component. You can do this so that the tab buttons are rendered within an App Bar. This provides a container for your tab buttons—by default, there is nothing surrounding them.

How to do it...

Let's say that you have a `Tabs` component with three `Tab` buttons. Instead of rendering the tabs so that they look as though they're floating on the screen, you can wrap them in an `AppBar` component to give them a contained look and feel. Here's the code:

```
import React, { useState } from 'react';

import { withStyles } from '@material-ui/core/styles';
import AppBar from '@material-ui/core/AppBar';
import Tabs from '@material-ui/core/Tabs';
import Tab from '@material-ui/core/Tab';
import Typography from '@material-ui/core/Typography';

const styles = theme => ({
  root: {
    flexGrow: 1,
    backgroundColor: theme.palette.background.paper
  },
  tabContent: {
    padding: theme.spacing.unit * 2
  }
});

function AppBarIntegration({ classes }) {
  const [value, setValue] = useState(0);

  const onChange = (e, value) => {
    setValue(value);
  };

  return (
    <div className={classes.root}>
      <AppBar position="static">
        <Tabs value={value} onChange={onChange}>
          <Tab label="Item One" />
          <Tab label="Item Two" />
          <Tab label="Item Three" />
        </Tabs>
      </AppBar>
      {value === 0 && (
        <Typography component="div" className={classes.tabContent}>
          Item One
        </Typography>
      )}
      {value === 1 && (
        <Typography component="div" className={classes.tabContent}>
```

```
        Item Two
      </Typography>
    )}
    {value === 2 && (
      <Typography component="div" className={classes.tabContent}>
        Item Three
      </Typography>
    )}
    </div>
  );
}
```

```
export default withStyles(styles)(AppBarIntegration);
```

When the screen first loads, you'll see the following:

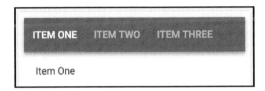

When you click on one of the tab buttons, the selected tab changes, along with the content underneath the tabs. For example, clicking on the **ITEM THREE** tab results in this:

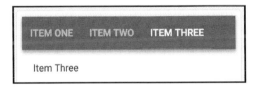

How it works...

The `Tabs` and `Tab` components are rendered inside the `AppBar` component. Usually, `AppBar` has a `Toolbar` component as its child, but `Tab` can work too:

```
<AppBar position="static">
  <Tabs value={value} onChange={onChange}>
    <Tab label="Item One" />
    <Tab label="Item Two" />
    <Tab label="Item Three" />
  </Tabs>
</AppBar>
```

Your component has a `value` state that is used to keep track of the selected tab. The `onChange()` handler is used to update this state; it gets set to the current index of the selected tab. Then, you can use the `value` state to determine which content to render below the `AppBar` component:

```
{value === 0 && (
  <Typography
    component="div"
    className={classes.tabContent}
  >
    Item One
  </Typography>
)}
{value === 1 && (
  <Typography
    component="div"
    className={classes.tabContent}
  >
    Item Two
  </Typography>
)}
{value === 2 && (
  <Typography
    component="div"
    className={classes.tabContent}
  >
    Item Three
  </Typography>
)}
```

If the first tab is selected, then the value is `0` and the `Item One` text is rendered. The same logic follows for the other two tabs.

There's more...

If you want tabs but you don't want the indicator that's rendered underneath the text, you can set it to be the same color as the `AppBar` component. This is done using the `indicatorColor` property, as follows:

```
<Tabs
  value={value}
  onChange={this.onChange}
  indicatorColor="primary"
>
  <Tab label="Item One" />
```

```
    <Tab label="Item Two" />
    <Tab label="Item Three" />
</Tabs>
```

By setting the `indicatorColor` value to `primary`, the indicator should now be the same color as the `AppBar` component:

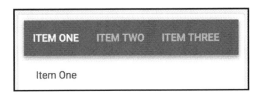

See also

- `Tabs` API documentation: `https://material-ui.com/api/tabs/`
- `Tabs` demos: `https://material-ui.com/demos/tabs/`

Tab alignment

The `Tabs` component has two properties to help you align your tab buttons. The `centered` property centers the tabs, while the `fullWidth` property spreads out the tabs.

How to do it...

Let's say that you have three basic tabs using the following code:

```
import React, { useState } from 'react';

import { withStyles } from '@material-ui/core/styles';
import Tabs from '@material-ui/core/Tabs';
import Tab from '@material-ui/core/Tab';

const styles = theme => ({
  root: {
    flexGrow: 1,
    backgroundColor: theme.palette.background.paper
  }
});
```

```
function TabAlignment({ classes }) {
  const [value, setValue] = useState(0);

  const onChange = (e, value) => {
    setValue(value);
  };

  return (
    <div className={classes.root}>
      <Tabs value={value} onChange={onChange}>
        <Tab label="Item One" />
        <Tab label="Item Two" />
        <Tab label="Item Three" />
      </Tabs>
    </div>
  );
}

export default withStyles(styles)(TabAlignment);
```

Here's what you should see when the screen first loads:

```
┌──────────────────────────────────────────────────────────┐
│                                                            │
│   ITEM ONE    ITEM TWO    ITEM THREE                       │
│   ───────────                                              │
└──────────────────────────────────────────────────────────┘
```

By default, tabs are aligned to the left. You can center your tabs by setting the `centered` property, as follows:

```
<Tabs value={value} onChange={onChange} centered>
  <Tab label="Item One" />
  <Tab label="Item Two" />
  <Tab label="Item Three" />
</Tabs>
```

Here's what centered tabs look like:

```
┌──────────────────────────────────────────────────────────┐
│                                                            │
│              ITEM ONE    ITEM TWO    ITEM THREE            │
│              ───────────                                   │
└──────────────────────────────────────────────────────────┘
```

When your tabs are centered, all of the empty space goes to the left and right of the tabs. The alternative is setting the `variant` property to `fullWidth`:

```
<Tabs value={value} onChange={onChange} variant="fullWidth">
  <Tab label="Item One" />
  <Tab label="Item Two" />
  <Tab label="Item Three" />
</Tabs>
```

Here's what full width tabs look like:

The tabs are centered, but they're spaced evenly to cover the width of the screen.

How it works...

The `centered` property is just a convenient way of specifying the `justifyContent` style on the `Tabs` component. Whenever there is a property to style Material-UI components in a specific way, you should use it instead of applying your own styles. Future versions of the library could include fixes that rely on the property that you'll miss out on.

Another reason to style components using the property is that Material-UI might behave differently depending on how other properties are set. For example, with the `Tabs` component, you can't set the `centered` property while the `scrollable` property is set to true; Material-UI checks for this and handles it.

The `fullWidth` value of the `variant` property is actually passed to the `Tab` component, which alters the styles it uses based on this value. The result is the even spacing of tabs within the container element.

You can set the `centered` and `variant` properties at the same time. However, `centered` isn't necessary if `variant` has a value of `fullWidth`. Using both is harmless though.

There's more...

The centered layout for tabs works well on smaller screens, while the full width layout looks good on larger screens. You can use Material-UI utilities that tell you about breakpoint changes. You can then use this information to change the alignment of your tabs.

Here's a modified version of this example:

```
import React, { useState } from 'react';
import compose from 'recompose/compose';

import { withStyles } from '@material-ui/core/styles';
import withWidth from '@material-ui/core/withWidth';
import Tabs from '@material-ui/core/Tabs';
import Tab from '@material-ui/core/Tab';

const styles = theme => ({
  root: {
    flexGrow: 1,
    backgroundColor: theme.palette.background.paper
  }
});

function TabAlignment({ classes, width }) {
  const [value, setValue] = useState(0);

  const onChange = (e, value) => {
    setValue(value);
  };

  return (
    <div className={classes.root}>
      <Tabs
        value={value}
        onChange={onChange}
        variant={['xs', 'sm'].includes(width) ? null : 'fullWidth'}
        centered
      >
        <Tab label="Item One" />
        <Tab label="Item Two" />
        <Tab label="Item Three" />
      </Tabs>
    </div>
  );
}
```

```
export default compose(
  withWidth(),
  withStyles(styles)
)(TabAlignment);
```

Now when you resize your screen, the alignment properties of the grid can change in response to breakpoint changes. Let's break down these changes from the bottom up, starting with the `variant` property value:

```
variant={['xs', 'sm'].includes(width) ? null : 'fullWidth'}
```

The value will be `fullWidth` if the `width` property is anything but the xs or sm breakpoint. In other words, if it's a larger screen, the value will be `fullWidth`.

Next, you need the width property to be passed to your component somehow. You can use the `withWidth()` utility from Material-UI. It works like `withStyles()` in that it returns a new component with new properties assigned to it. The component returned by `withWidth()` will update its `width` prop any time the breakpoint changes. For example, if the user resizes their screen from sm to md, this will trigger a width change and `fullWidth` will change from false to true.

To use the `withWidth()` component—along with the `withStyles()` component—you can use the `compose()` function from `recompose`. This function makes your code more readable when you're applying several higher-order functions that decorate your component:

```
export default compose(
  withWidth(),
  withStyles(styles)
)(TabAlignment);
```

You could call `withWidth(withStyles(styles))(TabAlignment)` if you really don't want to use `recompose`, but as a general rule, I like to use it any time more than one higher-order function is involved.

See also

- `Tabs` demos: https://material-ui.com/demos/tabs/
- `Tabs` API documentation: https://material-ui.com/api/tabs/
- **Tools for composing React components:** https://github.com/acdlite/recompose/

Rendering tabs based on state

Tabs in your React application might be driven by data. If so, you can set tab data in the state of your component to have them render initially and update if anything changes.

How to do it...

Let's say that you have some data that determines the tabs to render in your app. You can set this data in the state of your component and use it to render the `Tab` components, as well as the tab content when tab selections are made. Here's the code:

```
import React, { useState } from 'react';

import { makeStyles } from '@material-ui/styles';
import Tabs from '@material-ui/core/Tabs';
import Tab from '@material-ui/core/Tab';
import Typography from '@material-ui/core/Typography';

const useStyles = makeStyles(theme => ({
  root: {
    flexGrow: 1,
    backgroundColor: theme.palette.background.paper
  },
  tabContent: {
    padding: theme.spacing(2)
  }
}));

export default function RenderingTabsBasedOnState() {
  const classes = useStyles();
  const [tabs, setTabs] = useState([
    {
      active: true,
      label: 'Item One',
      content: 'Item One Content'
    },
    {
      active: false,
      label: 'Item Two',
      content: 'Item Two Content'
    },
    {
      active: false,
      label: 'Item Three',
      content: 'Item Three Content'
```

```
    }
  ]);

  const onChange = (e, value) => {
    setTabs(
      tabs
        .map(tab => ({ ...tab, active: false }))
        .map((tab, index) => ({
          ...tab,
          active: index === value
        }))
    );
  };

  const active = tabs.findIndex(tab => tab.active);
  const content = tabs[active].content;

  return (
    <div className={classes.root}>
      <Tabs value={active} onChange={onChange}>
        {tabs
          .map(tab => (
            <Tab
              key={tab.label}
              label={tab.label}
            />
          ))}
      </Tabs>
      <Typography component="div" className={classes.tabContent}>
        {content}
      </Typography>
    </div>
  );
}
```

When you first load the screen, you'll see the following:

If you click on the **ITEM TWO** tab, here's what you'll see:

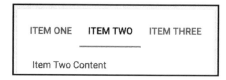

How it works...

Let's start by looking at the state of your component that drives the tabs that are rendered:

```
const [tabs, setTabs] = useState([
  {
    active: true,
    label: 'Item One',
    content: 'Item One Content'
  },
  {
    active: false,
    label: 'Item Two',
    content: 'Item Two Content'
  },
  {
    active: false,
    label: 'Item Three',
    content: 'Item Three Content'
  }
]);
```

The tabs state is an array, and each object within it represents a tab to be rendered. The active Boolean property determines which tab is active. The label property is what is rendered as the actual tab button and the content is rendered below the tabs when the tab is clicked on.

Next, let's take a look at the markup used to render the tabs and the content:

```
<Tabs value={active} onChange={onChange}>
  {tabs.map(tab => <Tab label={tab.label} />)}
</Tabs>
<Typography component="div" className={classes.tabContent}>
  {content}
</Typography>
```

Instead of manually rendering `Tab` components, you're iterating over the `tabs` state to render each tab. For the selected content, you now only have to render one `Typography` component that references `content`.

Let's take a look at the two `active` and `content` values, as follows:

```
const active = tabs.findIndex(tab => tab.active);
const content = tabs[active].content;
```

The `active` constant is the index of the active tab. This value is passed to the `value` property of the `Tabs` component. It's also used by the `content` value—the content of the active tab. Both of these constants simplify the markup that your component needs to render.

There's more...

Now that you're controlling your tabs with `state`, you can control more aspects of your rendered tabs. For instance, you could add `disabled` and `hidden` states to each tab. You could also place an `icon` property to render in your tab state. Here's a new version of the `tabs` state:

```
const [tabs, setTabs] = useState([
  {
    active: true,
    label: 'Home',
    content: 'Home Content',
    icon: <HomeIcon />
  },
  {
    active: false,
    label: 'Settings',
    content: 'Settings Content',
    icon: <SettingsIcon />
  },
  {
    active: false,
    disabled: true,
    label: 'Search',
    content: 'Search Content',
    icon: <SearchIcon />
  },
  {
    active: false,
    hidden: true,
    label: 'Add',
```

```
      content: 'AddContent',
      icon: <AddIcon />
    }
  ]);
```

Now you have the ability to render `disabled` tabs that cannot be clicked on—as is the case with the **SEARCH** tab. You can also hide tabs completely by setting `hidden` to `true`—as is the case with the **Add** tab. Every tab now has an icon as well. Let's see what this looks like when you load the screen:

The icons for every tab are rendered as expected, even for the **SEARCH** tab, which has been marked as `disabled`. There's no **Add** tab because it was marked as `hidden`. Let's take a look at the changes to the `Tabs` markup that were necessary to accommodate these new state values:

```
<Tabs value={active} onChange={onChange}>
  {tabs
    .filter(tab => !tab.hidden)
    .map(tab => (
      <Tab
        key={tab.label}
        disabled={tab.disabled}
        icon={tab.icon}
        label={tab.label}
      />
    ))}
</Tabs>
```

The `disabled` and `icon` properties of `Tab` are passed directly from the tab in your component state. The `filter()` call was added to remove tabs that are marked as hidden.

See also

- `Tabs` API documentation: `https://material-ui.com/api/tabs/`
- `Tabs` demos: `https://material-ui.com/demos/tabs/`

Abstracting tab content

If your application uses tabs in several places, you can create abstractions that simplify the markup involved with rendering tabs and tab content. Instead of having tab content defined outside of the tabs component, why not have everything be self-contained and easier to read?

How to do it...

Let's say that your app uses tabs in several places throughout your app, and you want to simplify the markup used to create the tabs and the tab content. In the places where you use tabs, you just want to be able to render the content and not have to worry about handing state for the active tab. Here's some code that creates two new components that simplify the **JavaScript XML (JSX)** required for rendering tab content:

```
import React, { Fragment, Children, useState } from 'react';

import { withStyles } from '@material-ui/core/styles';
import Tabs from '@material-ui/core/Tabs';
import Tab from '@material-ui/core/Tab';
import Typography from '@material-ui/core/Typography';

const styles = theme => ({
  root: {
    flexGrow: 1,
    backgroundColor: theme.palette.background.paper
  },
  tabContent: {
    padding: theme.spacing(2)
  }
});

function TabContainer({ children }) {
  const [value, setValue] = useState(0);

  const onChange = (e, value) => {
    setValue(value);
  };

  return (
    <Fragment>
      <Tabs value={value} onChange={onChange}>
        {Children.map(children, child => (
          <Tab label={child.props.label} />
        ))}
```

```
        </Tabs>
        {Children.map(children, (child, index) =>
          index === value ? child : null
        )}
      </Fragment>
    );
}

const TabContent = withStyles(styles)(({ classes, children }) => (
    <Typography component="div" className={classes.tabContent}>
      {children}
    </Typography>
));

const AbstractingTabContent = withStyles(styles)(({ classes }) => (
    <div className={classes.root}>
      <TabContainer>
        <TabContent label="Item One">Item One Content</TabContent>
        <TabContent label="Item Two">Item Two Content</TabContent>
        <TabContent label="Item Three">Item Three Content</TabContent>
      </TabContainer>
    </div>
));

export default AbstractingTabContent;
```

When you load the screen, you'll see three tabs rendered with the first tab selected by default. The content of the first tab is also visible. The following screenshot shows what it looks like:

How it works...

Let's start by looking at the markup used to render the tabs in this following example:

```
<TabContainer>
  <TabContent label="Item One">Item One Content</TabContent>
  <TabContent label="Item Two">Item Two Content</TabContent>
  <TabContent label="Item Three">Item Three Content</TabContent>
</TabContainer>
```

This markup is much more concise than using the `Tab` and `Tabs` components directly. This approach also handles rendering the content of the selected tab. Everything is self-contained with this approach.

Next, let's take a look at the `TabContainer` component:

```
function TabContainer({ children }) {
  const [value, setValue] = useState(0);

  const onChange = (e, value) => {
    setValue(value);
  };

  return (
    <Fragment>
      <Tabs value={value} onChange={onChange}>
        {Children.map(children, child => (
          <Tab label={child.props.label} />
        ))}
      </Tabs>
      {Children.map(children, (child, index) =>
        index === value ? child : null
      )}
    </Fragment>
  );
}
```

The `TabContainer` component handles the state of the selected tab and changing the state when a different tab is selected. This component renders a `Fragment` component so that it can place the selected tab content after the `Tabs` component. It's using `Children.map()` to render the individual `Tab` components. The label of the tab comes from the `label` property of the child. In this example, there are three children (`TabContent`). The next call to `Children.map()` renders the content of the selected tab. This is based on the `value` state—if the child index matches, it's the `active` content. Otherwise, it gets mapped to `null` and nothing is rendered.

Lastly, let's take a look at the `TabContent` component:

```
const TabContent = withStyles(styles)(({ classes, children }) => (
  <Typography component="div" className={classes.tabContent}>
    {children}
  </Typography>
));
```

`TabContent` takes care of styling the `Typography` component and renders the child text within. Although the `label` property is passed to `TabContent`, it doesn't actually use it; instead, it's used by `TabContainer` when rendering tabs.

There's more...

You can add a `value` property to the `TabsContainer` component so that you can set whichever tab to activate initially. For example, you might want the second tab to be `active` instead of the first tab when the screen first loads. To do this, you'll have to add a default property value for `value`, call `setValue()` if the `value` state hasn't been set yet, and remove `value` from the initial state:

```
function TabContainer({ children, value: valueProp }) {
  const [value, setValue] = useState();

  const onChange = (e, value) => {
    setValue(value);
  };

  if (value === undefined) {
    setValue(valueProp);
  }

  return (
    <Fragment>
      <Tabs value={value} onChange={onChange}>
        {Children.map(children, child => (
          <Tab label={child.props.label} />
        ))}
      </Tabs>
      {Children.map(children, (child, index) =>
        index === value ? child : null
      )}
    </Fragment>
  );
}

TabContainer.defaultProps = {
  value: 0
};
```

The default property is necessary because the `value` state is now undefined by default. The `setValue()` method is called if the `value` state is undefined. If it is, then you can set it by passing it the `value` property value.

Now, you can pass this property to your component to change the initially-active tab:

```
<TabContainer value={1}>
  <TabContent label="Item One">Item One Content</TabContent>
  <TabContent label="Item Two">Item Two Content</TabContent>
  <TabContent label="Item Three">Item Three Content</TabContent>
</TabContainer>
```

The value property is set to 1. It's a zero-based index, which means that the second tab will be active by default:

When the user starts clicking on other tabs, the `value` state updates as expected—only the initially-active tab is impacted by this change.

See also

- `Tabs` API documentation: https://material-ui.com/api/tabs/
- `Tabs` demos: https://material-ui.com/demos/tab/
- Working with React child components: https://reactjs.org/docs/react-api.html#reactchildren

Tab navigation with routes

You can base your tab content on routes in a routing solution, such as `react-router`. To do this, you have to make your tab buttons into links, and you need to have `Route` components below the `Tabs` component to render the current URL.

How to do it...

Let's say that your app has three URLs and you want tabs as the navigation mechanism to navigate between the routes. The first step is turning the `Tab` buttons into links. The second step is having `Route` components render the appropriate tab content, based on which one was clicked on. Here's the code:

```
import React, { useState } from 'react';
import { Route, Link } from 'react-router-dom';

import { withStyles } from '@material-ui/core/styles';
import AppBar from '@material-ui/core/AppBar';
import Tabs from '@material-ui/core/Tabs';
import Tab from '@material-ui/core/Tab';
import Typography from '@material-ui/core/Typography';

const styles = theme => ({
  root: {
    flexGrow: 1,
    backgroundColor: theme.palette.background.paper
  },
  tabContent: {
    padding: theme.spacing(2)
  }
});

function TabNavigationWithRoutes({ classes }) {
  const [value, setValue] = useState(0);

  const onChange = (e, value) => {
    setValue(value);
  };

  return (
    <div className={classes.root}>
      <AppBar position="static">
        <Tabs value={value} onChange={onChange}>
          <Tab label="Item One" component={Link} to="/" />
          <Tab label="Item Two" component={Link} to="/page2" />
          <Tab label="Item Three" component={Link} to="/page3" />
        </Tabs>
      </AppBar>
      <Route
        exact
        path="/"
        render={() => (
          <Typography component="div" className={classes.tabContent}>
```

```
            Item One
          </Typography>
        )}
    />
    <Route
      exact
      path="/page2"
      render={() => (
        <Typography component="div" className={classes.tabContent}>
          Item Two
        </Typography>
      )}
    />
    <Route
      exact
      path="/page3"
      render={() => (
        <Typography component="div" className={classes.tabContent}>
          Item Three
        </Typography>
      )}
    />
  </div>
);
}

export default withStyles(styles)(TabNavigationWithRoutes);
```

When you load the screen, the first tab should be selected and the first tab content should be rendered:

If you click on the **ITEM TWO** tab, you'll be taken to the /page2 URL. This results in the active Route component changing the tab content, and the changed tab state changes the selected tab:

How it works...

The state portion of your component remains the same as any other component that uses the Tabs component. The onChange event changes the value state, which is passed to Tabs as a property to mark the selected tab.

Let's take a closer look at the Tab components:

```
<Tabs value={value} onChange={onChange}>
  <Tab label="Item One" component={Link} to="/" />
  <Tab label="Item Two" component={Link} to="/page2" />
  <Tab label="Item Three" component={Link} to="/page3" />
</Tabs>
```

A major difference with this implementation compared to something more standard is that you're using Link as the component property value. The Link component, from react-router-dom, is used to make the tab button into a link that the router will process. The to property is actually passed to Link, which is how it knows where the link should take the user.

Below the Tabs component are the routes that render the tab content, based on the tab that the user has clicked on. Let's take a look at one of these Routes:

```
<Route
  exact
  path="/"
  render={() => (
    <Typography
      component="div"
      className={classes.tabContent}
    >
      Item One
    </Typography>
  )}
/>
```

The content that is rendered below the tab is based on the current URL, not the value state of your component. The value state is only used to control the state of the selected tab.

There's more...

Given that the active tab depends on the active route, you could completely remove any tab-related state. First, you create a TabContainer component to render the Tabs component:

```
const TabContainer = ({ value }) => (
  <AppBar position="static">
    <Tabs value={value}>
      <Tab label="Item One" component={Link} to="/" />
      <Tab label="Item Two" component={Link} to="/page2" />
      <Tab label="Item Three" component={Link} to="/page3" />
    </Tabs>
  </AppBar>
);
```

Instead of supplying an onChange() handler to the Tabs component, the value property is passed from TabContainer. Now, you can render this component in each Route component, passing the appropriate value property:

```
const TabNavigationWithRoutes = withStyles(styles)(({ classes }) => (
  <div className={classes.root}>
    <Route
      exact
      path="/"
      render={() => (
        <Fragment>
          <TabContainer value={0} />
          <Typography component="div" className={classes.tabContent}>
            Item One
          </Typography>
        </Fragment>
      )}
    />
    <Route
      exact
      path="/page2"
      render={() => (
        <Fragment>
          <TabContainer value={1} />
          <Typography component="div" className={classes.tabContent}>
            Item Two
          </Typography>
        </Fragment>
      )}
    />
    <Route
```

```
      exact
      path="/page3"
      render={() => (
        <Fragment>
          <TabContainer value={2} />
          <Typography component="div" className={classes.tabContent}>
            Item Three
          </Typography>
        </Fragment>
      )}
    />
  </div>
));

export default TabNavigationWithRoutes;
```

There's no more confusing the component state with the current `Route` and how the two interact. Everything is handled by the route.

See also

- Tabs API documentation: https://material-ui.com/api/tabs/
- Tabs demos: https://material-ui.com/demos/tabs/
- React Router documentation: https://reacttraining.com/react-router/

5

Expansion Panels - Group Content into Panel Sections

In this chapter, you'll learn about the following:

- Stateful expansion panels
- Formatting panel headers
- Scrollable panel content
- Lazy loading panel content

Introduction

Expansion panels are containers for your content. Usually, screens in your Material-UI applications are divided into sections so that users can mentally organize the information that they're looking at. The `ExpansionPanel` component is one way that you can create these sections. You can even combine expansion panels with other organizational components, such as tabs, to provide a consistent organizational layout for your users.

Stateful expansion panels

You can use component the state to control every aspect of your expansion panels. For example, each panel could be represented as an object in an array, where each object has panel title and panel content properties. There are other aspects you can control, such as visibility and disabled panels.

How to do it...

Let's say that your component has a state for rendering expansion panels. The panels themselves are objects in an array. Here's the code to do this:

```
import React, { useState, Fragment } from 'react';

import ExpansionPanel from '@material-ui/core/ExpansionPanel';
import ExpansionPanelSummary from '@material-
ui/core/ExpansionPanelSummary';
import ExpansionPanelDetails from '@material-
ui/core/ExpansionPanelDetails';
import Typography from '@material-ui/core/Typography';
import ExpandMoreIcon from '@material-ui/icons/ExpandMore';

export default function StatefulExpansionPanels() {
  const [panels] = useState([
    {
      title: 'First Panel Title',
      content: 'First panel content...'
    },
    {
      title: 'Second Panel Title',
      content: 'Second panel content...'
    },
    {
      title: 'Third Panel Title',
      content: 'Third panel content...'
    },
    {
      title: 'Fourth Panel Title',
      content: 'Fourth panel content...'
    }
  ]);

  return (
    <Fragment>
      {panels
        .filter(panel => !panel.hidden)
        .map((panel, index) => (
          <ExpansionPanel
            key={index}
            disabled={panel.disabled}
          >
            <ExpansionPanelSummary expandIcon={<ExpandMoreIcon />}>
              <Typography>{panel.title}</Typography>
            </ExpansionPanelSummary>
            <ExpansionPanelDetails>
```

```
            <Typography>{panel.content}</Typography>
          </ExpansionPanelDetails>
        </ExpansionPanel>
      ))}
    </Fragment>
  );
}
```

When you load the screen, here's what you'll see:

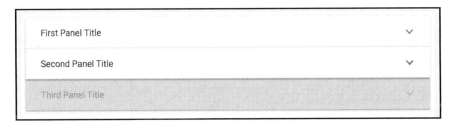

Here's what the first two panels look like when they're expanded:

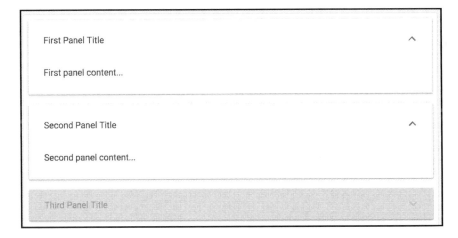

The third panel cannot be expanded because it's disabled.

How it works...

The state defines everything about expansion panels. This includes the panel `title`, the panel `content` that's displayed when the panel is expanded, the `disabled` property, and whether or not the panel is `hidden`:

```
const [panels] = useState([
  {
    title: 'First Panel Title',
    content: 'First panel content...'
  },
  {
    title: 'Second Panel Title',
    content: 'Second panel content...'
  },
  {
    title: 'Third Panel Title',
    content: 'Third panel content...'
  },
  {
    title: 'Fourth Panel Title',
    content: 'Fourth panel content...'
  }
]);
```

The `disabled` property marks the panel as disabled. This means that the user can see the panel `title`, but it cannot be expanded. It's also visually marked as not being expandable. The `hidden` property ensures that the panel isn't rendered at all. This is useful for cases when you don't want the user to know about it at all.

Next, let's look at the code that renders each panel based on the component state:

```
{panels
  .filter(panel => !panel.hidden)
  .map((panel, index) => (

    }>
      {panel.title}


      {panel.content}


  ))}
```

The `filter()` call removes panels from the array that have the `hidden` property set to true.

An alternative to using a `hidden` property to hide panels is removing them completely from the array. It really depends on personal preference—toggling a property value versus adding and removing values from an array.

Each panel is mapped to `ExpansionPanel` components using `map()`. The expansion panel uses an `ExpansionPanelSummary` component for the title and the content goes into the `ExpansionPanelDetails` component.

There's more...

You can also use state to control whether or not a panel is expanded. For example, you can use `ExpansionPanel` components to create an *accordion* widget—there's always one panel open, and opening another panel closes anything that's open.

The first step is to add an `expanded` state to determine which panel is open at any given time:

```
const [expanded, setExpanded] = useState(0);
const [panels] = useState([
  {
    title: 'First Panel Title',
    content: 'First panel content...'
  },
  {
    title: 'Second Panel Title',
    content: 'Second panel content...'
  },
  {
    title: 'Third Panel Title',
    content: 'Third panel content...'
  },
  {
    title: 'Fourth Panel Title',
    content: 'Fourth panel content...'
  }
]);
```

The expanded state defaults to 0, meaning that the first panel is expanded by default. As the expanded panels change, the expanded state changes to reflect the index of the expanded panel. Next, you'll add an onChange handler for the ExpansionPanel component:

```
const onChange = expanded => () => {
  setExpanded(expanded);
};
```

This is a higher-order function—it takes the index of the panel you want to expand and returns a function that sets the expanded state when the given panel is clicked on. Finally, you can add the new expanded state and the onChange handler to the ExpansionPanel component:

```
<ExpansionPanel
  key={index}
  expanded={index === expanded}
  disabled={panel.disabled}
  onChange={onChange(index)}
>
  <ExpansionPanelSummary expandIcon={<ExpandMoreIcon />}>
    <Typography>{panel.title}</Typography>
  </ExpansionPanelSummary>
  <ExpansionPanelDetails>
    <Typography>{panel.content}</Typography>
  </ExpansionPanelDetails>
</ExpansionPanel>
```

The expanded property is based on the index of the current panel, equaling the expanded state of your component. If they're equal, the panel is expanded. The onChange handler is also assigned to ExpansionPanel, which changes the expanded state when the panel is clicked on.

See also

- ExpansionPanel **demos:** https://material-ui.com/demos/expansion-panels/
- ExpansionPanel **API documentation:** https://material-ui.com/api/expansion-panel/
- ExpansionPanelSummary **API documentation:** https://material-ui.com/api/expansion-panel-summary/
- ExpansionPanelDetails **API documentation:** https://material-ui.com/api/expansion-panel-details/

Formatting panel headers

Headers in ExpansionPanel components can be formatted. Typically, the Typography component is used to render text within an expansion panel header. This means that you can use properties of Typography to customize the way that your expansion panel headers appear.

How to do it...

Let's say that you want the text within your ExpansionPanel headers to stand out relative to the text in the content section of each panel. You can change the variant property of the Typography component in the ExpansionPanelSummary component. Here's the code to do it:

```
import React, { Fragment } from 'react';

import ExpansionPanel from '@material-ui/core/ExpansionPanel';
import ExpansionPanelSummary from '@material-
ui/core/ExpansionPanelSummary';
import ExpansionPanelDetails from '@material-
ui/core/ExpansionPanelDetails';
import Typography from '@material-ui/core/Typography';

import ExpandMoreIcon from '@material-ui/icons/ExpandMore';

const FormattingPanelHeaders = () => (
  <Fragment>
    <ExpansionPanel>
      <ExpansionPanelSummary expandIcon={<ExpandMoreIcon />}>
        <Typography variant="subtitle1">Devices</Typography>
      </ExpansionPanelSummary>
      <ExpansionPanelDetails>
        <Typography>Devices content...</Typography>
      </ExpansionPanelDetails>
    </ExpansionPanel>
    <ExpansionPanel>
      <ExpansionPanelSummary expandIcon={<ExpandMoreIcon />}>
        <Typography variant="subtitle1">Networks</Typography>
      </ExpansionPanelSummary>
      <ExpansionPanelDetails>
        <Typography>Networks content...</Typography>
      </ExpansionPanelDetails>
    </ExpansionPanel>
    <ExpansionPanel>
      <ExpansionPanelSummary expandIcon={<ExpandMoreIcon />}>
```

```
        <Typography variant="subtitle1">Storage</Typography>
      </ExpansionPanelSummary>
      <ExpansionPanelDetails>
        <Typography>Storage content...</Typography>
      </ExpansionPanelDetails>
    </ExpansionPanel>
  </Fragment>
);

export default FormattingPanelHeaders;
```

Here's what the panels look like when the screen loads:

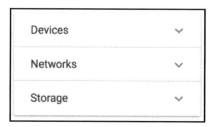

Here's what the panels look like when they're expanded:

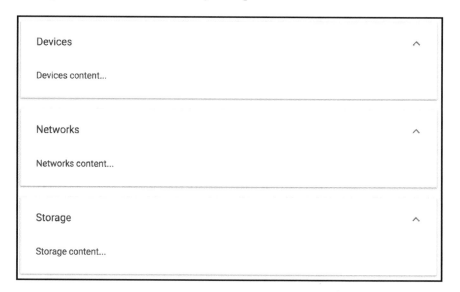

How it works...

To make the heading text stand out relative to the text in the `ExpansionPanelDetails` component, you only had to change the `variant` property of the `Typography` component used in the header. In this case, you're using the `subtitle1` variant, but there are a number of other variants that you can use here.

There's more...

In addition to formatting header text, you can add other components, such as icons. Let's modify the example to include icons for each panel header. First, you'll import the icons that you need:

```
import DevicesIcon from 'material-ui/icons/Devices';
import NetworkWifiIcon from 'material-ui/icons/NetworkWifi';
import StorageIcon from '@material-ui/icons/Storage';
```

Then, you'll add a new icon style that adds space between the icon and text in the panel header:

```
const styles = theme => ({
  icon: {
    marginRight: theme.spacing(1)
  }
});
```

Lastly, here's the markup to include the icons that you've imported in the appropriate panel header:

```
<Fragment>
  <ExpansionPanel>
    <ExpansionPanelSummary expandIcon={<ExpandMoreIcon />}>
      <DevicesIcon className={classes.icon} />
      <Typography variant="subtitle1">Devices</Typography>
    </ExpansionPanelSummary>
    <ExpansionPanelDetails>
      <Typography>Devices content...</Typography>
    </ExpansionPanelDetails>
  </ExpansionPanel>
  <ExpansionPanel>
    <ExpansionPanelSummary expandIcon={<ExpandMoreIcon />}>
      <NetworkWifiIcon className={classes.icon} />
      <Typography variant="subtitle1">Networks</Typography>
    </ExpansionPanelSummary>
```

```
      <ExpansionPanelDetails>
        <Typography>Networks content...</Typography>
      </ExpansionPanelDetails>
    </ExpansionPanel>
    <ExpansionPanel>
      <ExpansionPanelSummary expandIcon={<ExpandMoreIcon />}>
        <StorageIcon className={classes.icon} />
        <Typography variant="subtitle1">Storage</Typography>
      </ExpansionPanelSummary>
      <ExpansionPanelDetails>
        <Typography>Storage content...</Typography>
      </ExpansionPanelDetails>
    </ExpansionPanel>
  </Fragment>
```

The icon comes before the `Typography` component in the `ExpansionPanelSummary` component. Here's what the panels look like now:

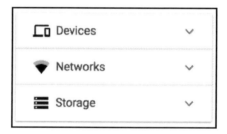

Here's what they look like when they're expanded:

By combining iconography and typography, you can make the headers of your expansion panels stand out, making your content easier to navigate.

See also

- ExpansionPanel **demos:** https://material-ui.com/demos/expansion-panels/
- ExpansionPanel **API documentation:** https://material-ui.com/api/expansion-panel/
- ExpansionPanelSummary **API documentation:** https://material-ui.com/api/expansion-panel-summary/
- ExpansionPanelDetails **API documentation:** https://material-ui.com/api/expansion-panel-details/

Scrollable panel content

The height of an ExpansionPanel component, when expanded, changes so that all of the content is visible on the screen. In cases where you have a lot of content in your panels, this isn't ideal because the panel headers aren't visible to the user. Instead of having to scroll down the entire page, you can make the content within the panel scrollable.

How to do it...

Let's say that you have three panels, each with several paragraphs of text. Rather than having each panel adjust its height to accommodate the content, you can make the panels a fixed height and scrollable. Here's the code:

```
import React, { Fragment } from 'react';

import { withStyles } from '@material-ui/core/styles';
import ExpansionPanel from '@material-ui/core/ExpansionPanel';
import ExpansionPanelSummary from '@material-
ui/core/ExpansionPanelSummary';
import ExpansionPanelDetails from '@material-
ui/core/ExpansionPanelDetails';
import Typography from '@material-ui/core/Typography';

import ExpandMoreIcon from '@material-ui/icons/ExpandMore';

const styles = theme => ({
```

```
    panelDetails: {
      flexDirection: 'column',
      height: 150,
      overflow: 'auto'
    }
});

const IpsumContent = () => (
  <Fragment>
    <Typography paragraph>
      Lorem ipsum dolor sit amet, consectetur adipiscing elit. Integer
      ultricies nibh ut ipsum placerat, eget egestas leo imperdiet.
      Etiam consectetur mollis ultrices. Fusce eu eros a dui maximus
      rutrum. Aenean at dolor eu nunc ultricies placerat. Sed finibus
      porta sapien eget euismod. Donec eget tortor non turpis
      hendrerit euismod. Phasellus at commodo augue. Maecenas
      scelerisque augue at mattis pharetra. Aenean fermentum sed neque
      id feugiat.
    </Typography>

    <Typography paragraph>
      Aliquam erat volutpat. Donec sit amet venenatis leo. Nullam
      tincidunt diam in nisi pretium, sit amet tincidunt nisi aliquet.
      Proin quis justo consectetur, congue nisi nec, pharetra erat. Ut
      volutpat pulvinar neque vitae vestibulum. Phasellus nisl risus,
      dapibus at sapien in, aliquam tempus tellus. Integer accumsan
      tortor id dolor lacinia, et pulvinar est porttitor. Mauris a est
      vitae arcu iaculis dictum. Sed posuere suscipit ultricies.
      Vivamus a lacus in dui vehicula tincidunt.
    </Typography>

    <Typography paragraph>
      In ut velit laoreet, blandit nisi id, tempus mi. Mauris interdum
      in turpis vel tempor. Vivamus tincidunt turpis vitae porta
      dignissim. Quisque condimentum augue arcu, quis tincidunt erat
      luctus sit amet. Sed quis ligula malesuada, sollicitudin nisl
      nec, molestie tellus. Donec commodo consequat gravida. Mauris in
      rhoncus tellus, eget posuere risus. Pellentesque eget lectus
      lorem. Lorem ipsum dolor sit amet, consectetur adipiscing elit.
      Integer condimentum, sapien varius vulputate lobortis, urna elit
      vestibulum ligula, sit amet interdum lectus augue ac eros.
      Vestibulum lorem ante, tincidunt eget faucibus id, placerat non
      est. Vivamus pretium consectetur nunc at imperdiet. Nullam eu
      elit dui. In imperdiet magna ac dui aliquam gravida. Aenean
      ipsum ex, fermentum eu pretium quis, posuere et velit.
    </Typography>
  </Fragment>
);
```

```
const ScrollablePanelContent = withStyles(styles)(({ classes }) => (
  <Fragment>
    <ExpansionPanel>
      <ExpansionPanelSummary expandIcon={<ExpandMoreIcon />}>
        <Typography>First</Typography>
      </ExpansionPanelSummary>
      <ExpansionPanelDetails className={classes.panelDetails}>
        <IpsumContent />
      </ExpansionPanelDetails>
    </ExpansionPanel>
    <ExpansionPanel>
      <ExpansionPanelSummary expandIcon={<ExpandMoreIcon />}>
        <Typography>Second</Typography>
      </ExpansionPanelSummary>
      <ExpansionPanelDetails className={classes.panelDetails}>
        <IpsumContent />
      </ExpansionPanelDetails>
    </ExpansionPanel>
    <ExpansionPanel>
      <ExpansionPanelSummary expandIcon={<ExpandMoreIcon />}>
        <Typography>Third</Typography>
      </ExpansionPanelSummary>
      <ExpansionPanelDetails className={classes.panelDetails}>
        <IpsumContent />
      </ExpansionPanelDetails>
    </ExpansionPanel>
  </Fragment>
));

export default ScrollablePanelContent;
```

The paragraph content in the `Typography` components has been truncated for brevity—you can view the full text in the GitHub repository for this book.

Here's what it looks like when the first panel is expanded:

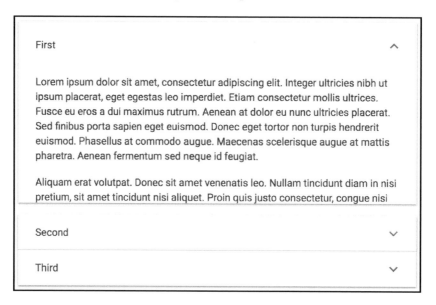

If you move your mouse pointer over the content of the expanded panel, you can now scroll the content to the bottom of the paragraph, within the panel. Here's what it looks like when the content has been scrolled to the bottom:

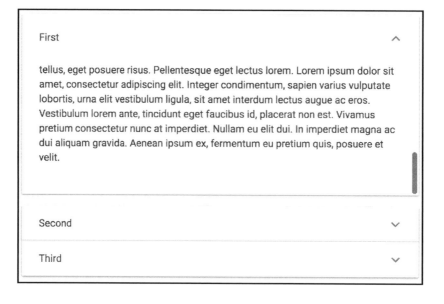

How it works...

The `IpsumContent` component is just a convenience component that holds paragraphs of content so that you don't have to repeat it in every panel. Let's start by looking at the styles used in this example:

```
const styles = theme => ({
  panelDetails: {
    flexDirection: 'column',
    height: 150,
    overflow: 'auto'
  }
});
```

Panel content uses flex box styles to lay out its content. It flows according to row direction by default, so you have to set the `flexDirection` style to `column` if you want the content to flow in a top-down direction. Next, you can set a fixed height for your panel content—in this case, it's `150px`. Finally, the `overflow` style set to `auto` will enable vertical scrolling for the panel content.

You can then apply the `panelDetails` class to each of your `ExpansionPanelContent` components:

```
<ExpansionPanelDetails className={classes.panelDetails}>
  <IpsumContent />
</ExpansionPanelDetails>
```

See also

- `ExpansionPanel` **demos:** https://material-ui.com/demos/expansion-panels/
- `ExpansionPanel` **API documentation:** https://material-ui.com/api/expansion-panel/
- `ExpansionPanelSummary` **API documentation:** https://material-ui.com/api/expansion-panel-summary/
- `ExpansionPanelDetails` **API documentation:** https://material-ui.com/api/expansion-panel-details/

Lazy loading panel content

If you're rendering expansion panels that are all collapsed by default, you don't have to populate the `ExpansionPanelDetails` component up front. Instead, you can wait for the user to expand the panel—then you can make whatever API calls you need in order to render the content.

How to do it...

Let's say that you have an API function that fetches content based on an index value. For example, if the first panel is expanded, the `index` value will be 0. You need to be able to call this function when the panel is expanded, supplying the corresponding `index` value. Here's what the code looks like:

```
import React, { useState, Fragment } from 'react';

import ExpansionPanel from '@material-ui/core/ExpansionPanel';
import ExpansionPanelSummary from '@material-
ui/core/ExpansionPanelSummary';
import ExpansionPanelDetails from '@material-
ui/core/ExpansionPanelDetails';
import Typography from '@material-ui/core/Typography';
import ExpandMoreIcon from '@material-ui/icons/ExpandMore';

const fetchPanelContent = index =>
  new Promise(resolve =>
    setTimeout(
      () =>
        resolve(
          [
            'First panel content...',
            'Second panel content...',
            'Third panel content...',
            'Fourth panel content...'
          ][index]
        ),
      1000
    )
  );

export default function LazyLoadingPanelContent() {
  const [panels, setPanels] = useState([
    { title: 'First Panel Title' },
    { title: 'Second Panel Title' },
    { title: 'Third Panel Title' },
```

```
        { title: 'Fourth Panel Title' }
    ]);

    const onChange = index => e => {
      if (!panels[index].content) {
        fetchPanelContent(index).then(content => {
          const newPanels = [...panels];
          newPanels[index] = { ...newPanels[index], content };
          setPanels(newPanels);
        });
      }
    };

    return (
      <Fragment>
        {panels.map((panel, index) => (
          <ExpansionPanel key={index} onChange={onChange(index)}>
            <ExpansionPanelSummary expandIcon={<ExpandMoreIcon />}>
              <Typography>{panel.title}</Typography>
            </ExpansionPanelSummary>
            <ExpansionPanelDetails>
              <Typography>{panel.content}</Typography>
            </ExpansionPanelDetails>
          </ExpansionPanel>
        ))}
      </Fragment>
    );
}
```

Here's what the four panels look like when the screen first loads:

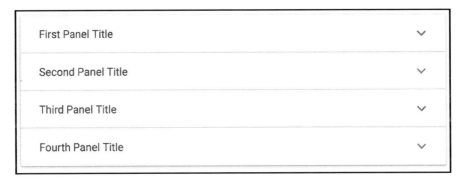

Try expanding the first panel. It expands right away but, for about one second, there's nothing there. Then the content appears:

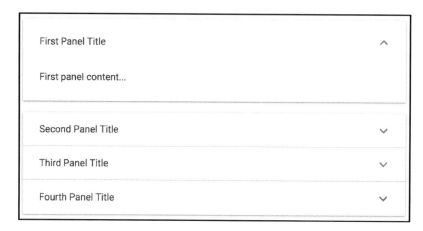

How it works...

Let's start with the fetchPanelContent() API function:

```
const fetchPanelContent = index =>
  new Promise(resolve =>
    setTimeout(
      () =>
        resolve(
          [
            'First panel content...',
            'Second panel content...',
            'Third panel content...',
            'Fourth panel content...'
          ][index]
        ),
      1000
    )
  );
```

Since this is just a mock, it returns a promise directly. It uses setTimeout() to simulate latency, similar to what you would experience using a real API. The promise resolves with the string value that's looked up from an array, based on the index argument.

Next, let's look at the `onChange` handler function that's called when `ExpansionPanel` expands:

```
const onChange = index => (e) => {
  if (!panels[index].content) {
    fetchPanelContent(index).then(content => {
      const newPanels = [...panels];
      newPanels[index] = { ...newPanels[index], content };
      setPanels(newPanels);
    });
  }
};
```

First, this function checks if the panel that's expanded has any `content` in its state. If not, you know that you have to fetch it by calling `fetchPanelContent()`. When the returned promise resolves, you can call `setPanels()` to update the panels array and set the content at the appropriate index.

The rest of your component just renders the `ExpansionPanel` components based on the panels array, using the `content` state as the panel content. When content is updated, it is reflected in the rendered content.

There's more...

There are a couple of improvements that you could make with this example. First, you could show a progress indicator within the panel while the content is loading so that the user knows that something is happening. The second improvement can be made both when the panel expands and when it collapses—this should be avoided.

Let's start with the progress indicator. For this, you'll need a utility component and a style for the `ExpansionPanelDetails` component:

```
const MaybeProgress = ({ loading }) =>
  loading ? <LinearProgress /> : null;

const useStyles = makeStyles(theme => ({
  panelDetails: { flexDirection: 'column' }
}));
```

The `MaybeProgress` component takes a `loading` property that, when true, results in a `LinearProgress` component. Otherwise, nothing is rendered. The `flexDirection` style is set to `column`; otherwise, the `LinearProgress` component won't display. Now let's modify the markup rendered by `LazyLoadingPanelContent` so it uses these two additions:

```
return (
  <Fragment>
    {panels.map((panel, index) => (
      <ExpansionPanel key={index} onChange={onChange(index)}>
        <ExpansionPanelSummary expandIcon={<ExpandMoreIcon />}>
          <Typography>{panel.title}</Typography>
        </ExpansionPanelSummary>
        <ExpansionPanelDetails className={classes.panelDetails}>
          <MaybeProgress loading={!panel.content} />
          <Typography>{panel.content}</Typography>
        </ExpansionPanelDetails>
      </ExpansionPanel>
    ))}
  </Fragment>
);
```

The `panelDetails` class is now used by the `ExpansionPanelDetails` component. The first child of this component is now `MaybeProgress`. The loading property is true until the API call populates the content state for the given panel. This means that the progress indicator will be visible until the content loads.

Here's what the first panel looks like when expanded, before the content has loaded:

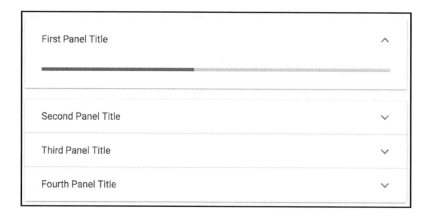

Once loaded, the content is rendered in place of the progress indicator. Finally, let's make sure that the API call to load content isn't made when the panel is collapsing. This requires an adjustment to the onChange() handler:

```
const onChange = index => (e, expanded) => {
  if (!panels[index].content && expanded) {
    fetchPanelContent(index).then(content => {
      const newPanels = [...panels];
      newPanels[index] = { ...newPanels[index], content };
      setPanels(newPanels);
    });
  }
};
```

The second argument passed to this function, expanded, tells you whether or not the panel is expanding. If this value is false, you know that the panel is collapsed and that the API call shouldn't be made. This condition has been added to look for content that has already been loaded for the panel.

See also

- ExpansionPanel **demos:** https://material-ui.com/demos/expansion-panels/
- ExpansionPanel **API documentation:** https://material-ui.com/api/expansion-panel/
- ExpansionPanelSummary **API documentation:** https://material-ui.com/api/expansion-panel-summary/
- ExpansionPanelDetails **API documentation:** https://material-ui.com/api/expansion-panel-details/

6
Lists - Display Simple Collection Data

In this chapter, you'll cover the following recipes:

- Using state to render list items
- List icons
- List avatars and text
- List sections
- Nested lists
- List controls
- Scrolling lists

Introduction

The `List` component in Material-UI is used to render data collections. Lists are like tables, only simpler. If you need to display an array of users, for example, you can render them in a list, showing only the most relevant data, instead of several properties in a tabular format. Material-UI lists are generic and provide a lot of flexibility.

Using state to render list items

The data source used to render `List` components often comes from the state of your component. A collection—usually an array of objects—is mapped to `ListItem` components. As the objects in this array change, the Material-UI list items change on the screen.

How to do it...

Let's say that you have an array of three objects that you need to display as a list on one of your screens. You can add this array to the state of your component, then map each array item to a `ListItem` component. Here's the code:

```
import React, { useState } from 'react';

import List from '@material-ui/core/List';
import ListItem from '@material-ui/core/ListItem';
import ListItemText from '@material-ui/core/ListItemText';

export default function UsingStatetoRenderListItems() {
  const [items, setItems] = useState([
    { name: 'First Item', timestamp: new Date() },
    { name: 'Second Item', timestamp: new Date() },
    { name: 'Third Item', timestamp: new Date() }
  ]);

  return (
    <List>
      {items.map((item, index) => (
        <ListItem key={index} button dense>
          <ListItemText
            primary={item.name}
            secondary={item.timestamp.toLocaleString()}
          />
        </ListItem>
      ))}
    </List>
  );
}
```

Here's what you'll see when you first load the screen:

First Item
9/26/2018, 12:12:28 PM

Second Item
9/26/2018, 12:12:28 PM

Third Item
9/26/2018, 12:12:28 PM

How it works...

Let's start by looking at the items state:

```
const [items, setItems] = useState([
  { name: 'First Item', timestamp: new Date() },
  { name: 'Second Item', timestamp: new Date() },
  { name: 'Third Item', timestamp: new Date() }
]);
```

The name property is the primary text, and the timestamp property is the secondary text for each list item. Next, let's look at the List markup that transforms this state into rendered list items:

```
<List>
  {items.map((item, index) => (
    <ListItem key={index} button dense>
      <ListItemText
        primary={item.name}
        secondary={item.timestamp.toLocaleString()}
      />
    </ListItem>
  ))}
</List>
```

The ListItem component has two Boolean properties passed to it – button and dense. The button property makes the list item behave like a button. For example, if you move your mouse pointer over an item in the list, you'll see the hover styles applied to it. The dense property removes extra padding from the list item. Without this property, the list takes up more space on the screen.

The ListItemText component uses the primary and secondary properties to render the name and timestamp properties respectively. The primary text is meant to stand out relative to the secondary information displayed in the item – in this case, the timestamp.

There's more...

This example could have used props instead of state, because the items never changed. Let's modify it so that the user can select items from the list. Here's what the new List markup looks like:

```
<List>
  {items.map((item, index) => (
    <ListItem
```

```
              key={index}
              button
              dense
              selected={item.selected}
              onClick={onClick(index)}
          >
            <ListItemText
              primary={item.name}
              secondary={item.timestamp.toLocaleString()}
              primaryTypographyProps={{
                color: item.selected ? 'primary' : undefined
              }}
            />
          </ListItem>
        ))}
      </List>
```

The selected property passed to the ListItem component will apply selected styles to the item when true. This value comes from the item.selected state, which is false by default for every item (nothing is selected). Next, the ListItem component has an onClick handler.

The ListItemText component also has styles applied to it based on the selected state of the item. Behind the scenes, item text is rendered using the Typography component. You can use the primaryTypographyProps property to pass properties to the Typography component. In this case, you're changing the color of the text to primary when it's selected.

Let's look at the onClick() handler as follows:

```
      const onClick = index => () => {
        const item = items[index];
        const newItems = [...items];

        newItems[index] = { ...item, selected: !item.selected };
        setItems(newItems);
      };
```

This is a higher-order function, which returns an event handler function based on the index argument. It toggles the selected state for the item at the given index.

The onClick property isn't a ListItem property. It's a button property. Since you've set the button property to true, ListItem uses a button property and passes it to your onClick property.

Here's what the list looks like when **First Item** is selected:

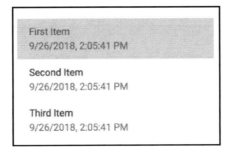

The change to the background color is caused by the selected property of `ListItem`. The change to the text color is caused by the `primaryTypographyProps` property of `ListItemText`.

See also

- `List` demos: https://material-ui.com/demos/lists/
- `Typography` API documentation: https://material-ui.com/api/typography/

List icons

`ListItem` components have first-class support for icons. By rendering icons in each list item, you can make it clear to the user what types of objects are displayed in the list.

How to do it...

Let's say that you have an array of user objects that you want to render in a `List`. You could render each item with a user icon to make it clear what each item in the list is. The code for this is as follows:

```
import React, { useState } from 'react';

import List from '@material-ui/core/List';
import ListItem from '@material-ui/core/ListItem';
import ListItemText from '@material-ui/core/ListItemText';
import ListItemIcon from '@material-ui/core/ListItemIcon';
```

```
import AccountCircleIcon from '@material-ui/icons/AccountCircle';

export default function ListIcons() {
  const [items, setItems] = useState([
    { name: 'First User' },
    { name: 'Second User' },
    { name: 'Third User' }
  ]);

  return (
    <List>
      {items.map((item, index) => (
        <ListItem key={index} button>
          <ListItemIcon>
            <AccountCircleIcon />
          </ListItemIcon>
          <ListItemText primary={item.name} />
        </ListItem>
      ))}
    </List>
  );
}
```

When you load the screen, this is what the list should look like:

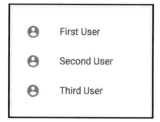

How it works...

The ListItemIcon component can be used as a child of ListItem components. In the previous example, it comes before the text, so it ends up to the left of the item text:

```
<ListItem button key={index}>
  <ListItemIcon>
    <AccountCircleIcon />
  </ListItemIcon>
  <ListItemText primary={item.name} />
</ListItem>
```

You could place the icon after the text as well:

```
<ListItem button key={index}>
  <ListItemText primary={item.name} />
  <ListItemIcon>
    <AccountCircleIcon />
  </ListItemIcon>
</ListItem>
```

Here's how it looks:

There's more...

You can mark `ListItem` components as selected by setting the `selected` property to `true`. You can also change the icon to give a better visual indication that an item has been selected. Here's the updated code:

```
import React, { useState } from 'react';

import List from '@material-ui/core/List';
import ListItem from '@material-ui/core/ListItem';
import ListItemText from '@material-ui/core/ListItemText';
import ListItemIcon from '@material-ui/core/ListItemIcon';

import AccountCircleIcon from '@material-ui/icons/AccountCircle';
import CheckCircleOutlineIcon from '@material-ui/icons/CheckCircleOutline';

const MaybeSelectedIcon = ({ selected, Icon }) =>
  selected ? <CheckCircleOutlineIcon /> : <Icon />;

export default function ListIcons() {
  const [items, setItems] = useState([
    { name: 'First User' },
    { name: 'Second User' },
    { name: 'Third User' }
  ]);
```

```
const onClick = index => () => {
  const item = items[index];
  const newItems = [...items];

  newItems[index] = { ...item, selected: !item.selected };
  setItems(newItems);
};

return (
  <List>
    {items.map((item, index) => (
      <ListItem
        key={index}
        button
        selected={item.selected}
        onClick={onClick(index)}
      >
        <ListItemText primary={item.name} />
        <ListItemIcon>
          <MaybeSelectedIcon
            selected={item.selected}
            Icon={AccountCircleIcon}
          />
        </ListItemIcon>
      </ListItem>
    ))}
  </List>
);
}
```

Here's what the list looks like with **First User** selected:

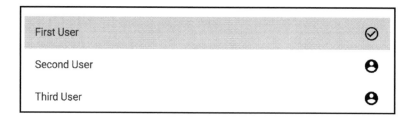

The icon for the selected items changes into a circled checkmark. Let's break down the changes that were introduced to make this happen, starting with the MaybeSelectedIcon component:

```
const MaybeSelectedIcon = ({ selected, Icon }) =>
  selected ? <CheckCircleOutlineIcon /> : <Icon />;
```

This component will render either `CheckCircleOutlineIcon` or the `Icon` component that is passed in as a property. This depends on the `selected` property. Next, let's look at how this component is used inside `ListItemIcon`:

```
<ListItemIcon>
  <MaybeSelectedIcon
    selected={item.selected}
    Icon={AccountCircleIcon}
  />
</ListItemIcon>
```

When a list item is clicked on, the `selected` state for that item is toggled. Then, the `selected` state is passed to `MaybeSelectedIcon`. The `AccountCircleIcon` component is the icon that's rendered when the list item isn't selected, because it's passed to the `Icon` property.

See also

- `List` **demos:** https://material-ui.com/demos/lists/
- `ListItemIcon` **API documentation:** https://material-ui.com/api/list-item-icon/

List avatars and text

If your list items have `primary` and `secondary` text, using an icon on its own can be less visually appealing than with an avatar surrounding the icon. It fills the space within the list item better.

How to do it...

Let's say that you have four categories of messages that can be displayed by your app. To access a given category, the user clicks on one of the list items. To help the user understand the categories, you'll use icons. And to make the icons stand out against the `primary` and `secondary` text of the list item, you'll wrap it with an `Avatar` component. Here's the code:

```
import React, { useState } from 'react';
import clsx from 'clsx';

import Avatar from '@material-ui/core/Avatar';
```

```
import List from '@material-ui/core/List';
import ListItem from '@material-ui/core/ListItem';
import ListItemText from '@material-ui/core/ListItemText';
import ListItemIcon from '@material-ui/core/ListItemIcon';

import MarkunreadIcon from '@material-ui/icons/Markunread';
import PriorityHighIcon from '@material-ui/icons/PriorityHigh';
import LowPriorityIcon from '@material-ui/icons/LowPriority';
import DeleteIcon from '@material-ui/icons/Delete';

export default function ListAvatarsAndText({ classes }) {
  const [items] = useState([
    {
      name: 'Unread',
      updated: '2 minutes ago',
      Icon: MarkunreadIcon,
      notifications: 1
    },
    {
      name: 'High Priority',
      updated: '30 minutes ago',
      Icon: PriorityHighIcon
    },
    {
      name: 'Low Priority',
      updated: '3 hours ago',
      Icon: LowPriorityIcon
    },
    { name: 'Junk', updated: '6 days ago', Icon: DeleteIcon }
  ]);

  return (
    <List>
      {items.map(({ Icon, ...item }, index) => (
        <ListItem button>
          <ListItemIcon>
            <Avatar>
              <Icon />
            </Avatar>
          </ListItemIcon>
          <ListItemText
            primary={item.name}
            secondary={item.updated}
          />
        </ListItem>
      ))}
    </List>
```

```
  );
}
```

Here's what the list looks like when rendered:

The circle that surrounds the icon is the `Avatar` component, and it helps the icon stand out. Here's what this list looks like without avatars:

It's the same content and the same icons, but because of the height of the list item text, there's a lot of excess space surrounding the icon. The `Avatar` component helps fill this space while drawing attention to the icon.

How it works...

The `Avatar` component is used on icons with a circular shape. The color of the circle comes from the theme palette – the shade of grey used depends on whether the theme is light or dark. The icon itself is passed as the child element:

```
<ListItemIcon>
  <Avatar>
    <Icon />
  </Avatar>
</ListItemIcon>
```

There's more...

If you use an `Avatar` with the icons in your list items, you can change the color of the `Avatar` and you can apply a badge to indicate unacknowledged actions to be taken. Let's modify the example so that each item in the items state can have a `notifications` property; that is, a number representing the number of unread messages for the category. If this number is greater than 0, you can change the `Avatar` color and display number of `notifications` in a badge. Here's what the result looks like:

The first item in the list has an `Avatar` that's using the primary `theme` color and a badge showing the number of `notifications`. The rest of the items don't have any `notifications`, so the `Avatar` color uses the default, and the badge isn't displayed.

Let's see how this is done, starting with the styles:

```
const styles = theme => ({
  activeAvatar: {
    backgroundColor: theme.palette.primary[theme.palette.type]
  }
});
```

The `activeAvatar` style is applied to the `Avatar` component when the `notifications` state is a number greater than 0. It looks up the primary `theme` color based on the theme type (light or dark). Next, let's look at the state of the first item in the items array:

```
{
  name: 'Unread',
  updated: '2 minutes ago',
  Icon: MarkunreadIcon,
  notifications: 1
}
```

Because the `notifications` value is 1, the color of the avatar changes, and the badge is displayed. Lastly, let's see how all of this comes together in the component markup using the `Badge` and `Avatar` components:

```
<Badge
  color={item.notifications ? 'secondary' : undefined}
  badgeContent={
    item.notifications ? item.notifications : null
  }
>
  <Avatar
    className={clsx({
      [classes.activeAvatar]: item.notifications
    })}
  >
    <Icon />
  </Avatar>
</Badge>
```

The `color` property of `Badge` is based on the `notifications` state of the item being greater than 0. If it is, the primary color is used. If it isn't, `undefined` is passed to `Badge`. In this case, this is necessary so that an empty badge circle doesn't show up when there aren't any notifications.

Passing `undefined` as a property value is equivalent to not setting the property at all.

Next, the `badgeContent` property is set based on the `notifications` state of the item. If it's not greater than 0, then you don't want any value set. Finally, setting the color of the `Avatar` component uses `clsx()` to apply the `activeAvatar` class if the `notifications` state for the item is greater than 0.

See also

- `Badge` **demos:** `https://material-ui.com/demos/badges/`
- `Avatar` **demos:** `https://material-ui.com/demos/avatars/`
- `List` **demos:** `https://material-ui.com/demos/lists/`

List sections

Once your lists have more than just a few items in them, you might want to consider organizing the items into sections. To do this, you split your lists into several smaller lists, which are stacked on top of one another with a divider in between them.

How to do it...

Let's say that you have several list items that can be divided into three sections. You can use three `List` components to group your items into their respective sections, and use a `Divider` component to visually indicate the section boundary for the user. Here's what the code looks like:

```
import React, { Fragment } from 'react';

import List from '@material-ui/core/List';
import ListItem from '@material-ui/core/ListItem';
import ListItemText from '@material-ui/core/ListItemText';
import Divider from '@material-ui/core/Divider';

const ListSections = () => (
  <Fragment>
    <List>
```

```
      <ListItem>
        <ListItemText primary="First" />
      </ListItem>
      <ListItem>
        <ListItemText primary="Second" />
      </ListItem>
    </List>
    <Divider />
    <List>
      <ListItem>
        <ListItemText primary="Third" />
      </ListItem>
      <ListItem>
        <ListItemText primary="Fourth" />
      </ListItem>
    </List>
    <Divider />
    <List>
      <ListItem>
        <ListItemText primary="Fifth" />
      </ListItem>
      <ListItem>
        <ListItemText primary="Sixth" />
      </ListItem>
    </List>
  </Fragment>
));

export default ListSections;
```

Here's what the rendered list looks like:

How it works...

Each section is its own `List` component, with its own `ListItem` components. The `Divider` component separates the lists. For example, the first section looks like this:

```
<List>
  <ListItem>
    <ListItemText primary="First" />
  </ListItem>
  <ListItem>
    <ListItemText primary="Second" />
  </ListItem>
</List>
```

There's more...

Instead of having a `Divider` component separate your list sections, you can use `Typography` to label your sections. This could help your users make sense of the items in each section:

```
<Fragment>
  <Typography variant="title">First Section</Typography>
  <List>
    <ListItem>
      <ListItemText primary="First" />
    </ListItem>
    <ListItem>
      <ListItemText primary="Second" />
    </ListItem>
  </List>
  <Typography variant="title">Second Section</Typography>
  <List>
    <ListItem>
      <ListItemText primary="Third" />
    </ListItem>
    <ListItem>
      <ListItemText primary="Fourth" />
    </ListItem>
  </List>
  <Typography variant="title">Third Section</Typography>
  <List>
    <ListItem>
      <ListItemText primary="Fifth" />
    </ListItem>
    <ListItem>
```

```
        <ListItemText primary="Sixth" />
      </ListItem>
    </List>
  </Fragment>
```

Here's what the list looks like now:

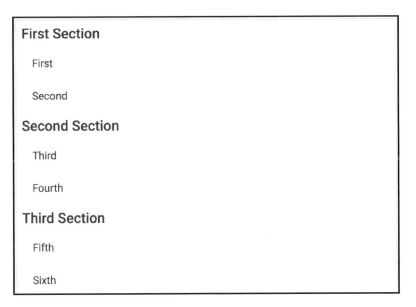

See also

- List **demos:** https://material-ui.com/demos/lists/
- Typography **API documentation:** https://material-ui.com/api/typography/

Nested lists

Lists can be nested. This is useful when you have a large number of items to render. Instead of showing everything all at once, you can only display those item categories. Then the user can click on these categories to display the items.

How to do it...

Let's say that you have two item categories. When the user clicks on a category, the items in that category should be displayed. Here's the code to do this, by using the `List` component:

```
import React, { useState, Fragment } from 'react';

import List from '@material-ui/core/List';
import ListItem from '@material-ui/core/ListItem';
import ListItemText from '@material-ui/core/ListItemText';
import ListItemIcon from '@material-ui/core/ListItemIcon';
import Collapse from '@material-ui/core/Collapse';

import ExpandLessIcon from '@material-ui/icons/ExpandLess';
import ExpandMoreIcon from '@material-ui/icons/ExpandMore';
import InboxIcon from '@material-ui/icons/Inbox';
import MailIcon from '@material-ui/icons/Mail';
import ContactsIcon from '@material-ui/icons/Contacts';
import ContactMailIcon from '@material-ui/icons/ContactMail';

const ExpandIcon = ({ expanded }) =>
  expanded ? <ExpandLessIcon /> : <ExpandMoreIcon />;

export default function NestedLists() {
  const [items, setItems] = useState([
    {
      name: 'Messages',
      Icon: InboxIcon,
      expanded: false,
      children: [
        { name: 'First Message', Icon: MailIcon },
        { name: 'Second Message', Icon: MailIcon }
      ]
    },
    {
      name: 'Contacts',
      Icon: ContactsIcon,
      expanded: false,
      children: [
        { name: 'First Contact', Icon: ContactMailIcon },
        { name: 'Second Contact', Icon: ContactMailIcon }
      ]
    }
  ]);

  const onClick = index => () => {
```

```
    const newItems = [...items];
    const item = items[index];

    newItems[index] = { ...item, expanded: !item.expanded };

    setItems(newItems);
  };

  return (
    <List>
      {items.map(({ Icon, ...item }, index) => (
        <Fragment key={index}>
          <ListItem button onClick={onClick(index)}>
            <ListItemIcon>
              <Icon />
            </ListItemIcon>
            <ListItemText primary={item.name} />
            <ExpandIcon expanded={item.expanded} />
          </ListItem>
          <Collapse in={item.expanded}>
            {item.children.map(child => (
              <ListItem key={child.name} button dense>
                <ListItemIcon>
                  <child.Icon />
                </ListItemIcon>
                <ListItemText primary={child.name} />
              </ListItem>
            ))}
          </Collapse>
        </Fragment>
      ))}
    </List>
  );
}
```

When you first load the screen, you'll see the following:

If you click on each of these categories, you'll see the following:

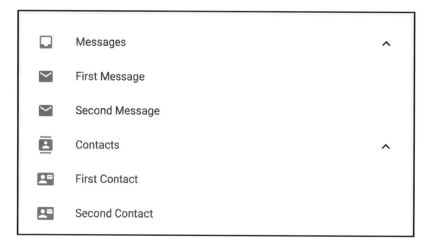

How it works...

When you click on a category, the down arrow icon changes to an up arrow. Beneath the category, the list items belonging to that category are displayed. Let's break down what's happening in this code, starting with the component state:

```
const [items, setItems] = useState([
  {
    name: 'Messages',
    Icon: InboxIcon,
    expanded: false,
    children: [
      { name: 'First Message', Icon: MailIcon },
      { name: 'Second Message', Icon: MailIcon }
    ]
  },
  {
    name: 'Contacts',
    Icon: ContactsIcon,
    expanded: false,
    children: [
      { name: 'First Contact', Icon: ContactMailIcon },
      { name: 'Second Contact', Icon: ContactMailIcon }
    ]
  }
]);
```

Each object in the items array represents a list category. In this case, the categories are Messages and Contacts. The Icon property is the icon component to render for the category. The expanded property determines the state of the expand arrow icon, and whether or not the items in the category should be displayed.

The children array contains the items that belong to the category. They have a name and an Icon property just like the category items, because they're all rendered using ListItem components.

Next, let's look at the markup used to render each category and its child items:

```
<Fragment key={index}>
  <ListItem button onClick={onClick(index)}>
    <ListItemIcon>
      <Icon />
    </ListItemIcon>
    <ListItemText primary={item.name} />
    <ExpandIcon expanded={item.expanded} />
  </ListItem>
  <Collapse in={item.expanded}>
    {item.children.map(child => (
      <ListItem key={child.name} button dense>
        <ListItemIcon>
          <child.Icon />
        </ListItemIcon>
        <ListItemText primary={child.name} />
      </ListItem>
    ))}
  </Collapse>
</Fragment>
```

The category ListItem component has an onClick handler that toggles the expanded state of the category. Next, the Collapse component is used to control the visibility of the child items of the category, based on the value of expanded.

There's more...

You can improve on the appearance of your nested list by differentiating the appearance of the sub-items. Right now, the only difference between the category items and subitems is that the category items have expand and collapse arrows.

Typically, list items are indented to indicate that they're part of another item in the hierarchy. Let's create a style that will allow you to indent subitems:

```
const useStyles = makeStyles(theme => ({
  subItem: { paddingLeft: theme.spacing(3) }
}));
```

The `paddingLeft` style property will shift everything in the list item to the right. Now, let's apply this class to `subItem` while also making the item smaller than the category items:

```
<ListItem
  key={child.name}
  className={classes.subItem}
  button
  dense
>
  <ListItemIcon>
    <child.Icon />
  </ListItemIcon>
  <ListItemText primary={child.name} />
</ListItem>
```

By adding the `dense` and the `className` properties to `ListItem`, your users should be more easily able to differentiate between the category and its subitems:

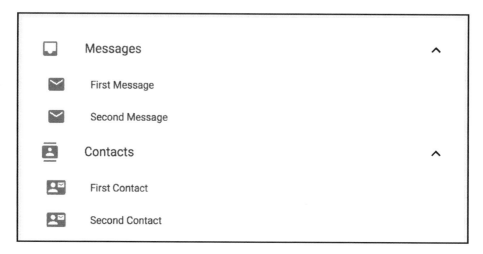

See also

- List **demos:** https://material-ui.com/demos/lists/
- Collapse **API documentation:** https://material-ui.com/api/collapse/

List controls

List items can be clickable, resulting in a change in state, or a link being followed, or something else entirely. This is the primary action of the item. You can have secondary actions on lists called controls. These are common actions that you might perform, depending on the type of item.

How to do it...

Let's say that you have a list of devices. When you click on a list item, it might take you to a details page for the device. Each device has Bluetooth connectivity that can be toggled on or off. This is a good candidate secondary action to render in the item. Here's the code to do this:

```
import React, { useState } from 'react';

import List from '@material-ui/core/List';
import ListItem from '@material-ui/core/ListItem';
import ListItemText from '@material-ui/core/ListItemText';
import ListItemIcon from '@material-ui/core/ListItemIcon';
import ListItemSecondaryAction from '@material-
ui/core/ListItemSecondaryAction';
import IconButton from '@material-ui/core/IconButton';

import BluetoothIcon from '@material-ui/icons/Bluetooth';
import BluetoothDisabledIcon from '@material-ui/icons/BluetoothDisabled';
import DevicesIcon from '@material-ui/icons/Devices';

const MaybeBluetoothIcon = ({ bluetooth }) =>
  bluetooth ? <BluetoothIcon /> : <BluetoothDisabledIcon />;

export default function ListControls() {
  const [items, setItems] = useState([
    {
      name: 'Device 1',
      bluetooth: true,
```

```
        Icon: DevicesIcon
      },
      {
        name: 'Device 2',
        bluetooth: true,

        Icon: DevicesIcon
      },
      {
        name: 'Device 3',
        bluetooth: true,

        Icon: DevicesIcon
      }
    ]);

    const onBluetoothClick = index => () => {
      const newItems = [...items];
      const item = items[index];

      newItems[index] = { ...item, bluetooth: !item.bluetooth };

      setItems(newItems);
    };

    return (
      <List>
        {items.map(({ Icon, ...item }, index) => (
          <ListItem key={index} button>
            <ListItemIcon>
              <Icon />
            </ListItemIcon>
            <ListItemText primary={item.name} />
            <ListItemSecondaryAction>
              <IconButton
                onClick={onBluetoothClick(index, 'bluetooth')}
              >
                <MaybeBluetoothIcon bluetooth={item.bluetooth} />
              </IconButton>
            </ListItemSecondaryAction>
          </ListItem>
        ))}
      </List>
    );
  }
```

Here's what the screen looks like when it first loads:

You can toggle the Bluetooth state of one of the items by clicking on the icon buttons. Here's what it looks like after toggling the Bluetooth state of the first item:

The Bluetooth icon has changed to indicate the `disabled` state. Clicking on the icon again will enable Bluetooth.

How it works...

Let's look at the markup that's used to render each list item:

```
<ListItem key={index} button>
  <ListItemIcon>
    <Icon />
  </ListItemIcon>
  <ListItemText primary={item.name} />
  <ListItemSecondaryAction>
    <IconButton
      onClick={onBluetoothClick(index, 'bluetooth')}
    >
      <MaybeBluetoothIcon bluetooth={item.bluetooth} />
    </IconButton>
```

```
      </ListItemSecondaryAction>
    </ListItem>
```

The `ListItemSecondaryAction` component is used as a container for any controls in your list item. In this example, an `IconButton` is used as the control. It shows a different icon depending on the state of the item, using the `MaybeBluetoothIcon` component. The `onBluetoothClick()` function is used to return the event handler function for the item. Let's take a look at this function:

```
const onBluetoothClick = index => () => {
  const newItems = [...items];
  const item = items[index];

  newItems[index] = { ...item, bluetooth: !item.bluetooth };

  setItems(newItems);
};
```

The device item is looked up in the `items` array. Then, the Bluetooth state is toggled, and the new `items` array is returned to set as the new state. This results in the updated icon in the list item control.

There's more...

You can have more than one control in your list item. For example, let's say that in addition to toggling the Bluetooth state of a device, another common action for your users is toggling the `power` state of the device. When the device is powered off, the list item and the Bluetooth control should be displayed.

Avoid having too many controls as secondary actions in your list items. Doing so detracts from the convenience of having one or two common actions easily accessible by your users.

Let's start by adding a new `power` state to each item in your component state:

```
const [items, setItems] = useState([
  {
    name: 'Device 1',
    bluetooth: true,
    power: true,
    Icon: DevicesIcon
  },
  {
    name: 'Device 2',
    bluetooth: true,
```

```
      power: true,
      Icon: DevicesIcon
    },
    {
      name: 'Device 3',
      bluetooth: true,
      power: true,
      Icon: DevicesIcon
    }
  ]);
```

Next, let's create a toggle click handler that can handle updating both the Bluetooth and the power state of items:

```
const onToggleClick = (index, prop) => () => {
  const newItems = [...items];
  const item = items[index];

  newItems[index] = { ...item, [prop]: !item[prop] };

  setItems(newItems);
};
```

This is very similar to the `onBluetoothClick()` handler. Now, it accepts an additional prop argument. This is used to tell the function which property to update – `bluetooth` or `power`. Finally, let's look at the updated `ListItem` markup:

```
<ListItem key={index} disabled={!item.power} button>
  <ListItemIcon>
    <Icon />
  </ListItemIcon>
  <ListItemText primary={item.name} />
  <ListItemSecondaryAction>
    <IconButton
      onClick={onToggleClick(index, 'bluetooth')}
      disabled={!item.power}
    >
      <MaybeBluetoothIcon bluetooth={item.bluetooth} />
    </IconButton>
    <IconButton onClick={onToggleClick(index, 'power')}>
      <PowerSettingsNewIcon />
    </IconButton>
  </ListItemSecondaryAction>
</ListItem>
```

The changes can be summarized as follows:

- The `disabled` property of `ListItem` depends on the `power` state of the item.
- There's another `IconButton` control for toggling the `power` state of the item.
- The `onToggleClick()` function is used by both controls to toggle the state of the item.

Here's how the screen looks now, when first loaded:

When you click on the power icon, the list item and the Bluetooth button become disabled. Here's what it looks like when the first item is powered off:

See also

- `ListItemSecondaryAction` API documentation: `https://material-ui.com/api/list-item-secondary-action/`
- `IconButton` API documentation: `https://material-ui.com/api/icon-button/`

Scrolling lists

When your lists contain a limited number of items in them, you're safe to just iterate over the item data, and render `ListItem` components. This becomes a problem when you have the potential for lists with over 1,000 items in them. You can render these items fast enough, but having this many items in the **Document Object Model (DOM)** eats a lot of browser resources, and can lead to unpredictable performance challenges for the user. The solution is to virtualize your Material-UI lists using `react-virtualized`.

How to do it...

Let's say that you have a list of 1,000 items in it. You want to render these items inside a list with a fixed height. In order to provide predictable performance characteristics for your users, you only want to render items that are actually visible to the user as they scroll through the list. Here's the code:

```
import React, { useState } from 'react';
import { List as VirtualList, AutoSizer } from 'react-virtualized';

import { makeStyles } from '@material-ui/styles';
import List from '@material-ui/core/List';
import ListItem from '@material-ui/core/ListItem';
import ListItemText from '@material-ui/core/ListItemText';
import Paper from '@material-ui/core/Paper';

const useStyles = makeStyles(theme => ({
  list: {
    height: 300
  },
  paper: {
    margin: theme.spacing(3)
  }
}));

function* genItems() {
  for (let i = 1; i <= 1000; i++) {
    yield `Item ${i}`;
  }
}

export default function ScrollingLists() {
  const classes = useStyles();
  const [items] = useState([...genItems()]);
```

```
const rowRenderer = ({ index, isScrolling, key, style }) => {
  const item = items[index];

  return (
    <ListItem button key={key} style={style}>
      <ListItemText primary={isScrolling ? '...' : item} />
    </ListItem>
  );
};

return (
  <Paper className={classes.paper}>
    <List className={classes.list}>
      <AutoSizer disableHeight>
        {({ width }) => (
          <VirtualList
            width={width}
            height={300}
            rowHeight={50}
            rowCount={items.length}
            rowRenderer={rowRenderer}
          />
        )}
      </AutoSizer>
    </List>
  </Paper>
);
}
```

When you first load the screen, you'll see the following:

Item 1

Item 2

Item 3

Item 4

Item 5

Item 6

As you scroll through the list, here's what you'll see:

Lastly, here's what the bottom of the list looks like:

Item 995

Item 996

Item 997

Item 998

Item 999

Item 1000

How it works...

First, let's take a look at how the `items` state is generated. First, there's a `genItems()` generator function:

```
function* genItems() {
  for (let i = 1; i <= 1000; i++) {
    yield `Item ${i}`;
  }
}
```

Then, the spread operator is used to turn the generated `items` into an array for the component state:

```
const [items] = useState([...genItems()]);
```

Next, let's look at the `rowRenderer()` function:

```
const rowRenderer = ({ index, isScrolling, key, style }) => {
  const item = items[index];

  return (
    <ListItem button key={key} style={style}>
      <ListItemText primary={isScrolling ? '...' : item} />
    </ListItem>
  );
};
```

This function returns the `ListItem` component that should be rendered at the given index. Instead of manually mapping this component to `items`, the `List` component from `react-virtualized` orchestrates when to call it for you, based on how the user scrolls through the list.

The `key` and the `style` values that are passed to this function are required by `react-virtualized` in order to work correctly. For example, the `style` value is used to control the visibility of the item as scrolling happens. The `isScrolling` value is used to render different data while the list is actively being scrolled. For example, imagine that instead of just a text label within the list item, you also had an icon, along with other controls that are all based on state. Trying to render these things while scrolling is going on is expensive and wasteful. Instead, you can render something that's less resource intensive, such as a placeholder string: `'...'`.

Finally, let's examine the markup used to render this list:

```
<List className={classes.list}>
  <AutoSizer disableHeight>
    {({ width }) => (
      <VirtualList
        width={width}
        height={300}
        rowHeight={50}
        rowCount={items.length}
        rowRenderer={rowRenderer}
      />
    )}
  </AutoSizer>
</List>
```

The `List` component is the container for everything else. Next, the `AutoSizer` component from `react-virtualized` figures out the width of the list, which is needed as a `VirtualList` property.

`List` is imported from `react-virtualized` using the alias `VirtualList`. This is to avoid the naming conflict with `List` from `material-ui`. You could import `List` from `material-ui` as an alias instead, if you prefer.

The `List` component from `react-virtualized` also takes the height of the list, the height of each row, and the row count, in order to determine which rows to render. With this in place, you never have to worry about the performance of your application because of a list component with too many items.

See also

- React Virtualized documentation: `https://bvaughn.github.io/react-virtualized/`
- `List` demos: https://material-ui.com/demos/lists/

7
Tables - Display Complex Collection Data

In this chapter, you'll learn about the following topics:

- Stateful tables
- Sortable columns
- Filtering rows
- Selecting rows
- Row actions

Introduction

If your application needs to display tabular data, you can use the Material-UI `Table` component, along with all of its supporting components. Unlike grid components, which you might have seen or used in other React libraries, the Material-UI component is unopinionated. This means that you have to write your own code to control table data. On the plus side, the `Table` component stays out of your way and lets you implement things your own way.

Stateful tables

With `Table` components, it's rare that you'll have static markup that defines the row data of the table. Instead, component state will map to the rows that make up your table data. For example, you might have a component that fetches API data that you want displayed in a table.

How to do it...

Let's say that you have a component that fetches data from an API endpoint. When the data loads, you want to display the tabular data in a Material-UI Table component. Here's what the code looks like:

```
import React, { useState, useEffect } from 'react';

import { makeStyles } from '@material-ui/styles';
import Table from '@material-ui/core/Table';
import TableBody from '@material-ui/core/TableBody';
import TableCell from '@material-ui/core/TableCell';
import TableHead from '@material-ui/core/TableHead';
import TableRow from '@material-ui/core/TableRow';
import Paper from '@material-ui/core/Paper';

const fetchData = () =>
  new Promise(resolve => {
    const items = [
      {
        id: 1,
        name: 'First Item',
        created: new Date(),
        high: 2935,
        low: 1924,
        average: 2429.5
      },
      {
        id: 2,
        name: 'Second Item',
        created: new Date(),
        high: 439,
        low: 231,
        average: 335
      },
      {
        id: 3,
        name: 'Third Item',
        created: new Date(),
        high: 8239,
        low: 5629,
        average: 6934
      },
      {
        id: 4,
        name: 'Fourth Item',
        created: new Date(),
```

```
        high: 3203,
        low: 3127,
        average: 3165
      },
      {
        id: 5,
        name: 'Fifth Item',
        created: new Date(),
        high: 981,
        low: 879,
        average: 930
      }
    ];

    setTimeout(() => resolve(items), 1000);
  });

const usePaperStyles = makeStyles(theme => ({
  root: { margin: theme.spacing(2) }
}));

export default function StatefulTables() {
  const classes = usePaperStyles();

  const [items, setItems] = useState([]);

  useEffect(() => {
    fetchData().then(items => {
      setItems(items);
    });
  }, []);

  return (
    <Paper className={classes.root}>
      <Table>
        <TableHead>
          <TableRow>
            <TableCell>Name</TableCell>
            <TableCell>Created</TableCell>
            <TableCell align="right">High</TableCell>
            <TableCell align="right">Low</TableCell>
            <TableCell align="right">Average</TableCell>
          </TableRow>
        </TableHead>
        <TableBody>
          {items.map(item => {
            return (
              <TableRow key={item.id}>
```

```
            <TableCell component="th" scope="row">
              {item.name}
            </TableCell>
            <TableCell>{item.created.toLocaleString()}</TableCell>
            <TableCell align="right">{item.high}</TableCell>
            <TableCell align="right">{item.low}</TableCell>
            <TableCell align="right">{item.average}</TableCell>
          </TableRow>
        );
      })}
    </TableBody>
  </Table>
</Paper>
  );
}
```

When you load the screen, you'll see a table populated with data after one second:

Name	Created	High	Low	Average
First Item	10/16/2018, 1:15:40 PM	2935	1924	2429.5
Second Item	10/16/2018, 1:15:40 PM	439	231	335
Third Item	10/16/2018, 1:15:40 PM	8239	5629	6934
Fourth Item	10/16/2018, 1:15:40 PM	3203	3127	3165
Fifth Item	10/16/2018, 1:15:40 PM	981	879	930

How it works...

Let's start by looking at the fetchData() function, which resolves the data that is eventually set as the component state:

```
const fetchData = () =>
  new Promise(resolve => {
    const items = [
      {
```

```
          id: 1,
          name: 'First Item',
          created: new Date(),
          high: 2935,
          low: 1924,
          average: 2429.5
       },
       {
          id: 2,
          name: 'Second Item',
          created: new Date(),
          high: 439,
          low: 231,
          average: 335
       },
       ...
    ];

    setTimeout(() => resolve(items), 1000);
  });
```

This function returns a `Promise` that resolves an array of objects after one second. The idea is to simulate a function that calls a real API using `fetch()`.

 The objects shown in the array are truncated for brevity.

Next, let's look at the initial component state and what happens when your component is mounted:

```
const [items, setItems] = useState([]);

useEffect(() => {
  fetchData().then(items => {
    setItems(items);
  });
}, []);
```

The `items` state represents the table rows that are to be rendered within the `Table` component. When your component is mounted, the `fetchData()` call is made, and when the `Promise` resolves, the `items` state is set. Lastly, let's look at the markup that's responsible for rendering the table rows:

```
<Table>
  <TableHead>
```

```
        <TableRow>
          <TableCell>Name</TableCell>
          <TableCell>Created</TableCell>
          <TableCell align="right">High</TableCell>
          <TableCell align="right">Low</TableCell>
          <TableCell align="right">Average</TableCell>
        </TableRow>
      </TableHead>
      <TableBody>
        {items.map(item => {
          return (
            <TableRow key={item.id}>
              <TableCell component="th" scope="row">
                {item.name}
              </TableCell>
              <TableCell>{item.created.toLocaleString()}</TableCell>
              <TableCell align="right">{item.high}</TableCell>
              <TableCell align="right">{item.low}</TableCell>
              <TableCell align="right">{item.average}</TableCell>
            </TableRow>
          );
        })}
      </TableBody>
    </Table>
```

`Table` components typically have two children—a `TableHead` and a `TableBody` component. Inside `TableHead`, you'll find a `TableRow` component with several `TableCell` components. These are the table column headings. Inside `TableBody`, you'll see that the `items` state is mapped to `TableRow` and `TableCell` components. When the `items` state changes, the rows are changed too. You can already see this in action, because the `items` state defaults to an empty array. After the API data resolves, the `items` state changes and the rows are visible on the screen.

There's more...

One suboptimal aspect of this example is the user's experience while they wait for table data to load. Showing the column headers upfront is fine, since you know what they are ahead of time and the user might too. What's needed is some sort of indicator that the actual row data is, in fact, loading.

One way to fix this issue is to add a circular progress indicator underneath the column headers. This should help the user understand that not only are they waiting for data to load, but that it's the table row data specifically, thanks to the position of the progress indicator.

First, let's introduce a new component for displaying a `CircularProgress` component along with some new styles:

```
const usePaperStyles = makeStyles(theme => ({
  root: { margin: theme.spacing(2), textAlign: 'center' }
}));

const useProgressStyles = makeStyles(theme => ({
  progress: { margin: theme.spacing(2) }
}));

function MaybeLoading({ loading }) {
  const classes = useProgressStyles();
  return loading ? (
    <CircularProgress className={classes.progress} />
  ) : null;
}
```

There's a new `progress` style that's applied to the `CircularProgress` component. This adds `margin` to the progress indicator. The `textAlign` property has been added to the `root` style so that the progress indicator is horizontally centered within the `Paper` component. The `MaybeLoading` component renders the `CircularProgress` component if the `loading` property is `true`.

This means that you now have to keep track of the `loading` state of the API call. Here's the new state, which defaults to `true`:

```
const [loading, setLoading] = useState(true);
```

When the API call returns, you can set the `loading` state to `false`:

```
useEffect(() => {
  fetchData().then(items => {
    setItems(items);
    setLoading(false);
  });
}, []);
```

Lastly, you need to render the `MaybeLoading` component after the `Table` component:

```
<Paper className={classes.root}>
  <Table>
    ...
  </Table>
  <MaybeLoading loading={loading} />
</Paper>
```

Here's what your users will see while waiting for the table data to load:

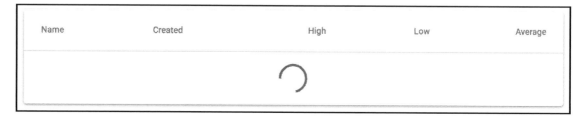

See also

- `Table` API documentation: https://material-ui.com/api/table/

Sortable columns

Material-UI tables have tools that help you implement sortable columns. If you're rendering a `Table` component in your application, your users will likely expect to be able to sort the table data by column.

How to do it...

When the users clicks on a column header, there should be a visual indication that table rows are now sorted by this column and the row order should change. When clicked on again, the column should appear in reverse order. Here's the code:

```
import React, { useState } from 'react';

import { makeStyles } from '@material-ui/styles';
import Table from '@material-ui/core/Table';
```

```
import TableBody from '@material-ui/core/TableBody';
import TableCell from '@material-ui/core/TableCell';
import TableHead from '@material-ui/core/TableHead';
import TableRow from '@material-ui/core/TableRow';
import TableSortLabel from '@material-ui/core/TableSortLabel';
import Paper from '@material-ui/core/Paper';

const comparator = (prop, desc = true) => (a, b) => {
  const order = desc ? -1 : 1;

  if (a[prop] < b[prop]) {
    return -1 * order;
  }

  if (a[prop] > b[prop]) {
    return 1 * order;
  }

  return 0 * order;
};

const useStyles = makeStyles(theme => ({
  root: { margin: theme.spacing(2), textAlign: 'center' }
}));

export default function SortableColumns() {
  const classes = useStyles();
  const [columns, setColumns] = useState([
    { name: 'Name', active: false },
    { name: 'Created', active: false },
    { name: 'High', active: false, numeric: true },
    { name: 'Low', active: false, numeric: true },
    { name: 'Average', active: false, numeric: true }
  ]);
  const [rows, setRows] = useState([
    {
      id: 1,
      name: 'First Item',
      created: new Date(),
      high: 2935,
      low: 1924,
      average: 2429.5
    },
    {
      id: 2,
      name: 'Second Item',
      created: new Date(),
      high: 439,
```

```
      low: 231,
      average: 335
    },
    {
      id: 3,
      name: 'Third Item',
      created: new Date(),
      high: 8239,
      low: 5629,
      average: 6934
    },
    {
      id: 4,
      name: 'Fourth Item',
      created: new Date(),
      high: 3203,
      low: 3127,
      average: 3165
    },
    {
      id: 5,
      name: 'Fifth Item',
      created: new Date(),
      high: 981,
      low: 879,
      average: 930
    }
  ]);

  const onSortClick = index => () => {
    setColumns(
      columns.map((column, i) => ({
        ...column,
        active: index === i,
        order:
          (index === i &&
            (column.order === 'desc' ? 'asc' : 'desc')) ||
          undefined
      }))
    );

    setRows(
      rows
        .slice()
        .sort(
          comparator(
            columns[index].name.toLowerCase(),
            columns[index].order === 'desc'
```

```
            )
          )
      );
    };

    return (
      <Paper className={classes.root}>
        <Table>
          <TableHead>
            <TableRow>
              {columns.map((column, index) => (
                <TableCell
                  key={column.name}
                  align={column.numeric ? 'right' : 'inherit'}
                >
                  <TableSortLabel
                    active={column.active}
                    direction={column.order}
                    onClick={onSortClick(index)}
                  >
                    {column.name}
                  </TableSortLabel>
                </TableCell>
              ))}
            </TableRow>
          </TableHead>
          <TableBody>
            {rows.map(row => (
              <TableRow key={row.id}>
                <TableCell component="th" scope="row">
                  {row.name}
                </TableCell>
                <TableCell>{row.created.toLocaleString()}</TableCell>
                <TableCell align="right">{row.high}</TableCell>
                <TableCell align="right">{row.low}</TableCell>
                <TableCell align="right">{row.average}</TableCell>
              </TableRow>
            ))}
          </TableBody>
        </Table>
      </Paper>
    );
  }
```

If you click on the **Name** column header, here's what you'll see:

Name ↓	Created	High	Low	Average
Fifth Item	10/19/2018, 1:23:44 AM	981	879	930
First Item	10/19/2018, 1:23:44 AM	2935	1924	2429.5
Fourth Item	10/19/2018, 1:23:44 AM	3203	3127	3165
Second Item	10/19/2018, 1:23:44 AM	439	231	335
Third Item	10/19/2018, 1:23:44 AM	8239	5629	6934

The column changes to indicate the sort order. If you click on the name column again, the sort order will reverse:

Name ↑	Created	High	Low	Average
Third Item	10/19/2018, 1:23:44 AM	8239	5629	6934
Second Item	10/19/2018, 1:23:44 AM	439	231	335
Fourth Item	10/19/2018, 1:23:44 AM	3203	3127	3165
First Item	10/19/2018, 1:23:44 AM	2935	1924	2429.5
Fifth Item	10/19/2018, 1:23:44 AM	981	879	930

How it works...

Let's break down the code used to render this table, starting with the markup used to render the column headers:

```
<TableHead>
  <TableRow>
    {columns.map((column, index) => (
      <TableCell
        key={column.name}
        align={column.numeric ? 'right' : 'inherit'}
      >
        <TableSortLabel
          active={column.active}
          direction={column.order}
          onClick={onSortClick(index)}
        >
          {column.name}
        </TableSortLabel>
      </TableCell>
    ))}
  </TableRow>
</TableHead>
```

Each column in the table is defined in the `columns` state. This array is mapped to `TableCell` components. Inside each `TableCell`, there's a `TableSortLabel` component. This component makes the column header text bold when it's the active column for sorting. It also adds the sort arrow to the right of the text. `TableSortLabel` takes `active`, `direction`, and `onClick` properties. The `active` property is based on the `active` state of the column, which changes when the column is clicked on. The `direction` property determines whether the rows are sorted in ascending or descending order for the given column. The `onClick` property takes an event handler that makes the necessary state changes when the column is clicked on. Here's the `onSortClick()` handler:

```
const onSortClick = index => () => {
  setColumns(
    columns.map((column, i) => ({
      ...column,
      active: index === i,
      order:
        (index === i &&
          (column.order === 'desc' ? 'asc' : 'desc')) ||
        undefined
    }))
  );
```

```
    setRows(
      rows
        .slice()
        .sort(
          comparator(
            columns[index].name.toLowerCase(),
            columns[index].order === 'desc'
          )
        )
    );
  };
```

This function takes an `index` argument—the column index—and returns a new function for the column. The returned function has two purposes:

1. To update the column state so that the correct column is marked as active and that it has the correct sort direction
2. To update the row state so that the table rows are in the correct order

Once these state changes have been made, the `active` column and the table rows will reflect them. The last piece of code to look at is the `comparator()` function. This is another higher-order function that takes the name of a column, and returns a new function that can be passed to `Array.sort()` to sort an array of objects by the given column:

```
const comparator = (prop, desc = true) => (a, b) => {
  const order = desc ? -1 : 1;

  if (a[prop] < b[prop]) {
    return -1 * order;
  }

  if (a[prop] > b[prop]) {
    return 1 * order;
  }

  return 0 * order;
};
```

This function is generic enough that you can use it with any tables in your app. In this case, the column name and order are passed to `comparator()` from the component state. As the state of the component changes, so too does the sorting behavior in `comparator()`.

There's more...

What if your data is already sorted by a particular column when it arrives from the API? If this is the case, you'll probably want to indicate which columns the rows are sorted by and in what direction, before the user starts interacting with the table.

To do so, you just need to change the default column state. For example, let's say that the **Average** column is sorted in descending order by default. Here's what your initial `column` state would look like:

```
const [columns, setColumns] = useState([
  { name: 'Name', active: false },
  { name: 'Created', active: false },
  { name: 'High', active: false, numeric: true },
  { name: 'Low', active: false, numeric: true },
  { name: 'Average', active: true, numeric: true }
]);
```

The **Average** column is now active by default. You didn't need to specify the order since the default is ascending. Here's what the table looks like when the screen first loads:

Name	Created	High	Low	↓ Average
First Item	10/23/2018, 3:37:37 PM	2935	1924	2429.5
Second Item	10/23/2018, 3:37:37 PM	439	231	335
Third Item	10/23/2018, 3:37:37 PM	8239	5629	6934
Fourth Item	10/23/2018, 3:37:37 PM	3203	3127	3165
Fifth Item	10/23/2018, 3:37:37 PM	981	879	930

See also

- Table **demos**: https://material-ui.com/demos/tables/

Filtering rows

Where there are tables, there's potential for too much information. This is why adding a search feature to your tables is a good idea. It allows the user to remove irrelevant rows from the table as they type.

How to do it...

Let's say that you have a table with lots of rows in it, meaning that the user is going to have a tough time scrolling through the entire table. To make things easier for them, you decide to add a search feature to your table that filters rows by checking whether the search text exists within the name column. Here's the code:

```
import React, { useState, useEffect, Fragment } from 'react';

import { makeStyles } from '@material-ui/styles';
import { withStyles } from '@material-ui/core/styles';
import Table from '@material-ui/core/Table';
import TableBody from '@material-ui/core/TableBody';
import TableCell from '@material-ui/core/TableCell';
import TableHead from '@material-ui/core/TableHead';
import TableRow from '@material-ui/core/TableRow';
import Paper from '@material-ui/core/Paper';
import CircularProgress from '@material-ui/core/CircularProgress';
import Input from '@material-ui/core/Input';
import InputLabel from '@material-ui/core/InputLabel';
import InputAdornment from '@material-ui/core/InputAdornment';
import FormControl from '@material-ui/core/FormControl';
import TextField from '@material-ui/core/TextField';

import SearchIcon from '@material-ui/icons/Search';

const fetchData = () =>
  new Promise(resolve => {
    const items = [
      {
        id: 1,
        name: 'First Item',
        created: new Date(),
        high: 2935,
        low: 1924,
        average: 2429.5
      },
      {
        id: 2,
```

```
      name: 'Second Item',
      created: new Date(),
      high: 439,
      low: 231,
      average: 335
    },
    {
      id: 3,
      name: 'Third Item',
      created: new Date(),
      high: 8239,
      low: 5629,
      average: 6934
    },
    {
      id: 4,
      name: 'Fourth Item',
      created: new Date(),
      high: 3203,
      low: 3127,
      average: 3165
    },
    {
      id: 5,
      name: 'Fifth Item',
      created: new Date(),
      high: 981,
      low: 879,
      average: 930
    }
  ];

  setTimeout(() => resolve(items), 1000);
});

const styles = theme => ({
  root: { margin: theme.spacing(2), textAlign: 'center' },
  progress: { margin: theme.spacing(2) },
  search: { marginLeft: theme.spacing(2) }
});
const useStyles = makeStyles(styles);

const MaybeLoading = withStyles(styles)(({ classes, loading }) =>
  loading ? <CircularProgress className={classes.progress} /> : null
);

export default function FilteringRows() {
  const classes = useStyles();
```

```
const [search, setSearch] = useState('');
const [items, setItems] = useState([]);
const [loading, setLoading] = useState(true);

useEffect(() => {
  fetchData().then(items => {
    setItems(items);
    setLoading(false);
  });
}, []);

const onSearchChange = e => {
  setSearch(e.target.value);
};

return (
  <Fragment>
    <TextField
      value={search}
      onChange={onSearchChange}
      className={classes.search}
      id="input-search"
      InputProps={{
        startAdornment: (
          <InputAdornment position="start">
            <SearchIcon />
          </InputAdornment>
        )
      }}
    />
    <Paper className={classes.root}>
      <Table>
        <TableHead>
          <TableRow>
            <TableCell>Name</TableCell>
            <TableCell>Created</TableCell>
            <TableCell align="right">High</TableCell>
            <TableCell align="right">Low</TableCell>
            <TableCell align="right">Average</TableCell>
          </TableRow>
        </TableHead>
        <TableBody>
          {items
            .filter(item => !search || item.name.includes(search))
            .map(item => {
              return (
                <TableRow key={item.id}>
                  <TableCell component="th" scope="row">
```

```
                    {item.name}
                  </TableCell>
                  <TableCell>
                    {item.created.toLocaleString()}
                  </TableCell>
                  <TableCell align="right">{item.high}</TableCell>
                  <TableCell align="right">{item.low}</TableCell>
                  <TableCell align="right">
                    {item.average}
                  </TableCell>
                </TableRow>
              );
            })}
          </TableBody>
        </Table>
        <MaybeLoading loading={loading} />
      </Paper>
    </Fragment>
  );
}
```

Here's what the table and search input fields look like when the screen first loads:

Q				
Name	Created	High	Low	Average
First Item	10/24/2018, 5:45:23 PM	2935	1924	2429.5
Second Item	10/24/2018, 5:45:23 PM	439	231	335
Third Item	10/24/2018, 5:45:23 PM	8239	5629	6934
Fourth Item	10/24/2018, 5:45:23 PM	3203	3127	3165
Fifth Item	10/24/2018, 5:45:23 PM	981	879	930

The search input is just above the table. Try typing in a filter string, such as **Fourth**—you should see the following:

If you delete the filter text from the search input, all rows in the table data will be rendered again.

How it works...

Let's start by looking at the state of the `FilteringRows` component:

```
const [search, setSearch] = useState('');
const [items, setItems] = useState([]);
const [loading, setLoading] = useState(true);
```

The search string is the actual filter that changes the rows that are rendered within the `Table` element. Next, let's look at the `TextField` component that renders the search input:

```
<TextField
  value={search}
  onChange={onSearchChange}
  className={classes.search}
  id="input-search"
  InputProps={{
    startAdornment: (
      <InputAdornment position="start">
        <SearchIcon />
      </InputAdornment>
    )
  }}
/>
```

The `onSearchChange()` function is responsible for maintaining the search state as the user types. You should render the search input component close to the table that it filters. In this example, the position of the search input feels like it belongs to the table.

Lastly, let's look at how the table rows are filtered and rendered:

```
<TableBody>
  {items
    .filter(item => !search || item.name.includes(search))
    .map(item => {
      return (
        <TableRow key={item.id}>
          <TableCell component="th" scope="row">
            {item.name}
          </TableCell>
          <TableCell>
            {item.created.toLocaleString()}
          </TableCell>
          <TableCell align="right">{item.high}</TableCell>
          <TableCell align="right">{item.low}</TableCell>
          <TableCell align="right">
            {item.average}
          </TableCell>
        </TableRow>
      );
    })}
</TableBody>
```

Instead of calling `map()` directly on the item's state, `filter()` is used to produce an array of items that match the search criteria. As the `search` state changes, the `filter()` call is repeated. The condition that checks whether the item matches what the user has typed checks to see whether the `name` property of the item contains the search string. But first, you have to make sure that the user is actually filtering. For example, if the search string is empty, every item should be returned. How the item is searched is specific to your application—you could search every item property if you wanted to.

See also

- `Table` demos: https://material-ui.com/demos/tables/

Selecting rows

Users often need to interact with specific rows in a table. For example, they might select a row and then perform an action that uses data from the selected row. Or, the user selects multiple rows, which produces new data related to their selection. With Material-UI tables, you can mark rows as selected using a single `TableRow` property.

How to do it...

In this example, let's assume that the user needs to be able to select multiple rows in your table. As rows are selected, another section on the screen is updated with data that reflects the selected rows. Let's start by looking at the `Card` component, which displays data from the selected table rows:

```
<Card className={classes.card}>
  <CardHeader title={`(${selections()}) rows selected`} />
  <CardContent>
    <Grid container direction="column">
      <Grid item>
        <Grid container justify="space-between">
          <Grid item>
            <Typography>Low</Typography>
          </Grid>
          <Grid item>
            <Typography>{selectedLow()}</Typography>
          </Grid>
        </Grid>
      </Grid>
      <Grid item>
        <Grid container justify="space-between">
          <Grid item>
            <Typography>High</Typography>
          </Grid>
          <Grid item>
            <Typography>{selectedHigh()}</Typography>
          </Grid>
        </Grid>
      </Grid>
      <Grid item>
        <Grid container justify="space-between">
          <Grid item>
            <Typography>Average</Typography>
          </Grid>
          <Grid item>
            <Typography>{selectedAverage()}</Typography>
          </Grid>
        </Grid>
      </Grid>
    </Grid>
  </CardContent>
</Card>
```

Let's take a look at the rest of the components now:

```
import React, { useState, Fragment } from 'react';

import { makeStyles } from '@material-ui/styles';
import Typography from '@material-ui/core/Typography';
import Grid from '@material-ui/core/Grid';
import Table from '@material-ui/core/Table';
import TableBody from '@material-ui/core/TableBody';
import TableCell from '@material-ui/core/TableCell';
import TableHead from '@material-ui/core/TableHead';
import TableRow from '@material-ui/core/TableRow';
import Paper from '@material-ui/core/Paper';
import Card from '@material-ui/core/Card';
import CardContent from '@material-ui/core/CardContent';
import CardHeader from '@material-ui/core/CardHeader';

const useStyles = makeStyles(theme => ({
  root: { margin: theme.spacing.unit * 2, textAlign: 'center' },
  card: { margin: theme.spacing.unit * 2, maxWidth: 300 }
}));

export default function SelectingRows() {
  const classes = useStyles();
  const [columns, setColumns] = useState([
    { name: 'Name', active: false },
    { name: 'Created', active: false },
    { name: 'High', active: false, numeric: true },
    { name: 'Low', active: false, numeric: true },
    { name: 'Average', active: true, numeric: true }
  ]);
  const [rows, setRows] = useState([
    {
      id: 1,
      name: 'First Item',
      created: new Date(),
      high: 2935,
      low: 1924,
      average: 2429.5
    },
    {
      id: 2,
      name: 'Second Item',
      created: new Date(),
      high: 439,
      low: 231,
      average: 335
    },
```

```
    {
      id: 3,
      name: 'Third Item',
      created: new Date(),
      high: 8239,
      low: 5629,
      average: 6934
    },
    {
      id: 4,
      name: 'Fourth Item',
      created: new Date(),
      high: 3203,
      low: 3127,
      average: 3165
    },
    {
      id: 5,
      name: 'Fifth Item',
      created: new Date(),
      high: 981,
      low: 879,
      average: 930
    }
  ]);

  const onRowClick = id => () => {
    const newRows = [...rows];
    const index = rows.findIndex(row => row.id === id);
    const row = rows[index];

    newRows[index] = { ...row, selected: !row.selected };
    setRows(newRows);
  };

  const selections = () => rows.filter(row => row.selected).length;

  const selectedLow = () =>
    rows
      .filter(row => row.selected)
      .reduce((total, row) => total + row.low, 0);

  const selectedHigh = () =>
    rows
      .filter(row => row.selected)
      .reduce((total, row) => total + row.high, 0);

  const selectedAverage = () => (selectedLow() + selectedHigh()) / 2;
```

```
return (
  <Fragment>
    <Card className={classes.card}>
      ...
    </Card>
    <Paper className={classes.root}>
      <Table>
        <TableHead>
          <TableRow>
            {columns.map(column => (
              <TableCell
                key={column.name}
                align={column.numeric ? 'right' : 'inherit'}
              >
                {column.name}
              </TableCell>
            ))}
          </TableRow>
        </TableHead>
        <TableBody>
          {rows.map(row => (
            <TableRow
              key={row.id}
              onClick={onRowClick(row.id)}
              selected={row.selected}
            >
              <TableCell component="th" scope="row">
                {row.name}
              </TableCell>
              <TableCell>{row.created.toLocaleString()}</TableCell>
              <TableCell align="right">{row.high}</TableCell>
              <TableCell align="right">{row.low}</TableCell>
              <TableCell align="right">{row.average}</TableCell>
            </TableRow>
          ))}
        </TableBody>
      </Table>
    </Paper>
  </Fragment>
);
}
```

Here's what the screen looks like when it first loads:

(0) rows selected

Low	0
High	0
Average	0

Name	Created	High	Low	Average
First Item	10/30/2018, 11:36:30 AM	2935	1924	2429.5
Second Item	10/30/2018, 11:36:30 AM	439	231	335
Third Item	10/30/2018, 11:36:30 AM	8239	5629	6934
Fourth Item	10/30/2018, 11:36:30 AM	3203	3127	3165
Fifth Item	10/30/2018, 11:36:30 AM	981	879	930

Now, you can try making some row selections. Here's what you'll see if you select the second and fourth rows:

(2) rows selected

Low	3358
High	3642
Average	3500

Name	Created	High	Low	Average
First Item	10/30/2018, 11:36:30 AM	2935	1924	2429.5
Second Item	10/30/2018, 11:36:30 AM	439	231	335
Third Item	10/30/2018, 11:36:30 AM	8239	5629	6934
Fourth Item	10/30/2018, 11:36:30 AM	3203	3127	3165
Fifth Item	10/30/2018, 11:36:30 AM	981	879	930

When you click on a table row, it changes visually so that the user can see that it is selected. Also note that the Card component contents change to reflect the selected rows. It also tells you how many rows are selected.

How it works...

The Card component relies on a few helper functions:

- selectedLow
- selectedHigh
- selectedAverage

The return values of these functions change when the table row selection changes. Let's take a closer look at how these values are computed:

```
const selectedLow = () =>
  rows
    .filter(row => row.selected)
    .reduce((total, row) => total + row.low, 0);

const selectedHigh = () =>
  rows
    .filter(row => row.selected)
    .reduce((total, row) => total + row.high, 0);

const selectedAverage = () => (selectedLow() + selectedHigh()) / 2;
```

The `selectedLow()` and `selectedHigh()` functions work the same way—they just operate on the `low` and `high` fields respectively. The `filter()` call is used to make sure that you're only working with selected rows. The `reduce()` call adds the values of the given field for the selected rows and returns the result as the property value. The `selectedAverage()` function uses the `selectedLow()` and `selectedHigh()` functions to compute a new average for the row selections.

Next, let's look at the handler that's called when a row is selected:

```
const onRowClick = id => () => {
  const newRows = [...rows];
  const index = rows.findIndex(row => row.id === id);
  const row = rows[index];

  newRows[index] = { ...row, selected: !row.selected };
  setRows(newRows);
};
```

The `onRowClick()` function finds the selected row in the `rows` state based on the `id` argument. Then, it toggles the selected state of the row. As a result, the computed properties that you just looked at are updated, and so is the appearance of the row itself:

```
<TableRow
  key={row.id}
  onClick={onRowClick(row.id)}
  selected={row.selected}
>
```

The `TableRow` component has a `selected` property, which changes the style of the row to mark it as selected.

See also

- Table **demos:** https://material-ui.com/demos/tables/

Row actions

Table rows often represent an object that you can perform actions on. For example, you might have a table of servers where each row represents a server that can be turned on or off. Instead of making your users click a link that takes them away from the table to perform an action, you can include common actions directly in each table row.

How to do it...

Let's say that you have a table with rows that have servers that can be turned on or off, depending on their current state. You want to include both of these actions as part of each table row, so that the user can more easily control their servers without spending lots of time navigating. The buttons also need to change their color and disabled state based on the state of the row.

Here's the code to do this:

```
import React, { useState } from 'react';

import { makeStyles } from '@material-ui/styles';
import Table from '@material-ui/core/Table';
import TableBody from '@material-ui/core/TableBody';
import TableCell from '@material-ui/core/TableCell';
import TableHead from '@material-ui/core/TableHead';
import TableRow from '@material-ui/core/TableRow';
import Paper from '@material-ui/core/Paper';
import IconButton from '@material-ui/core/IconButton';

import PlayArrowIcon from '@material-ui/icons/PlayArrow';
import StopIcon from '@material-ui/icons/Stop';

const useStyles = makeStyles(theme => ({
  root: { margin: theme.spacing(2), textAlign: 'center' },
  button: {}
}));

const StartButton = ({ row, onClick }) => (
  <IconButton
```

```
      onClick={onClick}
      color={row.status === 'off' ? 'primary' : 'default'}
      disabled={row.status === 'running'}
    >
      <PlayArrowIcon fontSize="small" />
    </IconButton>
  );

  const StopButton = ({ row, onClick }) => (
    <IconButton
      onClick={onClick}
      color={row.status === 'running' ? 'primary' : 'default'}
      disabled={row.status === 'off'}
    >
      <StopIcon fontSize="small" />
    </IconButton>
  );

  export default function RowActions() {
    const classes = useStyles();
    const [rows, setRows] = useState([
      {
        id: 1,
        name: 'First Item',
        status: 'running'
      },
      {
        id: 2,
        name: 'Second Item',
        status: 'off'
      },
      {
        id: 3,
        name: 'Third Item',
        status: 'off'
      },
      {
        id: 4,
        name: 'Fourth Item',
        status: 'running'
      },
      {
        id: 5,
        name: 'Fifth Item',
        status: 'off'
      }
    ]);
```

```
  const toggleStatus = id => () => {
    const newRows = [...rows];
    const index = rows.findIndex(row => row.id === id);
    const row = rows[index];

    newRows[index] = {
      ...row,
      status: row.status === 'running' ? 'off' : 'running'
    };
    setRows(newRows);
  };


  return (
    <Paper className={classes.root}>
      <Table>
        <TableHead>
          <TableRow>
            <TableCell>Name</TableCell>
            <TableCell>Status</TableCell>
            <TableCell>Actions</TableCell>
          </TableRow>
        </TableHead>
        <TableBody>
          {rows.map(row => {
            return (
              <TableRow key={row.id}>
                <TableCell component="th" scope="row">
                  {row.name}
                </TableCell>
                <TableCell>{row.status}</TableCell>
                <TableCell>
                  <StartButton
                    row={row}
                    onClick={toggleStatus(row.id)}
                  />
                  <StopButton
                    row={row}
                    onClick={toggleStatus(row.id)}
                  />
                </TableCell>
              </TableRow>
            );
          })}
        </TableBody>
      </Table>
    </Paper>
  );
}
```

Here's what the screen looks like when it first loads:

Depending on the status of the row data, the action buttons will show differently. For example, in the first row, the start button is disabled because `status` is `running`. The second row has a disabled stop button because the `status` is `off`. Let's try clicking on the stop button in the first row and the start button in the second row. Here's how the UI changes once this is done:

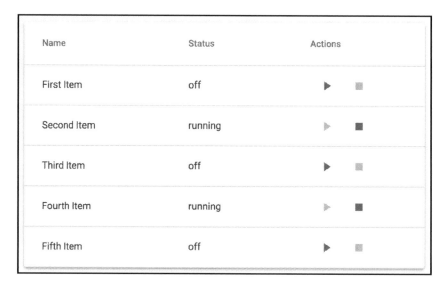

How it works...

Let's start by looking at the two components that are used as the row actions:

```
const StartButton = ({ row, onClick }) => (
  <IconButton
    onClick={onClick}
    color={row.status === 'off' ? 'primary' : 'default'}
    disabled={row.status === 'running'}
  >
    <PlayArrowIcon fontSize="small" />
  </IconButton>
);

const StopButton = ({ row, onClick }) => (
  <IconButton
    onClick={onClick}
    color={row.status === 'running' ? 'primary' : 'default'}
    disabled={row.status === 'off'}
  >
    <StopIcon fontSize="small" />
  </IconButton>
);
```

The StartButton and StopButton components are very similar. Both of these
components are rendered in every row of the table. There's the onClick property, a
function that changes the state of the row data when clicked. The color of the icon changes
based on the status of the row. Likewise, the disabled property changes based on the
status of the row.

Next, let's look at the toggleStatus() handler, which changes the status state of the row
when an action button is clicked:

```
const toggleStatus = id => () => {
  const newRows = [...rows];
  const index = rows.findIndex(row => row.id === id);
  const row = rows[index];

  newRows[index] = {
    ...row,
    status: row.status === 'running' ? 'off' : 'running'
  };
  setRows(newRows);
};
```

The StartButton and StopButton components both use the same handler function—it toggles the status value between running and off. Finally, let's look at the TableCell component where these row actions are rendered:

```
<TableCell>
  <StartButton
    row={row}
    onClick={toggleStatus(row.id)}
  />
  <StopButton
    row={row}
    onClick={toggleStatus(row.id)}
  />
</TableCell>
```

The row data is passed as the row property. The toggleStatus() function takes a row id argument and returns a new handler function that acts on this row.

See also

- Table demos: https://material-ui.com/demos/tables/

8
Cards - Display Detailed Information

In this chapter, you'll learn the following about Cards:

- Main content
- Card header
- Performing actions
- Presenting media
- Expandable cards

Introduction

Cards are a Material Design concept used to display specific information on a given subject. For example, the subject could be an object returned by an API endpoint. Or, the subject could just be part of a complex object—in this case, you can use multiple cards to organize information in a way that helps the user understand what they're looking at.

Main content

The main content of a `Card` component is where information concerning the subject is placed. The `CardContent` component is a child of `Card`, and you can use it to render other Material UI components, such as `Typography`.

How to do it...

Let's say that you're working on a detail screen for some type of entity, such as a blog post. You've decided to use a `Card` component to render some of the entity details since the entity is the subject under consideration. Here's the code that will render a `Card` component with information about a particular subject:

```
import React from 'react';

import { withStyles } from '@material-ui/core/styles';
import Card from '@material-ui/core/Card';
import CardContent from '@material-ui/core/CardContent';
import Typography from '@material-ui/core/Typography';

const styles = theme => ({
  card: {
    maxWidth: 400
  },
  content: {
    marginTop: theme.spacing(1)
  }
});

const MainContent = withStyles(styles)(({ classes }) => (
  <Card className={classes.card}>
    <CardContent>
      <Typography variant="h4">Subject Title</Typography>
      <Typography variant="subtitle1">
        A little more about subject
      </Typography>
      <Typography className={classes.content}>
        Even more information on the subject, contained within the
        card. You can fit a lot of information here, but don't try to
        overdo it.
      </Typography>
    </CardContent>
  </Card>
));

export default MainContent;
```

When you first load the screen, here's what you'll see:

Subject Title
A little more about subject

Even more information on the subject, contained within the card. You can fit a lot of information here, but don't try to overdo it.

The card's content is divided into three sections:

- **Subject Title**: Tells the user what they're looking at
- **Subtitle**: Gives the user a little more context
- **Content**: The main content of the subject

How it works...

This example uses the `CardContent` component as the key organizational unit within `Card`. Everything else is up to you. For example, the card in this example uses three `Typography` components to render three different styles of text as the card's content.

The first `Typography` component uses the `h4` variant and serves as the card's title. The second `Typography` component serves as the subtitle of the card and uses the `subtitle1` variant. Lastly, there's the main content of the card, which uses the `Typography` default font. There is a `marginTop` style set on this text so that it's not pushed up against the subtitle.

See also

- Card reference: `https://material-ui.com/demos/cards/`

Card header

The CardHeader component is used to render the header of a card. This includes the title text, as well as some other potential elements. The reason you might want to use a CardHeader component is so that you can let it handle the layout styles of the header and to keep the markup within your Card semantic.

How to do it...

Let's say that you're building a card component for users of your application. As the card header, you want to display the user's name. Instead of using a Typography component to render the title using a text variant, you could use a CardHeader component, placed adjacent to the CardContent component. Here's how the code appears:

```
import React from 'react';

import { withStyles } from '@material-ui/core/styles';
import Card from '@material-ui/core/Card';
import CardHeader from '@material-ui/core/CardHeader';
import CardContent from '@material-ui/core/CardContent';
import Typography from '@material-ui/core/Typography';
import Avatar from '@material-ui/core/Avatar';

import PersonIcon from '@material-ui/icons/Person';

const styles = theme => ({
  card: {
    maxWidth: 400
  }
});

const CardHeader = withStyles(styles)(({ classes }) => (
  <Card className={classes.card}>
    <CardHeader
      title="Ron Swanson"
      subheader="Legend"
      avatar={
        <Avatar>
          <PersonIcon />
        </Avatar>
      }
    />
    <CardContent>
      <Typography variant="caption">Joined 2009</Typography>
```

```
    <Typography>
        Some filler text about the user. There doesn't have to be a
        lot - just enough so that the text spans at least two lines.
    </Typography>
  </CardContent>
</Card>
));

export default CardHeader;
```

Here's what the screen looks like:

How it works...

Let's take a look at the markup used to render this card:

```
<Card className={classes.card}>
  <CardHeader title="Ron Swanson" />
  <CardContent>
    <Typography variant="caption">Joined 2009</Typography>
    <Typography>
        Some filler text about the user. There doesn't have to be a
        lot - just enough so that the text spans at least two lines.
    </Typography>
  </CardContent>
```

The CardHeader component is a sibling of CardContent. This makes the Card markup semantic, as opposed to having to declare the card header within CardContent. The CardHeader component takes a title string property, which is how the title of the card is rendered.

There's more...

You can add more than just a string to `CardHeader` components. You can also pass a sub-header string and an avatar to help users identify the subject in the card. Let's modify this example to add both of these things. First, here are the new component imports that you'll need to add:

```
import Avatar from '@material-ui/core/Avatar';
import PersonIcon from '@material-ui/icons/Person';
```

Next, here's the updated `CardHeader` markup:

```
<CardHeader
  title="Ron Swanson"
  subheader="Legend"
  avatar={
    <Avatar>
      <PersonIcon />
    </Avatar>
  }
/>
```

And here's what the result looks like:

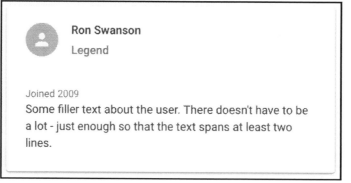

The `CardHeader` component handles alignment of the three header components—the avatar, the title, and the sub-header.

See also

- Card **demos:** https://material-ui.com/demos/cards/

Performing actions

Cards are used to display specific actions about a subject. Often, users take action on subjects, such as sending a contact a message or deleting a contact. `CardActions` components can be used by `Card` components to display actions that users can take on the subject.

How to do it...

Let's say that you're using a `Card` component to display a contact. In addition to showing information about the contact, you would like for your users to be able to take actions on contacts from within the card. For example, you could provide two actions—one to message the contact, and one to phone the contact. Here's the code to do this:

```
import React from 'react';

import { withStyles } from '@material-ui/core/styles';
import Card from '@material-ui/core/Card';
import CardHeader from '@material-ui/core/CardHeader';
import CardContent from '@material-ui/core/CardContent';
import CardActions from '@material-ui/core/CardActions';
import Typography from '@material-ui/core/Typography';
import Avatar from '@material-ui/core/Avatar';
import IconButton from '@material-ui/core/IconButton';
import PersonIcon from '@material-ui/icons/Person';
import ContactMailIcon from '@material-ui/icons/ContactMail';
import ContactPhoneIcon from '@material-ui/icons/ContactPhone';

const styles = theme => ({
  card: {
    maxWidth: 400
  }
});

const PerformingActions = withStyles(styles)(({ classes }) => (
  <Card className={classes.card}>
    <CardHeader
      title="Ron Swanson"
      subheader="Legend"
      avatar={
        <Avatar>
          <PersonIcon />
        </Avatar>
      }
    />
```

```
        <CardContent>
          <Typography variant="caption">Joined 2009</Typography>
          <Typography>
            Some filler text about the user. There doesn't have to be a
            lot - just enough so that the text spans at least two lines.
          </Typography>
        </CardContent>
        <CardActions disableActionSpacing>
          <IconButton>
            <ContactMailIcon />
          </IconButton>
          <IconButton>
            <ContactPhoneIcon />
          </IconButton>
        </CardActions>
      </Card>
  ));

  export default PerformingActions;
```

Here's what the card looks like when the screen first loads:

The two actions that users can take on the subject are rendered as icon buttons at the bottom of the card.

How it works...

The CardActions component handles aligning the button items inside of it, both horizontally, and making sure they're placed at the bottom of the card. The disableActionSpacing property removes the extra margin added by CardActions. Typically, you'll use this property any time you're using an IconButton component for your actions.

Let's take a closer look at the markup:

```
<CardActions disableActionSpacing>
  <IconButton>
    <ContactMailIcon />
  </IconButton>
  <IconButton>
    <ContactPhoneIcon />
  </IconButton>
</CardActions>
```

Like the other child components of Card, the CardActions component makes the overall card structure semantic, as it is a sibling of related card functionality. The items placed within CardActions can be anything you want, but common practice is to use icon buttons.

There's more...

You can change the alignment of the items in the CardActions component. Since it uses flexbox as its display, you can use any of the justify-content values. Here's an updated version that aligns the action buttons to the right of the card:

```
const styles = theme => ({
  card: {
    maxWidth: 400
  },
  actions: {
    justifyContent: 'flex-end'
  }
});

const PerformingActions = withStyles(styles)(({ classes }) => (
  <Card className={classes.card}>
    <CardHeader
      title="Ron Swanson"
      subheader="Legend"
```

```
        avatar={
          <Avatar>
            <PersonIcon />
          </Avatar>
        }
      />
      <CardContent>
        <Typography variant="caption">Joined 2009</Typography>
        <Typography>
          Some filler text about the user. There doesn't have to be a
          lot - just enough so that the text spans at least two lines.
        </Typography>
      </CardContent>
      <CardActions disableActionSpacing className={classes.actions}>
        <IconButton>
          <ContactMailIcon />
        </IconButton>
        <IconButton>
          <ContactPhoneIcon />
        </IconButton>
      </CardActions>
    </Card>
));

export default PerformingActions;
```

The `justify-content` **property is part of the** `actions` **style, which is then applied to the** `CardActions` **component. Here's what the result looks like:**

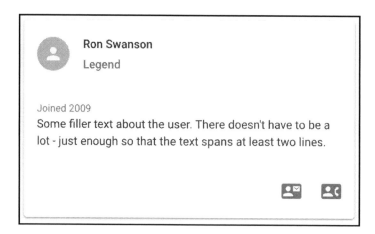

Here's another version showing `center` as the `justify-content` value:

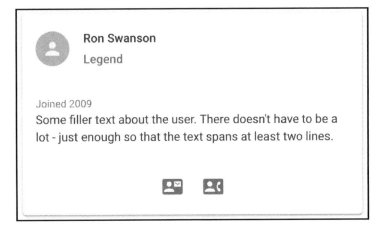

See also

- `Card` demos: `https://material-ui.com/demos/cards/`

Presenting media

Cards have built-in capabilities for displaying media. This includes things such as images and videos that become the focal point of the card.

How to do it...

Let's say that you have an image of the subject that the `Card` component is displaying. You can use the `CardMedia` component to render the image. You should use this component instead of something like `<img>` because it will handle a number of styling issues for you. Here's the code:

```
import React from 'react';

import { withStyles } from '@material-ui/core/styles';
import Card from '@material-ui/core/Card';
import CardHeader from '@material-ui/core/CardHeader';
import CardContent from '@material-ui/core/CardContent';
import CardMedia from '@material-ui/core/CardMedia';
```

```
import CardActions from '@material-ui/core/CardActions';
import Button from '@material-ui/core/Button';
import Typography from '@material-ui/core/Typography';

const styles = theme => ({
  card: {
    maxWidth: 322
  },
  media: {
    width: 322,
    height: 322
  }
});

const PresentingMedia = withStyles(styles)(({ classes }) => (
  <Card className={classes.card}>
    <CardHeader title="Grapefruit" subheader="Red" />
    <CardMedia
      className={classes.media}
      image="grapefruit-slice-332-332.jpg"
      title="Grapefruit"
    />
    <CardContent>
      <Typography>Mmmm. Grapefruit.</Typography>
    </CardContent>
  </Card>
));

export default PresentingMedia;
```

Here's what the card looks like when it's rendered:

How it works...

The CardMedia component is just like other components that make up cards – just another part. In this example, CardMedia is placed below CardHeader and above CardContent. But it doesn't have to be this way. You can rearrange the order of these components.

There's more...

You can rearrange your card items in a way that makes the most sense for your app. For example, your card with media might not have any content and you might want to display the header text at the bottom of the card, below the media, and with the text centered. Here's the modified code:

```
const styles = theme => ({
  card: {
    maxWidth: 322
  },
  media: {
    width: 322,
    height: 322
```

```
    },
    header: {
      textAlign: 'center'
    }
  });

  const PresentingMedia = withStyles(styles)(({ classes }) => (
    <Card className={classes.card}>
      <CardMedia
        className={classes.media}
        image="https://interactive-grapefruit-slice-332-332.jpg"
        title="Grapefruit"
      />
      <CardHeader
        className={classes.header}
        title="Grapefruit"
        subheader="Red"
      />
    </Card>
  ));

  export default PresentingMedia;
```

Here's what the resulting card looks like:

See also

- The img HTML tag reference: https://developer.mozilla.org/en-US/docs/Web/HTML/Element/img

Expandable cards

Sometimes, you can't fit everything into a card that you might want to. To accommodate, you can make your cards expandable, meaning that the user can click on an expand button to reveal additional content.

 If you're trying to fit too much content into a Card, making the card expandable just masks the problem. Instead, consider a different approach to displaying information about the subject in question. For example, maybe, instead of a card, the subject is worthy of its own page.

How to do it...

Let's see that there's additional content about a subject within a card that does the following:

- Takes up a little too much vertical space
- Isn't very important and doesn't need to be shown by default

You can deal with both of these challenges by putting the content into an expandable region of the card. Then, the vertical space isn't an issue and the user can look at the content if they deem it relevant. Here's an example that builds on an earlier example from this chapter to make part of the card content hidden by default:

```
import React, { useState } from 'react';

import { makeStyles } from '@material-ui/styles';
import Card from '@material-ui/core/Card';
import CardHeader from '@material-ui/core/CardHeader';
import CardContent from '@material-ui/core/CardContent';
import CardActions from '@material-ui/core/CardActions';
import Typography from '@material-ui/core/Typography';
import Avatar from '@material-ui/core/Avatar';
import IconButton from '@material-ui/core/IconButton';
import Collapse from '@material-ui/core/Collapse';
```

```
import PersonIcon from '@material-ui/icons/Person';
import ContactMailIcon from '@material-ui/icons/ContactMail';
import ContactPhoneIcon from '@material-ui/icons/ContactPhone';
import ExpandLessIcon from '@material-ui/icons/ExpandLess';
import ExpandMoreIcon from '@material-ui/icons/ExpandMore';

const useStyles = makeStyles(theme => ({
  card: {
    maxWidth: 400
  },
  expand: {
    marginLeft: 'auto'
  }
}));

const ExpandIcon = ({ expanded }) =>
  expanded ? <ExpandLessIcon /> : <ExpandMoreIcon />;

export default function ExpandableCards() {
  const classes = useStyles();
  const [expanded, setExpanded] = useState(false);

  const toggleExpanded = () => {
    setExpanded(!expanded);
  };

  return (
    <Card className={classes.card}>
      <CardHeader
        title="Ron Swanson"
        subheader="Legend"
        avatar={
          <Avatar>
            <PersonIcon />
          </Avatar>
        }
      />
      <CardContent>
        <Typography variant="caption">Joined 2009</Typography>
        <Typography>
          Some filler text about the user. There doesn't have to be a
          lot - just enough so that the text spans at least two lines.
        </Typography>
      </CardContent>
      <CardActions disableActionSpacing>
        <IconButton>
          <ContactMailIcon />
        </IconButton>
```

```
        <IconButton>
          <ContactPhoneIcon />
        </IconButton>
        <IconButton
          className={classes.expand}
          onClick={toggleExpanded}
        >
          <ExpandIcon expanded={expanded} />
        </IconButton>
      </CardActions>
      <Collapse in={expanded}>
        <CardContent>
          <Typography>
            Even more filler text about the user. It doesn't fit in
            the main content area of the card, so this is what the
            user will see when they click the expand button.
          </Typography>
        </CardContent>
      </Collapse>
    </Card>
  );
}
```

When you first load the screen, here's what the card looks like:

To the right of the action buttons in the card, there is now an expand button with a down arrow. If you click on the expand button, here's what the card looks like when it's expanded:

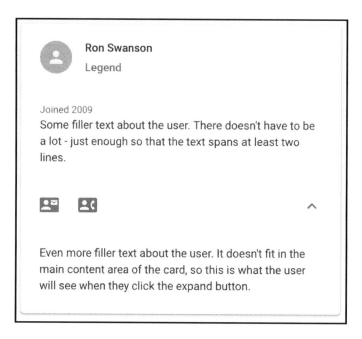

The expand icon has now changed to a collapse icon—clicking on it will collapse the card into its original state.

How it works...

Let's break down the additions in this example that added the expandable card region. First, there's the expand style:

```
expand: {
  marginLeft: 'auto'
}
```

This is used to align the expand/collapse icon button to the left of the other actions. Next, let's look at the ExpandIcon component:

```
const ExpandIcon = ({ expanded }) =>
  expanded ? <ExpandLessIcon /> : <ExpandMoreIcon />;
```

This utility component is used to render either the correct icon component, depending on the expanded state of the component. Next, let's take a look at the `toggleExpanded()` function:

```
const toggleExpanded = () => {
  setExpanded(!expanded);
};
```

This handler, when called, will toggle the expanded state. This state is then passed to the `ExpandIcon` component, which will render the appropriate icon. Next, let's take a closer look at the actions markup for this card:

```
<CardActions disableActionSpacing>
  <IconButton>
    <ContactMailIcon />
  </IconButton>
  <IconButton>
    <ContactPhoneIcon />
  </IconButton>
  <IconButton
    className={classes.expand}
    onClick={toggleExpanded}
  >
    <ExpandIcon expanded={expanded} />
  </IconButton>
</CardActions>
```

The expand/collapse button is the last `IconButton` component shown here. It's using the expand style, the `toggleExpanded()` click handler, and the expanded state. Finally, let's take a look at the card content that can be expanded and collapsed when the button is clicked on:

```
<Collapse in={expanded}>
  <CardContent>
    <Typography>
      Even more filler text about the user. It doesn't fit
      in the main content area of the card, so this is what
      the user will see when they click the expand button.
    </Typography>
  </CardContent>
</Collapse>
```

The `Collapse` component is used to show or hide the additional card content based on the expanded state. Note that the `CardContent` component is used here so that once the additional content is shown, it is styled consistently with the rest of the card content.

See also

- Card **demos:** https://material-ui.com/demos/cards/
- Card **API documentation:** https://material-ui.com/api/card/
- CardHeader **API documentation:** https://material-ui.com/api/card-header/
- CardContent **API documentation:** https://material-ui.com/api/card-content/
- CardActions **API documentation:** https://material-ui.com/api/card-actions/
- IconButton **API documentation:** https://material-ui.com/api/icon-button/
- Collapse **API documentation:** https://material-ui.com/api/collapse/

Snackbars - Temporary
Messages

9

In this chapter, you'll learn about the following:

- Snackbar content
- Controlling visibility with state
- Snackbar transitions
- Positioning Snackbars
- Error boundaries and error Snackbars
- Snackbars with actions
- Queuing Snackbars

Introduction

Material-UI comes with a `Snackbar` component that's used to display messages for users. These messages are brief, short-lived, and don't interfere with the main application components.

Snackbar content

Text is the most common form of Snackbar message content that you'll display for your users. Because of this, the Snackbar component makes it straightforward to set message content and display the snackbar.

How to do it...

The message property of the Snackbar component accepts a string value, or any other valid React element. Here's the code that shows you how to set the content of the Snackbar component and display it:

```
import React from 'react';
import Snackbar from '@material-ui/core/Snackbar';

const MySnackbarContent = () => <Snackbar open={true} message="Test" />;
export default MySnackbarContent;
```

When the page first loads, you'll see a snackbar that looks like this:

How it works...

By default, a snackbar is nothing fancy, but it renders your text content as specified in the message property. The open property is set to true because any other value hides the snackbar.

There's more...

The Snackbar components use SnackbackContent components to render the actual content that's displayed. In turn, SnackbarContent uses Paper, which uses Typography. It's kind of tricky to navigate through all of this indirection, but, thankfully, you don't have to. Instead, you can pass properties all the way to the Typography component from Snackbar via the ContentProps property.

Let's say that you wanted to use the h6 typography variant. Here's how you could do this:

```
import React from 'react';
import Snackbar from '@material-ui/core/Snackbar';

const MySnackbarContent () => (
  <Snackbar
    open={true}
    message="Test"
    ContentProps={{ variant: 'h6' }}
  />
);

export default MySnackbarContent;
```

Any properties that you want to pass to the component used by Paper can be set by
ContentProps. Here, you're passing the variant property—which results in the
following visual change:

The end result is larger text and a wider margin. The aim of this example isn't this
particular typography change, but rather the idea that you can customize Snackbar text
in the exact same way as you would Typography components.

You can put as many or as few components as you want into your
snackbar content. For example, you can pass child components to
Snackbar instead of in the message property. However, I would advise
keeping your snackbar content as simple as possible. The last place where
you want to go down a design rabbit hole is in a component that's already
been designed to handle simple text.

See also

- Snackbar demos: https://material-ui.com/demos/snackbars/
- Snackbar API documentation: https://material-ui.com/api/snackbar/

Controlling visibility with state

Snackbars are displayed in response to something. For example, if a new resource in your application is created, then using a `Snackbar` component to relay this information to the user is a good choice. If you need to control the state of your snackbars, then you need to add a state that controls the visibility of the snackbar.

How to do it...

The `open` property is used to control the visibility of the snackbar. All you need in order to control this property value is a state value that's passed to it. Then, when this state changes, so does the visibility of the snackbar. Here's some code that illustrates the basic idea of state-controlling snackbars:

```
import React, { Fragment, useState } from 'react';

import Button from '@material-ui/core/Button';
import Snackbar from '@material-ui/core/Snackbar';

export default function ControllingVisibilityWithState() {
  const [open, setOpen] = useState(false);

  const showSnackbar = () => {
    setOpen(true);
  };

  return (
    <Fragment>
      <Button variant="contained" onClick={showSnackbar}>
        Show Snackbar
      </Button>
      <Snackbar open={open} message="Visible Snackbar!" />
    </Fragment>
  );
}
```

When you first load the screen, all you'll see is a **SHOW SNACKBAR** button:

SHOW SNACKBAR

Clicking on this button shows the snackbar:

Visible Snackbar!

How it works...

The component has an `open` state that determines the visibility of the snackbar. The value of `open` is passed to the `open` property of `Snackbar`. When the user clicks on the **SHOW SNACKBAR** button, the `showSnackbar()` function sets the `open` state to true. As a result, the true value is passed to the `open` property of `Snackbar`.

There's more...

Once you've displayed a snackbar, you're going to need to be able to close it somehow. Once again, the `open` state can hide the snackbar. But how do you change the open state back to false? The typical pattern with snackbar messages is to have them appear only briefly, after which they're automatically hidden.

By passing two more properties to `Snackbar`, you can enhance this example so that the snackbar automatically hides itself after a certain time. Here's the updated code:

```
import React, { Fragment, useState } from 'react';

import Button from '@material-ui/core/Button';
import Snackbar from '@material-ui/core/Snackbar';

export default function ControllingVisibilityWithState() {
  const [open, setOpen] = useState(false);
  const showSnackbar = () => {
    setOpen(true);
  };
  const hideSnackbar = () => {
    setOpen(false);
  };

  return (
    <Fragment>
      <Button variant="contained" onClick={showSnackbar}>
        Show Snackbar
      </Button>
      <Snackbar
```

```
        open={open}
        onClose={hideSnackbar}
        autoHideDuration={5000}
        message="Visible Snackbar!"
      />
    </Fragment>
  );
}
```

A new function—hideSnackbar()—was added to the component. This is passed to the onClose property of Snackbar. The autoHideDuration component is the number of milliseconds that you want the snackbar to stay visible. In this example, after five seconds, the Snackbar component will call the function passed to its onClose property. This sets the open state to false, which is in turn passed to the open property of Snackbar.

See also

- Snackbar demos: https://material-ui.com/demos/snackbars/
- Snackbar API documentation: https://material-ui.com/api/snackbar/
- Button API documentation: https://material-ui.com/api/button/

Snackbar transitions

You can control the transitions used by Snackbar components when it is displayed and hidden. The Snackbar component directly supports transition customization through properties, so you don't have to spend too much time thinking about how to implement your snackbar transitions.

How to do it...

Let's say that you want to make it easier to change the transition used by snackbars throughout your application. You could create a thin wrapper component around Snackbar that takes care of setting the appropriate properties. Here's what the code looks like:

```
import React, { Fragment, useState } from 'react';

import Grid from '@material-ui/core/Grid';
import Button from '@material-ui/core/Button';
```

```
import Snackbar from '@material-ui/core/Snackbar';
import Slide from '@material-ui/core/Slide';
import Grow from '@material-ui/core/Grow';
import Fade from '@material-ui/core/Fade';

const MySnackbar = ({ transition, direction, ...rest }) => (
  <Snackbar
    TransitionComponent={
      { slide: Slide, grow: Grow, fade: Fade }[transition]
    }
    TransitionProps={{ direction }}
    {...rest}
  />
);

export default function SnackbarTransitions() {
  const [first, setFirst] = useState(false);
  const [second, setSecond] = useState(false);
  const [third, setThird] = useState(false);
  const [fourth, setFourth] = useState(false);

  return (
    <Fragment>
      <Grid container spacing={8}>
        <Grid item>
          <Button variant="contained" onClick={() => setFirst(true)}>
            Slide Down
          </Button>
        </Grid>
        <Grid item>
          <Button variant="contained" onClick={() => setSecond(true)}>
            Slide Up
          </Button>
        </Grid>
        <Grid item>
          <Button variant="contained" onClick={() => setThird(true)}>
            Grow
          </Button>
        </Grid>
        <Grid item>
          <Button variant="contained" onClick={() => setFourth(true)}>
            Fade
          </Button>
        </Grid>
      </Grid>
      <MySnackbar
        open={first}
        onClose={() => setFirst(false)}
```

```
        autoHideDuration={5000}
        message="Slide Down"
        transition="slide"
        direction="down"
      />
      <MySnackbar
        open={second}
        onClose={() => setSecond(false)}
        autoHideDuration={5000}
        message="Slide Up"
        transition="slide"
        direction="up"
      />
      <MySnackbar
        open={third}
        onClose={() => setThird(false)}
        autoHideDuration={5000}
        message="Grow"
        transition="grow"
      />
      <MySnackbar
        open={fourth}
        onClose={() => setFourth(false)}
        autoHideDuration={5000}
        message="Fade"
        transition="fade"
      />
    </Fragment>
  );
}
```

This code renders four buttons and four snackbars. When you first load the screen, you'll only see buttons:

Clicking on each of these buttons will display their corresponding `Snackbar` component at the bottom of the screen. If you pay attention to the transitions used when each of the snackbars is displayed, you'll notice the difference depending on the buttons you press. For example, clicking on the **Fade** button will use the `fade` transition, resulting in the following snackbar:

How it works...

Let's start by looking at the `MySnackbar` component that was created in this example:

```
const MySnackbar = ({ transition, direction, ...rest }) => (
  <Snackbar
    TransitionComponent={
      { slide: Slide, grow: Grow, fade: Fade }[transition]
    }
    TransitionProps={{ direction }}
    {...rest}
  />
);
```

There are two properties of interest here. The first is the `transition` string. This is used to look up the transition component to use. For example, the string `slide` will use the `Slide` component. The resulting component is used by the `TransitionComponent` property. The `Snackbar` components will use this component internally to apply the desired transition to your snackbars. The `direction` property is used with the `Slide` transition, which is why this property is passed to `TransitionProps`. These property values are passed directly to the component that's passed to `TransitionComponent`.

The alternative to using `TransitionProps` is to create a higher-order component that wraps its own property customization values. But since `Snackbar` is already set up to help you pass properties, there's no need to create yet another component if you want to avoid doing so.

Next, let's look at the component state and the functions that change it:

```
const [first, setFirst] = useState(false);
const [second, setSecond] = useState(false);
const [third, setThird] = useState(false);
const [fourth, setFourth] = useState(false);
```

The `first`, `second`, `third`, and `fourth` states correspond to their own `Snackbar` components. These state values control the visibility of each function, and their corresponding setter functions show or hide the snackbars.

Finally, let's look at two of the `MySnackbar` components being rendered:

```
<MySnackbar
  open={first}
  onClose={() => setFirst(false)}
  autoHideDuration={5000}
  message="Slide Down"
  transition="slide"
```

```
    direction="down"
  />
  <MySnackbar
    open={second}
    onClose={() => setSecond(false)}
    autoHideDuration={5000}
    message="Slide Up"
    transition="slide"
    direction="up"
  />
```

Both of these instances use the `slide` transition. However, the `direction` property is different for each. The `MySnackbar` abstraction makes it a little simpler for you to specify transitions and transition arguments.

See also

- Snackbar demos: `https://material-ui.com/demos/snackbars/`
- Snackbar API documentation: `https://material-ui.com/api/snackbar/`
- Slide API documentation: `https://material-ui.com/api/slide/`
- Grow API documentation: `https://material-ui.com/api/grow/`
- Fade API documentation: `https://material-ui.com/api/fade/`

Positioning snackbars

Material-UI Snackbar components have an `anchorOrigin` property that allows you to change the position of the snackbar when it's displayed. You might be fine using the default positioning of snackbars, but sometimes you'll need this level of customization to stay consistent with other parts of your application.

How to do it...

While you can't arbitrarily position snackbars on the screen, there are a number of options that allow you to change the position of the snackbar. Here's some code that allows you to play around with the `anchorOrigin` property values:

```
import React, { Fragment, useState } from 'react';

import { makeStyles } from '@material-ui/styles';
```

```
import Snackbar from '@material-ui/core/Snackbar';
import Radio from '@material-ui/core/Radio';
import RadioGroup from '@material-ui/core/RadioGroup';
import FormControlLabel from '@material-ui/core/FormControlLabel';
import FormControl from '@material-ui/core/FormControl';
import FormLabel from '@material-ui/core/FormLabel';

const useStyles = makeStyles(theme => ({
  formControl: {
    margin: theme.spacing(3)
  }
}));

export default function PositioningSnackbars() {
  const classes = useStyles();
  const [vertical, setVertical] = useState('bottom');
  const [horizontal, setHorizontal] = useState('left');

  const onVerticalChange = event => {
    setVertical(event.target.value);
  };

  const onHorizontalChange = event => {
    setHorizontal(event.target.value);
  };

  return (
    <Fragment>
      <FormControl
        component="fieldset"
        className={classes.formControl}
      >
        <FormLabel component="legend">Vertical</FormLabel>
        <RadioGroup
          name="vertical"
          className={classes.group}
          value={vertical}
          onChange={onVerticalChange}
        >
          <FormControlLabel
            value="top"
            control={<Radio />}
            label="Top"
          />
          <FormControlLabel
            value="bottom"
            control={<Radio />}
            label="Bottom"
```

```
              />
            </RadioGroup>
          </FormControl>
          <FormControl
            component="fieldset"
            className={classes.formControl}
          >
            <FormLabel component="legend">Horizontal</FormLabel>
            <RadioGroup
              name="horizontal"
              className={classes.group}
              value={horizontal}
              onChange={onHorizontalChange}
            >
              <FormControlLabel
                value="left"
                control={<Radio />}
                label="Left"
              />
              <FormControlLabel
                value="center"
                control={<Radio />}
                label="Center"
              />
              <FormControlLabel
                value="right"
                control={<Radio />}
                label="Right"
              />
            </RadioGroup>
          </FormControl>
          <Snackbar
            anchorOrigin={{
              vertical,
              horizontal
            }}
            open={true}
            message="Positioned Snackbar"
          />
        </Fragment>
      );
    }
```

When the screen first loads, you'll see controls for changing the position of the snackbar, and the Snackbar component in its default position:

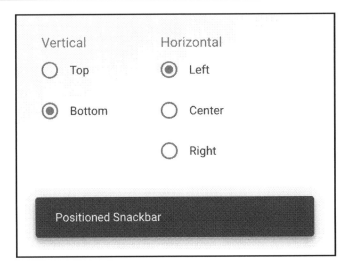

If you change any of the position control values, the snackbar will move to the new position. For example, if you changed the vertical anchor to top and the horizontal anchor to the right, here's what you'd see:

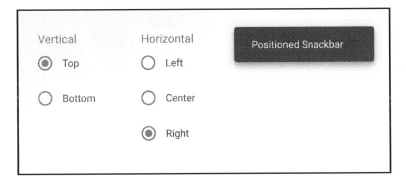

How it works...

The two radio button groups in this example are only used to illustrate the different position value combinations that are available. In a real application where you show snackbars, you wouldn't have the configurable state to change the positioning of your snackbars. Instead, you should think of a value passed to the `anchorOrigin` property as a configuration value that is set once during startup.

It isn't good to rely on state values, as is the case in this example:

```
<Snackbar
  anchorOrigin={{
    vertical,
    horizontal
  }}
  open={true}
  message="Positioned Snackbar"
/>
```

Instead, you would set the `anchorOrigin` values statically:

```
<Snackbar
  anchorOrigin={{
    vertical: 'top'
    horizontal: 'right'
  }}
  open={true}
  message="Positioned Snackbar"
/>
```

There's more...

Once you know where you want to position your snackbars, you can create your own `Snackbar` component that has the `anchorOrigin` values defined. Here's an example:

```
const MySnackbar = props => (
  <Snackbar
    anchorOrigin={{
      vertical: 'top',
      horizontal: 'right'
    }}
    {...props}
  />
);
```

Anywhere in your app that `MySnackbar` is used, the snackbars will be displayed in the top-right corner of the screen. Otherwise, `MySnackbar` is just like a regular `Snackbar` component.

See also

- Snackbar **demos:** https://material-ui.com/demos/snackbars/
- Snackbar **API documentation:** https://material-ui.com/api/snackbar/

Error boundaries and error snackbars

Error boundaries in React enable you to capture errors that happen when your components attempt to render. You can use the Snackbar components in your error boundaries to display captured errors. Furthermore, you can style snackbars so that errors are visually distinctive from normal messages.

How to do it...

Let's say that you have an error boundary at the top level of your application and you want to use the Snackbar component to display error messages to users. Here's an example that shows how you can do this:

```
import React, { Fragment, Component } from 'react';

import { withStyles } from '@material-ui/core/styles';
import Snackbar from '@material-ui/core/Snackbar';
import Button from '@material-ui/core/Button';

const styles = theme => ({
  error: {
    backgroundColor: theme.palette.error.main,
    color: theme.palette.error.contrastText
  }
});

const ErrorBoundary = withStyles(styles)(
  class extends Component {
    state = { error: null };

    onClose = () => {
      this.setState({ error: null });
    };

    componentDidCatch(error) {
      this.setState({ error });
    }
```

```
      render() {
        const { classes } = this.props;

        return (
          <Fragment>
            {this.state.error === null && this.props.children}
            <Snackbar
              open={Boolean(this.state.error)}
              message={
                this.state.error !== null && this.state.error.toString()
              }
              ContentProps={{ classes: { root: classes.error } }}
            />
          </Fragment>
        );
      }
    }
  );

const MyButton = () => {
  throw new Error('Random error');
};

export default () => (
  <ErrorBoundary>
    <MyButton />
  </ErrorBoundary>
);
```

When you load this screen, the `MyButton` component throws an error when it is rendered. Here's what you'll see:

Error: Random error

It explicitly throws an error so that you can see the error boundary mechanism in action. In a real application, the error could be triggered by any function that's called during the rendering process.

How it works...

Let's start by taking a closer look at the `ErrorBoundary` component. It has an `error` state that is initially null. The `componentDidCatch()` life cycle method changes this state when an error happens:

```
componentDidCatch(error) {
  this.setState({ error });
}
```

Next, let's take a closer look at the `render()` method:

```
render() {
  const { classes } = this.props;

  return (
    <Fragment>
      {this.state.error === null && this.props.children}
      <Snackbar
        open={Boolean(this.state.error)}
        message={
          this.state.error !== null && this.state.error.toString()
        }
        ContentProps={{ classes: { root: classes.error } }}
      />
    </Fragment>
  );
}
```

It uses the `error` state to determine whether children should be rendered. When the `error` state is non-null, it doesn't make sense to render child components because you'll be stuck in an infinite loop of error being thrown and handled. The `error` state is also used as the `open` property to determine whether the snackbar should be displayed, and as the message text.

The `ContentProps` property is used to style the snackbar so that it looks like an error. The `error` class uses `theme` values to change the background and text color:

```
const styles = theme => ({
  error: {
    backgroundColor: theme.palette.error.main,
    color: theme.palette.error.contrastText
  }
});
```

There's more...

The error boundary used in this example covered the entire application. This is good in the sense that you can blanket the entire application with error handling in one shot. But this is also bad, because the entire user interface vanishes, as the error boundary has no idea which component failed.

Because error boundaries are components, you can place as many of them as you like at any level of your component tree. This way, you can show Material-UI `error` snackbars while keeping the parts of the UI that haven't failed visible on the screen.

Let's change the scope of the error boundary used in the example. First, you can change the `MyButton` implementation so that it only throws an error when a Boolean property is `true`:

```
const MyButton = ({ label, throwError }) => {
  if (throwError) {
    throw new Error('Random error');
  }
  return <Button>{label}</Button>;
};
```

Now you can render a button with a given label. If `throwError` is `true`, then nothing is rendering due to the error. Next, let's change the markup of the example to include multiple buttons and multiple `error` boundaries:

```
export default () => (
  <Fragment>
    <ErrorBoundary>
      <MyButton label="First Button" />
    </ErrorBoundary>
    <ErrorBoundary>
      <MyButton label="Second Button" throwError />
    </ErrorBoundary>
  </Fragment>
);
```

The first button renders without any issues. However, if the error boundary were all-encompassing as was the case earlier, then this button wouldn't be displayed. The second button throws an error because the `throwError` property is true. Because this button has its own error boundary, it doesn't prevent other parts of the UI that are working fine from rendering. Here's what you'll see when you run the example now:

See also

- React `error` boundaries: `https://reactjs.org/docs/error-boundaries.html`
- `Snackbar` **demos:** `https://material-ui.com/demos/snackbars/`
- `Snackbar` API documentation: `https://material-ui.com/api/snackbar/`

Snackbars with actions

The purpose of Material-UI snackbars is to display brief messages for the user. Additionally, you can embed the next course of action for the user in the snackbar.

How to do it...

Let's say that you want a simple button in your snackbar that closes the snackbar. This could be useful for closing the snackbar before it automatically closes. Alternatively, you might want to require the user to explicitly acknowledge the message by having to close it manually. Here's the code to add a close button to a `Snackbar` component:

```
import React, { Fragment, useState } from 'react';
import { Route, Link } from 'react-router-dom';

import Snackbar from '@material-ui/core/Snackbar';
import Button from '@material-ui/core/Button';
import IconButton from '@material-ui/core/IconButton';
import Typography from '@material-ui/core/Typography';

import CloseIcon from '@material-ui/icons/Close';

export default function Snackbars() {
  const [open, setOpen] = useState(false);
```

```
    return (
      <Fragment>
        <Button onClick={() => setOpen(true)}>Do Something</Button>
        <Snackbar
          open={open}
          onClose={() => setOpen(false)}
          message="All done doing the thing"
          action={[
            <IconButton color="inherit" onClick={() => setOpen(false)}>
              <CloseIcon />
            </IconButton>
          ]}
        />
      </Fragment>
    );
  }
```

When the screen first loads, you'll only see a button:

DO SOMETHING

Clicking on this button will display the snackbar:

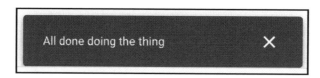

The close icon button on the right side of the snackbar, when clicked on, closes the snackbar.

How it works...

The close button is added to the `Snackbar` component via the `action` property, which accepts either a node or an array of nodes. The `SnackbarContent` component takes care of applying styles to align the actions within the snackbar.

There's more...

When users create new resources in your application, you probably want to let them know when the resource is created successfully. Snackbars are a good tool for this because they don't force the user away from anything that they might be in the middle of. What would be nice is if you included an action button in the snackbar that linked to the newly created resource.

Let's modify this example so that, when the user clicks on the **CREATE** button, they'll see a snackbar with the following:

- A brief message
- A close action
- A link to the new resource

Let's add routes from `react-router-dom` and then add the link to the snackbar. Here's the new markup:

```
<Fragment>
  <Route
    exact
    path="/"
    render={() => (
      <Button onClick={() => setOpen(true)}>create thing</Button>
    )}
  />
  <Route
    exact
    path="/thing"
    render={() => <Typography>The Thing</Typography>}
  />
  <Snackbar
    open={open}
    onClose={() => setOpen(false)}
    message="Finished creating thing"
    action={[
      <Button
        color="secondary"
        component={Link}
        to="/thing"
        onClick={() => setOpen(false)}
      >
        The Thing
      </Button>,
      <IconButton color="inherit" onClick={() => setOpen(false)}>
        <CloseIcon />
```

```
        </IconButton>
      ]}
    />
  </Fragment>
```

The first route is for the index page, so, when the screen first loads, the user will see the button that's rendered by this route:

CREATE THING

When you click on this button, you'll see the snackbar that includes a link to the newly-created resource:

Now you've given the user an easy way to navigate to the resource without disrupting what they're currently doing.

See also

- React router guide: `https://reacttraining.com/react-router/web/guides/quick-start`
- Snackbar demos: `https://material-ui.com/demos/snackbars/`
- Snackbar API documentation: `https://material-ui.com/api/snackbar/`
- Button API documentation: `https://material-ui.com/api/button/`
- IconButton API documentation: `https://material-ui.com/api/icon-button/`

Queuing snackbars

With larger Material-UI applications, you're likely to find yourself in a situation where more than one snackbar message is sent in a very short period of time. To deal with this, you can create a queue for all snackbar messages so that only the most recent notification is displayed, and so that the transitions are handled properly.

How to do it...

Let's say that you have several components throughout your application that need to send snackbar messages to your users. Having to manually render Snackbar components everywhere would be cumbersome—especially if all you're trying to do is display simple text snackbars.

One alternative approach is to implement a higher-order component that wraps your components with the ability to display messages by calling a function and then passing the text as the argument. Then, you can wrap any components that need the snackbar capability. Here's what the code looks like:

```
import React, { Fragment, useState } from 'react';

import Snackbar from '@material-ui/core/Snackbar';
import Button from '@material-ui/core/Button';
import IconButton from '@material-ui/core/IconButton';

import CloseIcon from '@material-ui/icons/Close';

const withMessage = Wrapped =>
  function WithMessage(props) {
    const [queue, setQueue] = useState([]);
    const [open, setOpen] = useState(false);
    const [message, setMessage] = useState('');

    const sendMessage = msg => {
      const newQueue = [...queue, msg];
      if (newQueue.length === 1) {
        setOpen(true);
        setMessage(msg);
      }
    };

    const onClose = () => {
      setOpen(false);
    };

    const onExit = () => {
      const [msg, ...rest] = queue;

      if (msg) {
        setQueue(rest);
        setOpen(true);
        setMessage(msg);
      }
    };
```

```
      return (
        <Fragment>
          <Wrapped message={sendMessage} {...props} />
          <Snackbar
            key={message}
            open={open}
            message={message}
            autoHideDuration={4000}
            onClose={onClose}
            onExit={onExit}
          />
        </Fragment>
      );
    };

  const QueuingSnackbars = withMessage(({ message }) => {
    const [counter, setCounter] = useState(0);

    const onClick = () => {
      const newCounter = counter + 1;
      setCounter(newCounter);
      message(`Message ${newCounter}`);
    };

    return <Button onClick={onClick}>Message</Button>;
  });

  export default QueuingSnackbars;
```

When the screen first loads, you'll see a message button. Clicking on it will display a snackbar message that looks like this:

Clicking on the message button again will clear the current snackbar by visually transitioning it off of the screen before transitioning the new snackbar onto the screen. Even if you click the button several times in rapid succession, everything works smoothly and you'll always see the latest message:

How it works...

Let's start by looking at the `QueuingSnackbars` component that renders the button that sends messages when clicked:

```
const QueuingSnackbars = withMessage(({ message }) => {
  const [counter, setCounter] = useState(0);

  const onClick = () => {
    const newCounter = counter + 1;
    setCounter(newCounter);
    message(`Message ${newCounter}`);
  };

  return <Button onClick={onClick}>Message</Button>;
});
```

The `withMessage()` wrapper provides the component with a `message()` function as a property. If you look at the `onClick()` handler, you can see the `message()` function in action.

Next, let's break down the `withMessage()` higher-order component. We'll start with the markup and work our way downward:

```
<Fragment>
  <Wrapped message={sendMessage} {...props} />
  <Snackbar
    key={message}
    open={open}
    message={message}
    autoHideDuration={4000}
    onClose={onClose}
    onExit={onExit}
  />
</Fragment>
```

The `Wrapped` component is the component that `withMessage()` was called on. It's passed the normal props that it would be called with normally, plus the `message()` function. Adjacent to this is the `Snackbar` component. There are two interesting properties that are worth pointing out here:

- key: This value is used internally by `Snackbar` to determine whether a new message is being displayed. It should be a unique value.
- onExit: This is called when the transition of a snackbar that is closing completes.

Next, let's look at the `sendMessage()` function:

```
const sendMessage = msg => {
  const newQueue = [...queue, msg];
  if (newQueue.length === 1) {
    setOpen(true);
    setMessage(msg);
  }
};
```

This function is called whenever a component wants to display a snackbar message. It puts the `message` string into the queue. If the message is the only item in the queue, then the `open` and `message` states are updated right away.

Next, let's look at the `onClose()` function. This is called when the snackbar is closed:

```
const onClose = () => {
  setOpen(false);
};
```

The only job of this function is to make sure that the open state is false.

Lastly, let's look at the `onExit()` function that's called when a snackbar has completed its exit transition:

```
const onExit = () => {
  const [msg, ...rest] = queue;

  if (msg) {
    setQueue(rest);
    setOpen(true);
    setMessage(msg);
  }
};
```

The fist message in the queue is assigned to the `message` constant. If there's a message, it becomes the active message state and the next snackbar is opened. The item is also removed from the queue at this point.

See also

- Snackbar **demos:** https://material-ui.com/demos/snackbars/
- Snackbar **API documentation:** https://material-ui.com/api/snackbar/
- Button **API documentation:** https://material-ui.com/api/button/
- IconButton **API documentation:** https://material-ui.com/api/icon-button/

10
Buttons - Initiating Actions

In this chapter, you'll learn about the following topics:

- Button variants
- Button emphasis
- Link buttons
- Floating actions
- Icon buttons
- Button sizes

Introduction

Buttons in Material-UI applications are used to initiate actions. The user clicks on a button and something happens. What happens when a button is activated is entirely up to you. Material-UI buttons range in complexity from simple text buttons to floating action buttons.

Button variants

The Material-UI `Button` component exists as one of three variants. These are as follows:

- `Text`
- `Outlined`
- `Contained`

How to do it...

Here's some code that renders three Button components, each explicitly setting their variant property:

```
import React from 'react';

import { withStyles } from '@material-ui/core/styles';
import Button from '@material-ui/core/Button';
import Grid from '@material-ui/core/Grid';

const styles = theme => ({
  container: {
    margin: theme.spacing(1)
  }
});

const ButtonVariants = withStyles(styles)(({ classes }) => (
  <Grid
    container
    direction="column"
    spacing={2}
    className={classes.container}
  >
    <Grid item>
      <Button variant="text">Text</Button>
    </Grid>
    <Grid item>
      <Button variant="outlined">Outlined</Button>
    </Grid>
    <Grid item>
      <Button variant="contained">Contained</Button>
    </Grid>
  </Grid>
));

export default ButtonVariants;
```

When you load the screen, here's what you'll see:

How it works...

The `variant` property controls the type of button that's rendered. The three variants can be used in different scenarios or contexts as you see fit. For example, **TEXT** buttons draw less attention if this is what you need. Conversely, **CONTAINED** buttons try to stand out as an obvious interaction point for the user.

The default variant is `text`. I find `Button` markup easier to read when you explicitly include the variant. This way, you or anyone else reading the code don't have to remember what the default `variant` is.

See also

- `Button` **demos:** https://material-ui.com/demos/buttons/
- `Button` **API documentation:** https://material-ui.com/api/button/

Button emphasis

The `color` and `disabled` properties of `Button` let you control the emphasis of a button relative to its surroundings. For example, you can specify that a button should use the `primary` color value. The emphasis of a button is the cumulative result of the `variant` and `color` properties. You can adjust both until the button has the appropriate emphasis.

There is no *right* level of emphasis. Use what makes sense in the context of your application.

How to do it...

Here's some code that shows the different color values that you can apply to Button components:

```
import React from 'react';

import { withStyles } from '@material-ui/core/styles';
import Button from '@material-ui/core/Button';
import Grid from '@material-ui/core/Grid';
import Typography from '@material-ui/core/Typography';

const styles = theme => ({
  container: {
    margin: theme.spacing(1)
  }
});

const ButtonEmphasis = withStyles(styles)(({ classes, disabled }) => (
  <Grid
    container
    direction="column"
    spacing={16}
    className={classes.container}
  >
    <Grid item>
      <Typography variant="h6">Default</Typography>
    </Grid>
    <Grid item>
      <Grid container spacing={16}>
        <Grid item>
          <Button variant="text" disabled={disabled}>
            Text
          </Button>
        </Grid>
        <Grid item>
          <Button variant="outlined" disabled={disabled}>
            Outlined
          </Button>
        </Grid>
        <Grid item>
          <Button variant="contained" disabled={disabled}>
            Contained
          </Button>
        </Grid>
      </Grid>
    </Grid>
    <Grid item>
```

```
      <Typography variant="h6">Primary</Typography>
  </Grid>
  <Grid item>
    <Grid container spacing={16}>
      <Grid item>
        <Button variant="text" color="primary" disabled={disabled}>
          Text
        </Button>
      </Grid>
      <Grid item>
        <Button
          variant="outlined"
          color="primary"
          disabled={disabled}
        >
          Outlined
        </Button>
      </Grid>
      <Grid item>
        <Button
          variant="contained"
          color="primary"
          disabled={disabled}
        >
          Contained
        </Button>
      </Grid>
    </Grid>
  </Grid>
  <Grid item>
    <Typography variant="h6">Secondary</Typography>
  </Grid>
  <Grid item>
    <Grid container spacing={16}>
      <Grid item>
        <Button
          variant="text"
          color="secondary"
          disabled={disabled}
        >
          Text
        </Button>
      </Grid>
      <Grid item>
        <Button
          variant="outlined"
          color="secondary"
          disabled={disabled}
```

```
      >
        Outlined
      </Button>
    </Grid>
    <Grid item>
      <Button
        variant="contained"
        color="secondary"
        disabled={disabled}
      >
        Contained
      </Button>
    </Grid>
  </Grid>
 </Grid>
</Grid>
));

export default ButtonEmphasis;
```

Here's what you'll see when the screen first loads:

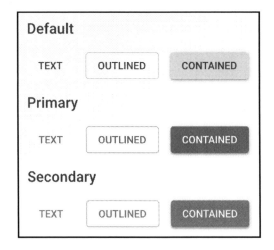

And if the `disabled` property is `true`, here's what you'll see:

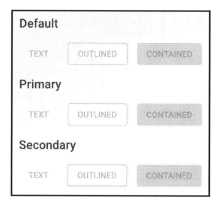

How it works...

This example serves to illustrate the combinatorial result of the `variant` and `color` properties. Alternatively, you can completely disable buttons and yet still control the `variant` aspect of their emphasis (the `color` property has no effect on disabled buttons).

The order of most to least emphatic `variant` values is as follows:

1. `contained`
2. `outlined`
3. `text`

The order of most to least emphatic `color` values is as follows:

1. `primary`
2. `secondary`
3. `default`

By combining these two property values, you can control the emphasis of your buttons. Sometimes, you really need a button to stand out, so you can combine `contained` and `primary`:

If you want your button to not stand out at all, you can combine the `text` variant with `default` color:

There's more...

If your button is placed in another Material-UI component, it can be difficult to ensure the correct color choice. For example, let's say that you have some buttons in an `AppBar` component, as follows:

```
<AppBar color={appBarColor}>
  <Toolbar>
    <Grid container spacing={16}>
      <Grid item>
        <Button variant="text" disabled={disabled}>
          Text
        </Button>
      </Grid>
      <Grid item>
        <Button variant="outlined" disabled={disabled}>
          Outlined
        </Button>
      </Grid>
      <Grid item>
        <Button variant="contained" disabled={disabled}>
          Contained
        </Button>
      </Grid>
    </Grid>
  </Toolbar>
</AppBar>
```

If the `AppBar` color value is `default`, here's what you'll see:

This doesn't actually look too bad because the buttons themselves are using the default color. But what happens if you change the `AppBar` color to `primary`:

The `contained` variant is the only button that even comes close to looking like it belongs in the App Bar. Let's modify the buttons so that they all use the `inherit` color property value, as follows:

```
<AppBar color={appBarColor}>
  <Toolbar>
    <Grid container spacing={16}>
      <Grid item>
        <Button
          variant="text"
          disabled={disabled}
          color="inherit"
        >
          Text
        </Button>
      </Grid>
      <Grid item>
        <Button
          variant="outlined"
          disabled={disabled}
          color="inherit"
        >
          Outlined
        </Button>
      </Grid>
      <Grid item>
        <Button
          variant="contained"
          disabled={disabled}
          color="inherit"
        >
          Contained
        </Button>
      </Grid>
    </Grid>
  </Toolbar>
</AppBar>
```

Now, your App Bar and buttons look like this:

The **TEXT** and **OUTLINE** buttons look much better now. They've inherited the theme font color from their parent component. The **CONTAINED** button actually looks worse, now that it's using `inherited` as its font color. This is because the background color of **CONTAINED** buttons doesn't change when inheriting colors. So instead, you have to change the color of **CONTAINED** buttons yourself.

Let's see whether we can automatically set the color of a **CONTAINED** button based on the color of its parent by implementing a function that returns the color to use:

```
function buttonColor(parentColor) {
  if (parentColor === 'primary') {
    return 'secondary';
  }

  if (parentColor === 'secondary') {
    return 'primary';
  }

  return 'default';
}
```

Now, you can use this `function` when you're setting the `color` of your `contained` buttons. Just make sure that you pass it the `color` of the parent as an argument, as follows:

```
<Button
  variant="contained"
  disabled={disabled}
  color={buttonColor(appBarColor)}
>
  Contained
</Button>
```

Now, if you change your App Bar color to `primary`, here's what your buttons look like:

Here's what your buttons look like if you change the App Bar color to `secondary`:

To quickly recap: **TEXT** and **OUTLINED** buttons can safely use `inherit` as a color. If you're working with **CONTAINED** buttons, you need to take extra steps to use the correct color, like you did with the `buttonColor()` function.

See also

- Button **demos:** https://material-ui.com/demos/buttons/
- Button **API documentation:** https://material-ui.com/api/button/
- AppBar **API documentation:** https://material-ui.com/api/app-bar/
- Toolbar **API documentation:** https://material-ui.com/api/toolbar/

Link buttons

Material-UI `Button` components can also be used as links to other locations in your app. The most common example is using a button as a link to a route declared using `react-router`.

How to do it...

Let's say that your application has three pages, and you need three buttons that link to each of them. You'll probably need buttons to link to them from arbitrary places too, as the application grows. Here's the code to do it:

```
import React from 'react';
import { Switch, Route, Link } from 'react-router-dom';

import { withStyles } from '@material-ui/core/styles';
import Grid from '@material-ui/core/Grid';
import Button from '@material-ui/core/Button';
import Typography from '@material-ui/core/Typography';

const styles = theme => ({
```

```
    content: {
      margin: theme.spacing(2)
    }
});

const LinkButtons = withStyles(styles)(({ classes }) => (
  <Grid container direction="column" className={classes.container}>
    <Grid item>
      <Grid container>
        <Grid item>
          <Button component={Link} to="/">
            Home
          </Button>
        </Grid>
        <Grid item>
          <Button component={Link} to="/page1">
            Page 1
          </Button>
        </Grid>
        <Grid item>
          <Button component={Link} to="/page2">
            Page 2
          </Button>
        </Grid>
      </Grid>
    </Grid>
    <Grid item className={classes.content}>
      <Switch>
        <Route
          exact
          path="/"
          render={() => <Typography>home content</Typography>}
        />
        <Route
          path="/page1"
          render={() => <Typography>page 1 content</Typography>}
        />
        <Route
          path="/page2"
          render={() => <Typography>page 2 content</Typography>}
        />
      </Switch>
    </Grid>
  </Grid>
));

export default LinkButtons;
```

The Storybook code that sets up this example to run includes a
`BrowserRouter` component. In your code, you'll need to include this
component as a parent of any of your `Route` components.

When the screen first loads, you'll see the following:

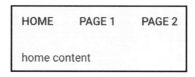

If you click on the **Page 2** button, you'll be taken to `/page2`, and the content will update
accordingly:

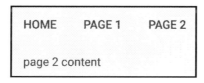

How it works...

When you use `react-router` as the router for your application, you can render links
using the `Link` component from `react-router-dom`. Since you want to render Material-
UI buttons in order to get the consistent Material-UI theme and user interaction behavior,
you can't render `Link` components directly. Instead, you can make the underlying `Button`
component a `Link` component, as follows:

```
<Button component={Link} to="/">
  Home
</Button>
```

By using the `component` property, you can tell the `Button` component to apply styles and
event handling logic to this component instead of the default. Then, any additional
properties that you would normally pass to `Link` are set on the `Button` component—which
forwards them to `Link`. For example, the `to` property isn't a `Button` property, so it gets
passed to `Link`, which requires it in order to work.

There's more...

One problem with this example is that there's no visual indication that a button links to the current URL. For example, when the app first loads the / URL, the **Home** button should stand out from the other buttons. One way to do this would be to change the color property to primary if the button is considered active.

You could use the NavLink component from react-router-dom. This component lets you set styles or class names that are only applied when the link is active. The challenge with doing this is that you only need to change a simple Button property when it is active. Having to maintain styles for active buttons seems like a bit much, especially if you want to make your UI easy to theme.

Instead, you can create a button abstraction that uses react-router tools to render the appropriate Button property when it's active, as follows:

```
const NavButton = ({ color, ...props }) => (
  <Switch>
    <Route
      exact
      path={props.to}
      render={() => (
        <Button color="primary" component={Link} {...props} />
      )}
    />
    <Route
      path="/"
      render={() => <Button component={Link} {...props} />}
    />
  </Switch>
);
```

The NavButton component uses Switch and Route components to determine the active route. It does this by comparing the to property passed to NavButton against the current URL. If a match is found, the Button component is rendered with the color property set to primary. Otherwise, no color is specified (if the first Route in Switch doesn't match, the second Route matches everything). Here's what the new component looks like in action:

```
<Grid container>
  <Grid item>
    <NavButton to="/">Home</NavButton>
  </Grid>
  <Grid item>
    <NavButton to="/page1">Page 1</NavButton>
  </Grid>
```

```
<Grid item>
  <NavButton to="/page2">Page 2</NavButton>
</Grid>
</Grid>
```

Here's what the screen looks like when it first loads:

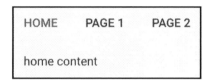

Because the initial URL is /, and the first `NavButton` component has a `to` property of /, the **Home** button color is marked as `primary`.

See also

- `Button` **demos:** `https://material-ui.com/demos/buttons/`
- `Button` **API documentation:** `https://material-ui.com/api/button/`
- **React Router Guide:** `https://reacttraining.com/react-router/web/guides/quick-start`

Floating actions

Some screens in your application will have one primary action. For example, if you're on a screen that lists items, the primary action might be to add a new item. If you're on an item details page, the primary action might be to edit the item. Material-UI provides a `Fab` component (floating action button) to show primary screen actions in a prominent way.

How to do it...

The common case for floating action buttons is to show the user a round button with an icon representing the action to perform, positioned in the bottom right of the screen. Also, the position of floating action buttons is `fixed`, meaning that as the user scrolls down the page, the primary action is always visible.

Let's write some code to `position` a floating action button at the bottom right of the screen that indicates an add action, as follows:

```
import React, { Fragment } from 'react';

import { withStyles } from '@material-ui/core/styles';
import Fab from '@material-ui/core/Fab';
import AddIcon from '@material-ui/icons/Add';

const styles = theme => ({
  fab: {
    margin: 0,
    top: 'auto',
    left: 'auto',
    bottom: 20,
    right: 20,
    position: 'fixed'
  }
});

const FloatingActions = withStyles(styles)(({ classes, fabColor }) => (
  <Fragment>
    <Fab className={classes.fab} color={fabColor}>
      <AddIcon />
    </Fab>
  </Fragment>
));

export default FloatingActions;
```

When you load the screen, you'll see the following in the bottom right-hand corner:

The component for this screen has a `fabColor` property that is used to set the color of the `Fab` component. Here's what the `primary` color looks like:

Lastly, here's what the floating action button looks like with secondary as the color:

How it works...

The Fab component is very similar to a Button component. In fact, you used to use Button to render floating action buttons, using the fab variant. The rounded styling of the button is handled by Fab. You just need to support the icon and any other button properties, such as onClick handlers. Additionally, you can include text in your floating action buttons. If you do, you should use the extended variant so that the shape of the button is styled correctly (flat top and bottom instead of rounded).

There's more...

Let's create a small abstraction for Fab components that applies the fab style and uses the correct variant. Since the extended variant is only useful when there's text in the button, you shouldn't have to remember to set it every time you want to use it. This can be especially confusing if your application has both icon and icon plus text floating action buttons.

Here's the code to implement the new Fab component:

```
const ExtendedFab = withStyles(styles)(({ classes, ...props }) => {
  const isExtended = React.Children.toArray(props.children).find(
    child => typeof child === 'string'
  );

  return (
    <Fab
      className={classes.fab}
      variant={isExtended && 'extended'}
      {...props}
    />
  );
});
```

The `className` property is set in the same way as before. The `variant` property is set to extended when `isExtended` is `true`. To figure this out, it uses the `React.Children.toArray()` function to convert the `children` property into a plain array. Then, the `find()` method looks for any text elements. If one is found, `isExtended` will be `true` and the `extended` variant is used.

Here's how the new `ExtendedFab` button can be used:

```
export default ({ fabColor }) => (
  <ExtendedFab color={fabColor}>
    Add
    <AddIcon />
  </ExtendedFab>
);
```

The `Add` text is placed before the `AddIcon` component. This `ExtendedFab` component has two children, and one of them is text, which means that the `extended` variant will be used. Here's what it looks like:

See also

- `Button` demos: https://material-ui.com/demos/buttons/
- `Fab` API documentation: https://material-ui.com/api/fab/

Icon buttons

Sometimes, you need a button that's just an icon. This is where the `IconButton` component comes in handy. You can pass it any icon component as a child, and then you have an icon button.

How to do it...

Icon buttons are especially useful when you're working with restricted screen real estate or when you want to visually show the toggled state of something. For example, it might be easier for a user to toggle the state of a microphone if the enabled/disabled state indicates the actual microphone.

Let's build on this idea and implement toggle controls for the microphone and volume in an app, using icon buttons. Here's the code:

```
import React, { useState } from 'react';

import IconButton from '@material-ui/core/IconButton';
import Grid from '@material-ui/core/Grid';

import MicIcon from '@material-ui/icons/Mic';
import MicOffIcon from '@material-ui/icons/MicOff';
import VolumeUpIcon from '@material-ui/icons/VolumeUp';
import VolumeOffIcon from '@material-ui/icons/VolumeOff';

export default function IconButtons({ iconColor }) {
  const [mic, setMic] = useState(true);
  const [volume, setVolume] = useState(true);

  return (
    <Grid container>
      <Grid item>
        <IconButton color={iconColor} onClick={() => setMic(!mic)}>
          {mic ? <MicIcon /> : <MicOffIcon />}
        </IconButton>
      </Grid>
      <Grid item>
        <IconButton
          color={iconColor}
          onClick={() => setVolume(!volume)}
        >
          {volume ? <VolumeUpIcon /> : <VolumeOffIcon />}
        </IconButton>
      </Grid>
    </Grid>
  );
}
```

When you first load the screen, here's what you'll see:

If you click on both icon buttons, here's what you'll see:

No matter the state of the microphone or volume, the user can still have a visual indication of the item and its state.

How it works...

The component for this screen maintains two pieces of state: `mic` and `volume`. Both of these are Booleans that control the icon that's displayed in the `IconButton` component:

```
const [mic, setMic] = useState(true);
const [volume, setVolume] = useState(true);
```

Then, based on these states, the icon is swapped as the `state` changes, giving useful visual feedback to the user:

```
<Grid item>
  <IconButton color={iconColor} onClick={() => setMic(!mic)}>
    {mic ? <MicIcon /> : <MicOffIcon />}
  </IconButton>
</Grid>
<Grid item>
  <IconButton
    color={iconColor}
    onClick={() => setVolume(!volume)}
  >
    {volume ? <VolumeUpIcon /> : <VolumeOffIcon />}
  </IconButton>
</Grid>
```

Additionally, the component for this screen takes an `iconColor` property, which can be either `default`, `primary`, or `secondary`. Here's what the `primary` color looks like:

See also

- `Button` **demos:** https://material-ui.com/demos/buttons/
- `IconButton` **API documentation:** https://material-ui.com/api/icon-button/

Button sizes

Material-UI buttons support tee shirt-style sizing. Rather than try to find the perfect size for your buttons, you can use one of the predefined sizes that comes closest to what you need.

How to do it...

If you need to adjust the size of your buttons, you can use `small`, `medium` (the default), or `large`. Here's an example of how to set the `size` of a `Button` component:

```
import React from 'react';

import Button from '@material-ui/core/Button';

export default function ButtonSizes({ size, color }) {
  return (
    <Button variant="contained" size={size} color={color}>
      Add
    </Button>
  );
}
```

Here's what the various sizes look like:

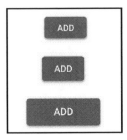

How it works...

The distinction between sizes is greatest between medium and large. Using a large button, in conjunction with other `Button` properties, such as `color` and `Icons`, can really make a button stand out.

There's more...

The one downside to using tee shirt sizes with buttons is when you combine text and icon images. The icon doesn't scale the same as the text, so the button never looks quite right, unless the medium default size is used.

Let's implement a button abstraction that makes it easier to use text buttons or icon buttons that can be resized consistently. Here's the code:

```
import React from 'react';

import Grid from '@material-ui/core/Grid';
import Button from '@material-ui/core/Button';
import IconButton from '@material-ui/core/IconButton';
import Fab from '@material-ui/core/Fab';

import AddIcon from '@material-ui/icons/Add';

const MyButton = ({ fab, ...props }) => {
  const [child] = React.Children.toArray(props.children);
  let ButtonComponent;

  if (React.isValidElement(child) && fab) {
    ButtonComponent = Fab;
  } else if (React.isValidElement(child)) {
```

```
        ButtonComponent = IconButton;
      } else {
        ButtonComponent = Button;
      }

      return <ButtonComponent {...props} />;
    };

    export default function ButtonSizes({ size, color }) {
      return (
        <Grid container spacing={16} alignItems="center">
          <Grid item>
            <MyButton variant="contained" size={size} color={color}>
              Add
            </MyButton>
          </Grid>
          <Grid item>
            <MyButton size={size} color={color}>
              <AddIcon />
            </MyButton>
          </Grid>
          <Grid item>
            <MyButton fab size={size} color={color}>
              <AddIcon />
            </MyButton>
          </Grid>
        </Grid>
      );
    }
```

Here's what the three buttons on the screen look like when the `size` property is set to `small`:

And here's the `large` size:

Let's break down what's going on in the MyButton component. It expects a single child node, which it gets by turning the children property into an array and assigning the first element to the child constant:

```
const [child] = React.Children.toArray(props.children);
```

The idea is to render the appropriate Button element, depending on the child element and the fab property. Here's how the correct component is assigned to ButtonComponent:

```
if (React.isValidElement(child) && fab) {
  ButtonComponent = Fab;
} else if (React.isValidElement(child)) {
  ButtonComponent = IconButton;
} else {
  ButtonComponent = Button;
}
```

If the child is an element and the fab property is true, then the Fab component is used. If the child is an element and fab is false, IconButton is used. Otherwise, Button is used. This means that you can pass either a valid icon element or text as a child to MyButton. Setting the size on any buttons rendered with this component will be consistent.

See also

- Button demos: https://material-ui.com/demos/buttons/
- Button API documentation: https://material-ui.com/api/button/
- IconButton API documentation: https://material-ui.com/api/icon-button/
- Fab API documentation: https://material-ui.com/api/fab/

11

Text - Collecting Text Input

In this chapter, you'll learn about the following topics:

- Controlling input with state
- Placeholder and helper text
- Validation and error display
- Password fields
- Multiline input
- Input adornments
- Input masking

Introduction

Material-UI has a flexible text input component that can be used in a variety of ways to collect user input. Its usages range from collecting simple one-liner text input to masked input adorned with icons.

Controlling input with state

The `TextField` component can be controlled by the React component, `state`, just like regular HTML text input elements. As with other types of form controls, the actual value is often the starting point—the state for each form control grows more complex as more functionality is added.

How to do it...

Just like any other text input element, you need to provide the `TextField` component with an `onChange` event handler that updates the state for the input. Without this handler, the value of the input won't change as the user types. Let's look at an example where three text fields are rendered and they're each controlled by their own piece of state:

```
import React, { useState } from 'react';

import { makeStyles } from '@material-ui/styles';
import TextField from '@material-ui/core/TextField';
import Grid from '@material-ui/core/Grid';

const useStyles = makeStyles(theme => ({
  container: { margin: theme.spacing.unit * 2 }
}));

export default function ControllingInputWithState() {
  const classes = useStyles();
  const [first, setFirst] = useState('');
  const [second, setSecond] = useState('');
  const [third, setThird] = useState('');

  return (
    <Grid container spacing={4} className={classes.container}>
      <Grid item>
        <TextField
          id="first"
          label="First"
          value={first}
          onChange={e => setFirst(e.target.value)}
        />
      </Grid>
      <Grid item>
        <TextField
          id="second"
          label="Second"
          value={second}
          onChange={e => setSecond(e.target.value)}
        />
      </Grid>
      <Grid item>
        <TextField
          id="third"
          label="Third"
          value={third}
          onChange={e => setThird(e.target.value)}
```

```
            />
          </Grid>
        </Grid>
      );
    }
```

When you first load the screen, here's what you'll see:

If you type in each of the text fields, you'll update the state of the component for the screen:

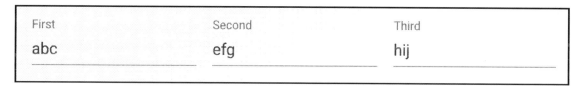

How it works...

The setter functions that are created with useState(): setFirst(), setSecond(), and setThird(), change the value of the TextField component by changing the state that's used by the component in the onChange event.

 The TextField component is a convenient abstraction that builds on other Material-UI components, such as FormControl and Input. You could achieve the exact same result by replacing TextField with each of these components. But all you would get is more code to maintain.

There's more...

What if, instead of only keeping the TextField value in the component state, you also kept the id and label information as well? It might seem confusing to store values that never change as a state, but the trade-off is that you can have the state data drive what's rendered by the component instead of having to repeat the same TextField components over and over.

First, let's change the shape of the component state, as follows:

```
const [inputs, setInputs] = useState([
  { id: 'first', label: 'First', value: '' },
  { id: 'second', label: 'Second', value: '' },
  { id: 'third', label: 'Third', value: '' }
]);
```

Instead of an object with string properties to hold the text field values, the `inputs` state is an array of objects. It's an array so that the component can iterate over the values while maintaining their order. Each object has everything necessary to render `TextField`. Let's look at the updated markup next:

```
<Grid container spacing={4} className={classes.container}>
  {inputs.map(input => (
    <Grid item key={input.id}>
      <TextField
        id={input.id}
        label={input.label}
        value={input.value}
        onChange={onChange}
      />
    </Grid>
  ))}
</Grid>
```

Each `Grid` item now maps to an element from the `inputs` array. If you need to add, remove, or change something about one of these text fields, you can do so by updating the state. Finally, let's see what the `onChange()` implementation looks like:

```
const onChange = ({ target: { id, value } }) => {
  const newInputs = [...inputs];
  const index = inputs.findIndex(input => input.id === id);

  newInputs[index] = { ...inputs[index], value };

  setInputs(newInputs);
};
```

The `onChange()` function updates an item in an array, the `inputs` array. First, it finds the `index` of the item to update, based on the text field `id`. Then, it updates the `value` property with the value of the text field.

The functionality is the exact same as before, with a different approach that requires less JSX markup.

See also

- `TextField` **demos:** https://material-ui.com/demos/text-fields/
- `TextField` **API documentation:** https://material-ui.com/api/text-field/

Placeholder and helper text

At a minimum, text fields should have a label so that the user knows what to type. But a label on its own can be downright confusing—especially if you have several text fields on the same screen. To help the user understand what to type, you can utilize `placeholder` and `helperText` in addition to `label`.

How to do it...

Let's write some code that showcases various `label`, `placeholder`, and `helperText` configurations you can use with the `TextField` component:

```
import React from 'react';

import { withStyles } from '@material-ui/core/styles';
import Grid from '@material-ui/core/Grid';
import TextField from '@material-ui/core/TextField';

const styles = theme => ({
  container: { margin: theme.spacing(2) }
});
const PlaceholderAndHelperText = withStyles(styles)(({ classes }) => (
  <Grid container spacing={4} className={classes.container}>
    <Grid item>
      <TextField label="The Value" />
    </Grid>
    <Grid item>
      <TextField placeholder="Example Value" />
    </Grid>
    <Grid item>
      <TextField helperText="Brief explanation of the value" />
    </Grid>
    <Grid item>
      <TextField
        label="The Value"
        placeholder="Example Value"
```

```
        helperText="Brief explanation of the value"
      />
    </Grid>
  </Grid>
));

export default PlaceholderAndHelperText;
```

Here's what the four text fields look like:

How it works...

Let's take a look at each of these text fields and break down their strengths and weaknesses.

First, there's a text field with a `label` component only:

```
<TextField label="The Value" />
```

When you only have `label`, it is displayed where the user would enter text:

When the user navigates to the text field and it receives focus, the `label` shrinks and moves out of the way:

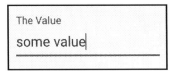

The next text field specifies placeholder text using the `placeholder` property:

```
<TextField placeholder="Example Value" />
```

The `placeholder` text should provide the user with an example of a valid value if possible:

> Example Value

When the user starts entering text, the `placeholder` value goes away:

> some value|

The next text field provides the `helperText` property with a value:

> Brief explanation of the value

The helper text of a text field is static in the sense that it's always visible and doesn't move, even after the user starts typing. Lastly, text fields can have all three properties that help the user figure out what value to provide:

- A label that tells the user what the value is
- Placeholder text that provides an example value
- Helper text that gives more of an explanation of why the value is needed

When you combine these three properties, you're increasing the likelihood that the user will understand what to type. When the text field is unfocused, the label and the helper text are visible:

> The Value
>
> Brief explanation of the value

When the text field receives focus, the label shrinks and the placeholder value is revealed:

> The Value
>
> Example Value
>
> Brief explanation of the value

See also

- `TextField` **demos:** https://material-ui.com/demos/text-fields/
- `TextField` **API documentation:** https://material-ui.com/api/text-field/

Validation and error display

Even with helper text, placeholders, and labels, users will inevitably enter something that's not quite right. It's not that they are trying to mess things up (some are, to be fair); it's that mistakes happen. When mistakes are made, text input fields need to be marked as being in an error state.

How to do it...

Let's say that you have two inputs: a phone number and an email address, and you want to make sure that the values provided by the user are correct.

 Please note: Validation isn't perfect. Thankfully, this piece can work, however, you need it to and you'll still get all of the Material-UI pieces.

Here's the code to do it:

```
import React, { useState } from 'react';

import { makeStyles } from '@material-ui/styles';
import Grid from '@material-ui/core/Grid';
import TextField from '@material-ui/core/TextField';

const useStyles = makeStyles(theme => ({
  container: { margin: theme.spacing(2) }
}));

export default function ValidationAndErrorDisplay() {
  const classes = useStyles();
  const [inputs, setInputs] = useState([
    {
      id: 'phone',
      label: 'Phone',
      placeholder: '999-999-9999',
      value: '',
```

```
        error: false,
        helperText: 'Any valid phone number will do',
        getHelperText: error =>
          error
            ? 'Woops. Not a valid phone number'
            : 'Any valid phone number will do',
        isValid: value =>
          /^[\+]?[(]?[0-9]{3}[)]?[-\s\.]?[0-9]{3}[-\s\.]?[0-9]{4,6}$/.test(
            value
          )
    },
    {
      id: 'email',
      label: 'Email',
      placeholder: 'john@acme.com',
      value: '',
      error: false,
      helperText: 'Any valid email address will do',
      getHelperText: error =>
        error
          ? 'Woops. Not a valid email address'
          : 'Any valid email address will do',
      isValid: value => /\S+@\S+\.\S+/.test(value)
    }
  ]);

  const onChange = ({ target: { id, value } }) => {
    const newInputs = [...inputs];
    const index = inputs.findIndex(input => input.id === id);
    const input = inputs[index];
    const isValid = input.isValid(value);

    newInputs[index] = {
      ...input,
      value: value,
      error: !isValid,
      helperText: input.getHelperText(!isValid)
    };

    setInputs(newInputs);
  };

  return (
    <Grid container spacing={4} className={classes.container}>
      {inputs.map(input => (
        <Grid item key={input.id}>
          <TextField
            id={input.id}
```

```
            label={input.label}
            placeholder={input.placeholder}
            helperText={input.helperText}
            value={input.value}
            onChange={onChange}
            error={input.error}
         />
      </Grid>
    ))}
   </Grid>
  );
}
```

The `ValidationAndErrorDisplay` component will render two `TextField` components on the screen. This is what they look like when the screen first loads:

The **Phone** and **Email** text fields are just regular text fields with labels, helper text, and placeholders. For example, when the **Phone** field receives focus, it looks like this:

As you start typing, the value of the text field is validated against a phone format regular expression. Here's what the field looks like when it has an invalid phone number value:

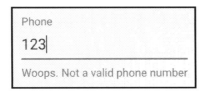

Then, once you have a valid phone number value, the state of the text field goes back to normal:

```
Phone

999-999-9999|

Any valid phone number will do
```

The **Email** field works the same way—the only difference is the regular expression used to validate the format of the value.

How it works...

Let's start by taking a look at the state of the `ValidationAndErrorDisplay` component:

```
const [inputs, setInputs] = useState([
  {
    id: 'phone',
    label: 'Phone',
    placeholder: '999-999-9999',
    value: '',
    error: false,
    helperText: 'Any valid phone number will do',
    getHelperText: error =>
      error
        ? 'Woops. Not a valid phone number'
        : 'Any valid phone number will do',
    isValid: value =>
      /^[\+]?[(]?[0-9]{3}[)]?[-\s\.]?[0-9]{3}[-\s\.]?[0-9]{4,6}$/.test(
        value
      )
  },
  {
    id: 'email',
    label: 'Email',
    placeholder: 'john@acme.com',
    value: '',
    error: false,
    helperText: 'Any valid email address will do',
    getHelperText: error =>
      error
        ? 'Woops. Not a valid email address'
        : 'Any valid email address will do',
    isValid: value => /\S+@\S+\.\S+/.test(value)
  }
]);
```

The inputs **array is mapped to** TextField **components by the** render() **method. Each object in this array has properties that map directly to the** TextField **component. For instance,** id, label, placeholder—these are all TextField **properties. The objects each have two functions that help with validating the text field values. First,** getHelperText() **returns either the default helper text, or error text that replaces the helper text if the** error **argument is true. The** isValid() **function validates the** value **argument against a regular expression and returns** true **if it matches.**

Next, let's look at the onChange() handler:

```
const onChange = ({ target: { id, value } }) => {
  const newInputs = [...inputs];
  const index = inputs.findIndex(input => input.id === id);
  const input = inputs[index];
  const isValid = input.isValid(value);

  newInputs[index] = {
    ...input,
    value: value,
    error: !isValid,
    helperText: input.getHelperText(!isValid)
  };

  setInputs(newInputs);
};
```

As the user types, this function updates the value state of the given text field. It also calls the isValid() function, passing it the updated value. The error state is set to true if the value is invalid. The helperText state is also updated using getHelperText(), which also depends on the validity of the value.

There's more...

What if this example could be modified so that you didn't have to store error messages as a state, or have a function to change the helper text of the text field? To do this, you could introduce a new TextField abstraction that handles setting the error property and changes the helperText component when the value is invalid. Here's the new component:

```
const MyTextField = ({ isInvalid, ...props }) => {
  const invalid = isInvalid(props.value);

  return (
    <TextField
```

```
        {...props}
        error={invalid}
        helperText={invalid || props.helperText}
      />
    );
};
```

Instead of having a function that returns `true` if the data is valid, the `MyTextField`
component expects an `isInvalid()` property that returns `false` if the data is valid and an
`error` message when it's `invalid`. Then, the `error` property can use this value, which
changes the color of the text field to indicate that it's in an error state and the `helperText`
property can use either the string that is returned by the `isInvalid()` function, or the
`helperText` property that was passed to the component.

Next, let's look at the state that the `ValidationAndErrorDisplay` component uses now:

```
const [inputs, setInputs] = useState([
  {
    id: 'phone',
    label: 'Phone',
    placeholder: '999-999-9999',
    value: '',
    helperText: 'Any valid phone number will do',
    isInvalid: value =>
      value === '' ||
      /^[\+]?[(]?[0-9]{3}[)]?[-\s\.]?[0-9]{3}[-\s\.]?[0-9]{4,6}$/.test(
        value
      )
        ? false
        : 'Woops. Not a valid phone number'
  },
  {
    id: 'email',
    label: 'Email',
    placeholder: 'john@acme.com',
    value: '',
    helperText: 'Any valid email address will do',
    isInvalid: value =>
      value === '' || /\S+@\S+\.\S+/.test(value)
        ? false
        : 'Woops. Not a valid email address'
  }
]);
```

The inputs no longer need the `getHelperText()` function or the `error` state. The `isInvalid()` function returns the error helper text when the value is invalid. Next, let's look at the `onChange()` handler:

```
const onChange = ({ target: { id, value } }) => {
  const newInputs = [...inputs];
  const index = inputs.findIndex(input => input.id === id);

  newInputs[index] = {
    ...inputs[index],
    value: value
  };

  setInputs(newInputs);
};
```

Now, it doesn't have to touch the `error` state, or worry about updating the helper text, or about calling any validation functions—this is all handled by `MyTextField` now.

See also

- `TextField` **demos:** https://material-ui.com/demos/text-fields/
- `TextField` **API documentation:** https://material-ui.com/api/text-field/

Password fields

Password fields are a special type of text input that hides the individual characters on the screen as they are typed. Material-UI `TextField` components support this type of field by changing the value of the `type` property.

How to do it...

Here's a simple example that changes a regular text input into a `password` input that prevents the value from displaying on the screen:

```
import React, { useState } from 'react';

import TextField from '@material-ui/core/TextField';

export default function PasswordFields() {
  const [password, setPassword] = useState('12345');

  const onChange = e => {
    setPassword(e.target.value);
  };

  return (
    <TextField
      type="password"
      label="Password"
      value={password}
      onChange={onChange}
    />
  );
}
```

Here's what the screen looks like when it first loads:

If you change the value of the **Password** field, any new characters remain hidden, even though the actual value typed is stored in the `password` state of the `PasswordFields` component.

How it works...

The `type` property tells the `TextField` component to use a password HTML `input` element. This is how the value remains hidden as the user types it, or if the field is pre-populated with a `password` value. Sometimes, **Password** fields can be autofilled.

There's more...

You can use the `autoComplete` property to control how password values are automatically filled by the browser. A common case for this value is to have the **Password** field automatically filled on a login screen once the **Username** field is filled. Here's an example of how you can use this property when you have **Username** and **Password** fields on the screen:

```
import React, { useState } from 'react';

import { makeStyles } from '@material-ui/styles';
import Grid from '@material-ui/core/Grid';
import TextField from '@material-ui/core/TextField';

const useStyles = makeStyles(theme => ({
  container: { margin: theme.spacing(2) }
}));

export default function PasswordFields() {
  const classes = useStyles();
  const [username, setUsername] = useState('');
  const [password, setPassword] = useState('');

  return (
    <Grid container spacing={4} className={classes.container}>
      <Grid item>
        <TextField
          id="username"
          label="Username"
          autoComplete="username"
          InputProps={{ name: 'username' }}
          value={username}
          onChange={e => setUsername(e.target.value)}
        />
      </Grid>
      <Grid item>
        <TextField
          id="password"
          type="password"
```

```
            label="Password"
            autoComplete="current-password"
            value={password}
            onChange={e => setPassword(e.target.value)}
          />
        </Grid>
      </Grid>
    );
  }
```

The first `TextField` component uses the `autoComplete` value of `username`. It also passes
`{ name: 'username' }` to `InputProps` so that the `name` property is set on the `<input>`
element. The reason you need to do this is so that, in the second `TextField` component,
the `autoComplete` value of `current-password` tells the browser to look up the password
based on the `username` field value.

 Not all browsers implement this functionality the same. In order for any
credentials to be automatically filled in text fields, they have to be saved
using the native browser credential remembering tool.

See also

- `TextField` demos: https://material-ui.com/demos/text-fields/
- `TextField` API documentation: https://material-ui.com/api/text-field/

Multiline input

For some fields, users need the ability to provide text values that span multiple lines. The
`multiline` property helps accomplish this goal.

How to do it...

Let's say that you have a field that could require multiple lines of text, provided by the
user. You can specify the `multiline` property to allow for this:

```
import React, { useState } from 'react';

import TextField from '@material-ui/core/TextField';
```

```
export default function MultilineInput() {
  const [multiline, setMultiline] = useState('');

  return (
    <TextField
      multiline
      value={multiline}
      onChange={e => setMultiline(e.target.value)}
    />
  );
}
```

The text field looks like a normal field when the screen first loads, because it has one row by default:

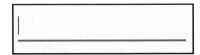

You can enter as many lines as you need to in this text field. New lines are started by pressing *Enter*:

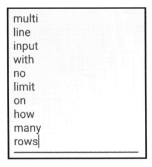

How it works...

The `multiline` Boolean property is used to indicate to the `TextField` component that `multiline` support is needed for the field. With the preceding example, you might run into a couple of issues if you're planning on using the `multiline` input in a crowded space, such as a screen with many other fields on it or in a dialog:

- The height of the field changes as the user presses *Enter*, adding more rows to the component. This might cause layout problems as other elements are moved around.

- If the field starts with one row and looks like a regular single-line text input, then the user might not realize that they can enter multiple lines of text in the field.

There's more...

To help prevent scenarios where a dynamically-sized `multiline` text field might cause problems, you can specify the number of rows used by a `multiline` text field. Here's an example of how to use the `rows` property:

```
<TextField
  multiline
  rows={5}
  label="Address"
  value={multiline}
  onChange={e => setMultiline(e.target.value)}
/>
```

Now, the text field will have exactly five rows:

If the user enters more than five lines of text, a vertical scrollbar will be displayed—the height of the text doesn't change and can't impact the layout of other surrounding components. You can impose the same type of height restriction on the `TextField` component by using the `rowsMax` property instead of `rows`. The difference is that the text field will start out with one row and will grow as the user adds new lines. But if you set `rowsMax` to 5, the text field will not exceed five rows.

See also

- `TextField` demos: `https://material-ui.com/demos/text-fields/`
- `TextField` API documentation: `https://material-ui.com/api/text-field/`

Input adornments

Material-UI `Input` components have properties that allow you to customize the way that they look and behave. The idea is that you can adorn inputs with other Material-UI components to extend the functionality of basic text inputs in a way that makes sense for the users of your application.

How to do it...

Let's say that your app has several screens that have password inputs. The users of your app like the ability to see passwords as they're typed. By default, values will be hidden, but if the input component itself had a button that toggles the visibility of the value, that would make your users happy.

Here's an example of a generic component that will adorn password fields with a visibility toggle button:

```
import React, { useState } from 'react';

import TextField from '@material-ui/core/TextField';
import IconButton from '@material-ui/core/IconButton';
import InputAdornment from '@material-ui/core/InputAdornment';

import VisibilityIcon from '@material-ui/icons/Visibility';
import VisibilityOffIcon from '@material-ui/icons/VisibilityOff';

function PasswordField() {
  const [visible, setVisible] = useState(false);

  const toggleVisibility = () => {
    setVisible(!visible);
  };

  return (
    <TextField
      type={visible ? 'text' : 'password'}
      InputProps={{
        endAdornment: (
          <InputAdornment position="end">
            <IconButton onClick={toggleVisibility}>
              {visible ? <VisibilityIcon /> : <VisibilityOffIcon />}
            </IconButton>
          </InputAdornment>
        )
      }}
```

```
      />
    );
  }

export default function InputAdornments() {
  const [password, setPassword] = useState('');

  return (
    <PasswordField
      value={password}
      onChange={e => setPassword(e.target.value)}
    />
  );
}
```

Here is what you'll see if you start typing without clicking on the toggle visibility button:

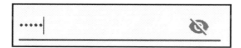

Here's what the **Password** field looks like if we click on the toggle visibility button:

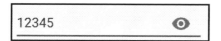

How it works...

Let's take a closer look at the `PasswordField` component:

```
function PasswordField() {
  const [visible, setVisible] = useState(false);

  const toggleVisibility = () => {
    setVisible(!visible);
  };

  return (
    <TextField
      type={visible ? 'text' : 'password'}
      InputProps={{
        endAdornment: (
          <InputAdornment position="end">
            <IconButton onClick={toggleVisibility}>
              {visible ? <VisibilityIcon /> : <VisibilityOffIcon />}
```

```
                </IconButton>
              </InputAdornment>
            )
          }}
        />
      );
    }
```

This component maintains a piece of state called `visible`. The reason that
`PasswordField` maintains this state instead of the parent component is because of the
separation of concerns principle. The parent component, for example, probably needs
access to the value of the password field. This value gets passed into `PasswordField` as a
property. However, only `PasswordField` cares about the `visibility` state. So, by
keeping it encapsulated within this component, you've simplified any code that uses
`PasswordField`.

The other valuable aspect of this abstraction is the adornment itself. The `type` property
changes as the `visible` state changes—this is the mechanism that reveals or hides the
password value. The `endAdornment` property is passed to the `Input` component that
`TextField` renders, passed via `InputProps`. This is how you can add components to the
field. In this example, you're adding an icon button to the right-hand side (end) of the
input. The icon here changes based on the visible state and, when clicked, the
`toggleVisible()` method is called to actually change the visible state.

There's more...

You can use input adornments for more than buttons that reveal the value of a password
field. For example, in a field that is validated, you can use input adornments to help
visualize the validation state of the field. Let's say that you need to validate an email field
as the user types. You could create an abstraction in the form of a component that changes
the color and the adornment of the component based on the result of validating what the
user has provided. Here's what that component looks like:

```
const ValidationField = props => {
  const { isValid, ...rest } = props;
  const empty = props.value === '';
  const valid = isValid(props.value);
  let startAdornment;

  if (empty) {
    startAdornment = null;
  } else if (valid) {
    startAdornment = (
```

```
        <InputAdornment position="start">
          <CheckCircleIcon color="primary" />
        </InputAdornment>
      );
    } else {
      startAdornment = (
        <InputAdornment position="start">
          <ErrorIcon color="error" />
        </InputAdornment>
      );
    }

    return (
      <TextField
        {...rest}
        error={!empty && !valid}
        InputProps={{ startAdornment }}
      />
    );
};
```

The idea with `ValidationField` is to take an `isValid()` function property and use it to test the value property. If it returns `true`, then `startAdornment` is a checkmark. If `isValid()` returns `false`, then `startAdornment` is a red *x*. Here's how the component is used:

```
<ValidationField
  label="Email"
  value={this.state.email}
  onChange={this.onEmailChange}
  isValid={v => /\S+@\S+\.\S+/.test(v)}
/>
```

The `ValidationField` component can be used almost identically to `TextField`. The one addition is the `isValid` property. Any state is handled outside of `ValidationField`, which means that `isValid()` is called any time the value changes, and will update the appearance of the component to reflect the validity of the data. By way of an added bonus: you don't actually have to store any kind of error state anywhere, because `ValidationField` derives everything that it needs from the value and `isValid` properties.

Here's what the field looks like with an invalid email address:

Here's what the field looks like with a valid email address:

See also

- `TextField` **demos:** https://material-ui.com/demos/text-fields/
- `TextField` **API documentation:** https://material-ui.com/api/text-field/
- `IconButton` **API documentation:** https://material-ui.com/api/icon-button/
- `InputAdornment` **API documentation:** https://material-ui.com/api/input-adornment/

Input masking

Some text inputs require values with a specific format. With Material-UI `TextField` components, you can add masking capabilities that help guide the user toward providing the correct format.

How to do it...

Let's say that you have phone number and email fields and you want to provide an input mask for each. Here's how you can use the `MaskedInput` component from `react-text-mask` with `TextField` components to add masking abilities:

```
import React, { Fragment, useState } from 'react';
import MaskedInput from 'react-text-mask';
import emailMask from 'text-mask-addons/dist/emailMask';

import { makeStyles } from '@material-ui/styles';
import TextField from '@material-ui/core/TextField';

const useStyles = makeStyles(theme => ({
  input: { margin: theme.spacing.unit * 3 }
}));

const PhoneInput = ({ inputRef, ...props }) => (
  <MaskedInput
```

```
        {...props}
        ref={ref => {
          inputRef(ref ? ref.inputElement : null);
        }}
        mask={[
          '(',
          /[1-9]/,
          /\d/,
          /\d/,
          ')',
          ' ',
          /\d/,
          /\d/,
          /\d/,
          '-',
          /\d/,
          /\d/,
          /\d/,
          /\d/
        ]}
        placeholderChar={'\u2000'}
    />
);

const EmailInput = ({ inputRef, ...props }) => (
    <MaskedInput
      {...props}
      ref={ref => {
        inputRef(ref ? ref.inputElement : null);
      }}
      mask={emailMask}
      placeholderChar={'\u2000'}
    />
);

export default function InputMasking() {
    const classes = useStyles();
    const [phone, setPhone] = useState('');
    const [email, setEmail] = useState('');

    return (
      <Fragment>
        <TextField
          label="Phone"
          className={classes.input}
          value={phone}
          onChange={e => setPhone(e.target.value)}
          InputProps={{ inputComponent: PhoneInput }}
```

```
      />
      <TextField
        label="Email"
        className={classes.input}
        value={email}
        onChange={e => setEmail(e.target.value)}
        InputProps={{ inputComponent: EmailInput }}
      />
    </Fragment>
  );
}
```

Here's what the screen looks like when it first loads:

Once you start typing a value into the **Phone** field, the format mask appears:

Here's what the completed value looks like—the user never has to type (,), or –:

Here's what the completed **Email** value looks like:

With the email input, the user will actually have to type @ and . because the mask doesn't know how many characters are in any part of the email address. It does, however, prevent the user from putting either of these characters in the wrong place.

How it works...

To make this work, you created a `PhoneInput` component and an `EmailInput` component. The idea of each is to provide a basic abstraction around the `MaskedInput` component. Let's take a closer look at each, starting with `PhoneInput`:

```
const PhoneInput = ({ inputRef, ...props }) => (
  <MaskedInput
    {...props}
    ref={ref => {
      inputRef(ref ? ref.inputElement : null);
    }}
    mask={[
      '(',
      /[1-9]/,
      /\d/,
      /\d/,
      ')',
      ' ',
      /\d/,
      /\d/,
      /\d/,
      '-',
      /\d/,
      /\d/,
      /\d/,
      /\d/
    ]}
    placeholderChar={'\u2000'}
  />
);
```

The properties that are passed to `PhoneInput` are forwarded to `MaskedInput` for the most part. The `ref` property needs to be set explicitly because it's named differently. The `placeholder` property is set to be whitespace. The `mask` property is the most important—this is what determines the pattern that the user sees as they start typing. The value passed to `mask` is an array with regular expressions and string characters. The string characters are what show up when the user starts typing—in the case of phone number, these are the `(`, `)`, and `-` characters. The regular expressions are the dynamic pieces that match against what the user types. With a phone number, any digit will do, but symbols and letters aren't allowed.

Let's look at the `EmailInput` component now:

```
const EmailInput = ({ inputRef, ...props }) => (
  <MaskedInput
    {...props}
    ref={ref => {
      inputRef(ref ? ref.inputElement : null);
    }}
    mask={emailMask}
    placeholderChar={'\u2000'}
  />
);
```

This follows the same approach as `PhoneInput`. The main difference is that, instead of passing an array of strings and regular expressions, the `emailMask` function (imported from `react-text-mask`) is used.

Now that you have these two masked inputs, you use them by passing them to the `inputComponent` property:

```
<TextField
  label="Phone"
  className={classes.input}
  value={phone}
  onChange={e => setPhone(e.target.value)}
  InputProps={{ inputComponent: PhoneInput }}
/>
<TextField
  label="Email"
  className={classes.input}
  value={email}
  onChange={e => setEmail(e.target.value)}
  InputProps={{ inputComponent: EmailInput }}
/>
```

See also

- `TextField` demos: https://material-ui.com/demos/text-fields/
- `TextField` API documentation: https://material-ui.com/api/text-field/
- React text mask: https://github.com/text-mask/text-mask

12

Autocomplete and Chips - Text Input Suggestions for Multiple Items

In this chapter, you will learn the following topics:

- Building an Autocomplete component
- Selecting Autocomplete suggestions
- API-driven Autocomplete
- Highlighting search results
- Standalone chip input

Introduction

Web applications typically provide autocomplete input fields when there are too many choices to select from. Autocomplete fields are like text input fields—as users starts typing, they are given a smaller list of choices based on what they've typed. Once the user is ready to make a selection, the actual input is filled with components called `Chips`—especially relevant when the user needs to be able to make multiple selections.

Building an Autocomplete component

Material-UI doesn't actually come with an `Autocomplete` component. The reason is that, since there are so many different implementations of autocomplete selection components in the React ecosystem already, it doesn't make sense to provide another one. Instead, you can pick an existing implementation and augment it with Material-UI components so that it can integrate nicely with your Material-UI application.

How to do it...

Let's say that you have a selector for a hockey team. But there are too many teams to reasonably fit in a simple select component—you need autocomplete capabilities. You can use the `Select` component from the `react-select` package to provide the autocomplete functionality that you need. You can use `Select` properties to replace key autocomplete components with Material-UI components so that the autocomplete matches the look and feel of the rest of your app.

Let's make a reusable `Autocomplete` component. The `Select` component allows you to replace certain aspects of the autocomplete experience. In particular, following are the components that you'll be replacing:

- `Control`: The text input component to use
- `Menu`: A menu with suggestions, displayed when the user starts typing
- `NoOptionsMessage`: The message that's displayed when there aren't any suggestions to display
- `Option`: The component used for each suggestion in `Menu`
- `Placeholder`: The placeholder text component for the text input
- `SingleValue`: The component for showing a value once it's selected
- `ValueContainer`: The component that wraps `SingleValue`
- `IndicatorSeparator`: Separates buttons on the right side of the autocomplete
- `ClearIndicator`: The component used for the button that clears the current value
- `DropdownIndicator`: The component used for the button that shows `Menu`

Each of these components is replaced with Material-UI components that change the look and feel of the autocomplete. Moreover, you'll have all of this as new `Autocomplete` components that you can reuse throughout your app.

Let's look at the result before diving into the implementation of each replacement component. Following is what you'll see when the screen first loads:

If you click on the down arrow, you'll see a menu with all the values, as follows:

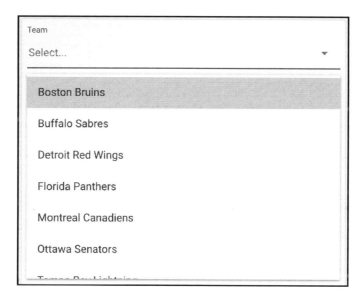

Try typing **tor** into the autocomplete text field, as follows:

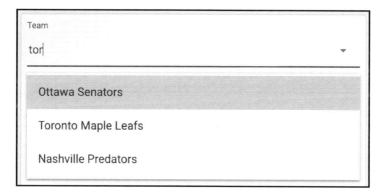

If you make a selection, the menu is closed and the text field is populated with the selected value, as follows:

You can change your selection by opening the menu and selecting another value, or you can clear the selection by clicking on the clear button to the right of the text.

How it works...

Let's break down the source by looking at the individual components that make up the Autocomplete component and replacing pieces of the Select component. Then, we'll look at the final Autocomplete component.

Text input control

Here's the source for the Control component:

```
const inputComponent = ({ inputRef, ...props }) => (
  <div ref={inputRef} {...props} />
);

const Control = props => (
  <TextField
    fullWidth
    InputProps={{
      inputComponent,
      inputProps: {
        className: props.selectProps.classes.input,
        inputRef: props.innerRef,
        children: props.children,
        ...props.innerProps
      }
    }}
    {...props.selectProps.textFieldProps}
  />
);
```

The `inputComponent()` function is a component that passes the `inputRef` value—a reference to the underlying input element—to the `ref` prop. Then, `inputComponent` is passed to `InputProps` to set the input component used by `TextField`. This component is a little bit confusing because it's passing references around and it uses a `helper` component for this purpose. The important thing to remember is that the job of `Control` is to set up the `Select` component to use a Material-UI `TextField` component.

Options menu

Here's the component that displays the autocomplete options when the user starts typing or clicks on the down arrow:

```
const Menu = props => (
  <Paper
    square
    className={props.selectProps.classes.paper}
    {...props.innerProps}
  >
    {props.children}
  </Paper>
);
```

The `Menu` component renders a Material-UI `Paper` component so that the element surrounding the options is themed accordingly.

No options available

Here's the `NoOptionsMessage` component. It is rendered when there aren't any autocomplete options to display, as follows:

```
const NoOptionsMessage = props => (
  <Typography
    color="textSecondary"
    className={props.selectProps.classes.noOptionsMessage}
    {...props.innerProps}
  >
    {props.children}
  </Typography>
);
```

This renders a `Typography` component with `textSecondary` as the `color` property value.

Individual option

Individual options that are displayed in the autocomplete menu are rendered using the
`MenuItem` component, as follows:

```
const Option = props => (
  <MenuItem
    buttonRef={props.innerRef}
    selected={props.isFocused}
    component="div"
    style={{
      fontWeight: props.isSelected ? 500 : 400
    }}
    {...props.innerProps}
  >
    {props.children}
  </MenuItem>
);
```

The `selected` and `style` properties alter the way that the item is displayed, based on the
`isSelected` and `isFocused` properties. The `children` property sets the value of the item.

Placeholder text

The `Placeholder` text of the `Autocomplete` component is shown before the user types
anything or makes a selection, as follows:

```
const Placeholder = props => (
  <Typography
    color="textSecondary"
    className={props.selectProps.classes.placeholder}
    {...props.innerProps}
  >
    {props.children}
  </Typography>
);
```

The Material-UI `Typography` component is used to theme the `Placeholder` text.

SingleValue

Once again, the Material-UI `Typography` component is used to render the selected value from the menu within the autocomplete input, as follows:

```
const SingleValue = props => (
  <Typography
    className={props.selectProps.classes.singleValue}
    {...props.innerProps}
  >
    {props.children}
  </Typography>
);
```

ValueContainer

The `ValueContainer` component is used to wrap the `SingleValue` component with a `div` and the `valueContainer` CSS class, as follows:

```
const ValueContainer = props => (
  <div className={props.selectProps.classes.valueContainer}>
    {props.children}
  </div>
);
```

IndicatorSeparator

By default, the `Select` component uses a pipe character as a separator between the buttons on the right side of the autocomplete menu. Since they're going to be replaced by Material-UI button components, this separator is no longer necessary, as follows:

```
const IndicatorSeparator = () => null;
```

By having the component return `null`, nothing is rendered.

Clear option indicator

This button is used to clear any selection made previously by the user, as follows:

```
const ClearIndicator = props => (
  <IconButton {...props.innerProps}>
    <CancelIcon />
  </IconButton>
);
```

The purpose of this component is to use the Material-UI `IconButton` component and to render a Material-UI icon. The click handler is passed in through `innerProps`.

Show menu indicator

Just like the `ClearIndicator` component, the `DropdownIndicator` component replaces the button used to show the autocomplete menu with an icon from Material-UI, as follows:

```
const DropdownIndicator = props => (
  <IconButton {...props.innerProps}>
    <ArrowDropDownIcon />
  </IconButton>
);
```

Styles

Here are the styles used by the various sub-components of the autocomplete:

```
const useStyles = makeStyles(theme => ({
  root: {
    flexGrow: 1,
    height: 250
  },
  input: {
    display: 'flex',
    padding: 0
  },
  valueContainer: {
    display: 'flex',
    flexWrap: 'wrap',
    flex: 1,
    alignItems: 'center',
    overflow: 'hidden'
  },
  noOptionsMessage: {
    padding: `${theme.spacing(1)}px ${theme.spacing(2)}px`
  },
  singleValue: {
    fontSize: 16
  },
  placeholder: {
    position: 'absolute',
    left: 2,
    fontSize: 16
  },
```

```
  paper: {
    position: 'absolute',
    zIndex: 1,
    marginTop: theme.spacing(1),
    left: 0,
    right: 0
  }
}));
```

The Autocomplete

Finally, following is the `Autocomplete` component that you can reuse throughout your application:

```
export default function Autocomplete(props) {
  const classes = useStyles();
  const [value, setValue] = useState(null);

  return (
    <div className={classes.root}>
      <Select
        value={value}
        onChange={v => setValue(v)}
        textFieldProps={{
          label: 'Team',
          InputLabelProps: {
            shrink: true
          }
        }}
        {...{ ...props, classes }}
      />
    </div>
  );
}

Autocomplete.defaultProps = {
  isClearable: true,
  components: {
    Control,
    Menu,
    NoOptionsMessage,
    Option,
    Placeholder,
    SingleValue,
    ValueContainer,
    IndicatorSeparator,
    ClearIndicator,
```

```
        DropdownIndicator
    },
    options: [
        { label: 'Boston Bruins', value: 'BOS' },
        { label: 'Buffalo Sabres', value: 'BUF' },
        { label: 'Detroit Red Wings', value: 'DET' },
        { label: 'Florida Panthers', value: 'FLA' },
        { label: 'Montreal Canadiens', value: 'MTL' },
        { label: 'Ottawa Senators', value: 'OTT' },
        { label: 'Tampa Bay Lightning', value: 'TBL' },
        { label: 'Toronto Maple Leafs', value: 'TOR' },
        { label: 'Carolina Hurricanes', value: 'CAR' },
        { label: 'Columbus Blue Jackets', value: 'CBJ' },
        { label: 'New Jersey Devils', value: 'NJD' },
        { label: 'New York Islanders', value: 'NYI' },
        { label: 'New York Rangers', value: 'NYR' },
        { label: 'Philadelphia Flyers', value: 'PHI' },
        { label: 'Pittsburgh Penguins', value: 'PIT' },
        { label: 'Washington Capitals', value: 'WSH' },
        { label: 'Chicago Blackhawks', value: 'CHI' },
        { label: 'Colorado Avalanche', value: 'COL' },
        { label: 'Dallas Stars', value: 'DAL' },
        { label: 'Minnesota Wild', value: 'MIN' },
        { label: 'Nashville Predators', value: 'NSH' },
        { label: 'St. Louis Blues', value: 'STL' },
        { label: 'Winnipeg Jets', value: 'WPG' },
        { label: 'Anaheim Ducks', value: 'ANA' },
        { label: 'Arizona Coyotes', value: 'ARI' },
        { label: 'Calgary Flames', value: 'CGY' },
        { label: 'Edmonton Oilers', value: 'EDM' },
        { label: 'Los Angeles Kings', value: 'LAK' },
        { label: 'San Jose Sharks', value: 'SJS' },
        { label: 'Vancouver Canucks', value: 'VAN' },
        { label: 'Vegas Golden Knights', value: 'VGK' }
    ]
};
```

The piece that ties all of the previous components together is the `components` property that's passed to `Select`. This is actually set as a `default` property in `Autocomplete`, so it can be further overridden. The value passed to `components` is a simple object that maps the component name to its implementation.

See also

- `Select` **components for React:** https://react-select.com/
- `Autocomplete` **demos:** https://material-ui.com/demos/autocomplete/
- `TextField` **API documentation:** https://material-ui.com/api/text-field/
- `Typography` **API documentation:** https://material-ui.com/api/typography/
- `Paper` **API documentation:** https://material-ui.com/api/paper/
- `MenuItem` **API documentation:** https://material-ui.com/api/menu-item/
- `IconButton` **API documentation:** https://material-ui.com/api/icon-button/

Selecting autocomplete suggestions

In the previous section, you built an `Autocomplete` component capable of selecting a single value. Sometimes, you need the ability to select multiple values from an `Autocomplete` component. The good news is that, with a few small additions, the component that you created in the previous section already does most of the work.

How to do it...

Let's walk through the additions that need to be made in order to support multi-value selection in the `Autocomplete` component, starting with the new `MultiValue` component, as follows:

```
const MultiValue = props => (
  <Chip
    tabIndex={-1}
    label={props.children}
    className={clsx(props.selectProps.classes.chip, {
      [props.selectProps.classes.chipFocused]: props.isFocused
    })}
    onDelete={props.removeProps.onClick}
    deleteIcon={<CancelIcon {...props.removeProps} />}
  />
);
```

The MultiValue component uses the Material-UI Chip component to render a selected value. In order to pass MultiValue to Select, add it to the components object that's passed to Select:

```
components: {
  Control,
  Menu,
  NoOptionsMessage,
  Option,
  Placeholder,
  SingleValue,
  MultiValue,
  ValueContainer,
  IndicatorSeparator,
  ClearIndicator,
  DropdownIndicator
},
```

Now you can use your Autocomplete component for single value selection, or for multi-value selection. You can add the isMulti property with a default value of true to defaultProps, as follows:

```
isMulti: true,
```

Now, you should be able to select multiple values from the autocomplete.

How it works...

Nothing looks different about the autocomplete when it's first rendered, or when you show the menu. When you make a selection, the Chip component is used to display the value. Chips are ideal for displaying small pieces of information like this. Furthermore, the close button integrates nicely with it, making it easy for the user to remove individual selections after they've been made.

Here's what the autocomplete looks like after multiple selections have been made:

Values that have been selected are removed from the menu.

See also

- Select components for React: `https://react-select.com/`
- `Autocomplete` demos: `https://material-ui.com/demos/autocomplete/`
- `TextField` API documentation: `https://material-ui.com/api/text-field/`
- `Typography` API documentation: `https://material-ui.com/api/typography/`
- `Paper` API documentation: `https://material-ui.com/api/paper/`
- `MenuItem` API documentation: `https://material-ui.com/api/menu-item/`
- `IconButton` API documentation: `https://material-ui.com/api/icon-button/`
- `Chip` API documentation: `https://material-ui.com/api/chip/`

API-driven Autocomplete

You can't always have your autocomplete data ready to render on the initial page load. Imagine trying to load hundreds or thousands of items before the user can interact with anything. The better approach is to keep the data on the server and supply an API endpoint with the autocomplete text as the user types. Then you only need to load a smaller set of data returned by the API.

How to do it...

Let's rework the example from the previous section. We'll keep all of the same autocomplete functionality, except that, instead of passing an array to the `options` property, we'll pass in an API function that returns a `Promise`. Here's the API function that mocks an API call that resolves a `Promise`:

```
const someAPI = searchText =>
  new Promise(resolve => {
    setTimeout(() => {
      const teams = [
        { label: 'Boston Bruins', value: 'BOS' },
        { label: 'Buffalo Sabres', value: 'BUF' },
```

```
            { label: 'Detroit Red Wings', value: 'DET' },
            ...
        ];

        resolve(
          teams.filter(
            team =>
              searchText &&
              team.label
                .toLowerCase()
                .includes(searchText.toLowerCase())
          )
        );
      }, 1000);
    });
```

This function takes a search string argument and returns a Promise. The same data that would otherwise be passed to the Select component in the options property is filtered here instead. Think of anything that happens in this function as happening behind an API in a real app. The returned Promise is then resolved with an array of matching items following a simulated latency of one second.

You also need to add a couple of components to the composition of the Select component (we're up to 13 now!), as follows:

```
const LoadingIndicator = () => <CircularProgress size={20} />;

const LoadingMessage = props => (
  <Typography
    color="textSecondary"
    className={props.selectProps.classes.noOptionsMessage}
    {...props.innerProps}
  >
    {props.children}
  </Typography>
);
```

The LoadingIndicator component is shown on the right the autocomplete text input. It's using the CircularProgress component from Material-UI to indicate that the autocomplete is doing something. The LoadingMessage component follows the same pattern as the other text replacement components used with Select in this example. The loading text is displayed when the menu is shown, but the Promise that resolves the options is still pending.

Lastly, there's the `Select` component. Instead of using `Select`, you need to use the `AsyncSelect` version, as follows:

```
import AsyncSelect from 'react-select/lib/Async';
```

Otherwise, `AsyncSelect` works the same as `Select`, as follows:

```
<AsyncSelect
  value={value}
  onChange={value => setValue(value)}
  textFieldProps={{
    label: 'Team',
    InputLabelProps: {
      shrink: true
    }
  }}
  {...{ ...props, classes }}
/>
```

How it works...

The only difference between a `Select` autocomplete and an `AsyncSelect` autocomplete is what happens while the request to the API is pending. Here is what the autocomplete looks like while this is happening:

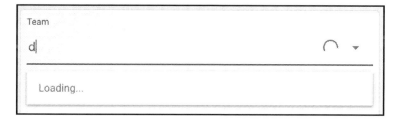

As the user types the `CircularProgress` component is rendered to the right, while the loading message is rendered in the menu using a `Typography` component.

See also

- Select components for React: https://react-select.com/
- Autocomplete demos: https://material-ui.com/demos/autocomplete/
- TextField API documentation: https://material-ui.com/api/text-field/

- `Typography` **API documentation:** https://material-ui.com/api/typography/
- `Paper` **API documentation:** https://material-ui.com/api/paper/
- `MenuItem` **API documentation:** https://material-ui.com/api/menu-item/
- `IconButton` **API documentation:** https://material-ui.com/api/icon-button/
- `Chip` **API documentation:** https://material-ui.com/api/chip/

Highlighting search results

When the user starts typing in an autocomplete and the results are displayed in the dropdown, it isn't always obvious how a given item matches the search criteria. You can help your users better understand the results by highlighting the matched portion of the string value.

How to do it...

You'll want to use two functions from the `autosuggest-highlight` package to help `highlight` the text presented in the autocomplete dropdown, as follows:

```
import match from 'autosuggest-highlight/match';
import parse from 'autosuggest-highlight/parse';
```

Now, you can build a new component that will render the item text, highlighting as and when necessary, as follows:

```
const ValueLabel = ({ label, search }) => {
  const matches = match(label, search);
  const parts = parse(label, matches);

  return parts.map((part, index) =>
    part.highlight ? (
      <span key={index} style={{ fontWeight: 500 }}>
        {part.text}
      </span>
    ) : (
      <span key={index}>{part.text}</span>
    )
  );
};
```

The end result is that ValueLabel renders an array of span elements, determined by the parse() and match() functions. One of the spans will be bolded if part.highlight is true. Now, you can use ValueLabel in the Option component, as follows:

```
const Option = props => (
  <MenuItem
    buttonRef={props.innerRef}
    selected={props.isFocused}
    component="div"
    style={{
      fontWeight: props.isSelected ? 500 : 400
    }}
    {...props.innerProps}
  >
    <ValueLabel
      label={props.children}
      search={props.selectProps.inputValue}
    />
  </MenuItem>
);
```

How it works...

Now, when you search for values in the autocomplete text input, the results will highlight the search criteria in each item, as follows:

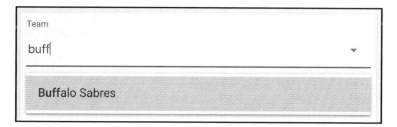

See also

- Autosuggest for React: https://github.com/moroshko/autosuggest-highlight
- Select components for React: https://react-select.com/
- Autocomplete demos: https://material-ui.com/demos/autocomplete/
- TextField API documentation: https://material-ui.com/api/text-field/

- `Typography` **API documentation:** https://material-ui.com/api/typography/
- `Paper` **API documentation:** https://material-ui.com/api/paper/
- `MenuItem` **API documentation:** https://material-ui.com/api/menu-item/
- `IconButton` **API documentation:** https://material-ui.com/api/icon-button/
- `Chip` **API documentation:** https://material-ui.com/api/chip/

Standalone chip input

Some applications require multi-value inputs but don't have a predefined list for the user to choose from. This rules out the possibility of using an autocomplete or a `select` component, for example, if you're asking the user for a list of names.

How to do it...

You can install the `material-ui-chip-input` package and use the `ChipInput` component, which brings together the `Chip` and `TextInput` components from Material-UI. The code is as follows:

```
import React, { useState } from 'react';

import { makeStyles } from '@material-ui/styles';
import ChipInput from 'material-ui-chip-input';

const useStyles = makeStyles(theme => ({
  chipInput: { minWidth: 300 }
}));

export default function StandaloneChipInput() {
  const classes = useStyles();
  const [values, setValues] = useState([]);

  const onAdd = chip => {
    setValues([...values, chip]);
  };

  const onDelete = (chip, index) => {
    setValues(values.slice(0, index).concat(values.slice(index + 1)));
  };

  return (
    <ChipInput
```

```
        className={classes.chipInput}
        helperText="Type name, hit enter to type another"
        value={values}
        onAdd={onAdd}
        onDelete={onDelete}
      />
    );
  }
```

When the screen first loads, the field looks like a regular text field that you can type in, as follows:

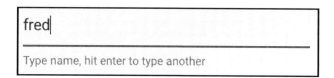

As the helper text indicates, you can hit *Enter* to add the item and enter more text, as follows:

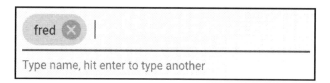

You can keep adding items to the field as you please, as follows:

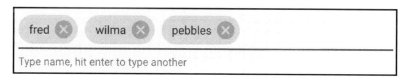

It's important that the helper text mentions the **enter** key. Otherwise, the user might not be able to figure out that they can enter multiple values.

How it works...

The state that holds the value of the `chip` input field is an array—because there are multiple values. The two actions involved with the `chip` input state are adding and removing strings from this array. Let's take a closer look at the `onAdd()` and `onDelete()` functions, as follows:

```
const onAdd = chip => {
  setValues([...values, chip]);
};

const onDelete = (chip, index) => {
  setValues(values.slice(0, index).concat(values.slice(index + 1)));
};
```

The `onAdd()` function adds the `chip` to the array, while the `onDelete()` function deletes the `chip` at the given `index`. The chips are deleted when the `Delete` icon in the chip is clicked on by the user. Lastly, let's look at the `ChipInput` component itself, as follows:

```
<ChipInput
  className={classes.chipInput}
  helperText="Type name, hit enter to type another"
  value={values}
  onAdd={onAdd}
  onDelete={onDelete}
/>
```

It's very similar to a `TextInput` component. It actually takes the same properties, such as `helperText`. It also takes additional properties not found in `TextInput`, such as `onAdd` and `onDelete`.

See also

- A Material-UI `ChipInput` component: https://www.npmjs.com/package/material-ui-chip-input

13

Selection - Make Selections from Choices

In this chapter, you'll learn about the following:

- Abstracting checkbox groups
- Customizing checkbox items
- Abstracting radio button groups
- Using radio button types
- Replacing checkboxes with switches
- Controlling selects with state
- Selecting multiple items

Introduction

Any application that includes user interactions involves user making selections. This could range from a simple on/off switch to selection with several items that allow more than one item to be selected. Material-UI has different selection components that best fit a given user scenario.

Abstracting checkbox groups

Checkboxes often provide the user with a group of related options that can be checked or unchecked. The Material-UI Checkbox component provides the base functionality, but you might want something a little more high level that can be reused throughout your application.

How to do it...

Let's create an abstraction for groups of checkbox options. Here's the code for a
CheckboxGroup **component:**

```
import React, { useState } from 'react';

import FormLabel from '@material-ui/core/FormLabel';
import FormControl from '@material-ui/core/FormControl';
import FormGroup from '@material-ui/core/FormGroup';
import FormControlLabel from '@material-ui/core/FormControlLabel';
import FormHelperText from '@material-ui/core/FormHelperText';
import Checkbox from '@material-ui/core/Checkbox';

const CheckboxGroup = ({ values, label, onChange }) => (
  <FormControl component="fieldset">
    <FormLabel component="legend">{label}</FormLabel>
    <FormGroup>
      {values.map((value, index) => (
        <FormControlLabel
          key={index}
          control={
            <Checkbox
              checked={value.checked}
              onChange={onChange(index)}
            />
          }
          label={value.label}
        />
      ))}
    </FormGroup>
  </FormControl>
);

export default function AbstractingCheckboxGroups() {
  const [values, setValues] = useState([
    { label: 'First', checked: false },
    { label: 'Second', checked: false },
    { label: 'Third', checked: false }
  ]);

  const onChange = index => ({ target: { checked } }) => {
    const newValues = [...values];
    const value = values[index];

    newValues[index] = { ...value, checked };

    setValues(newValues);
```

```
    };

    return (
      <CheckboxGroup
        label="Choices"
        values={values}
        onChange={onChange}
      />
    );
  }
```

When you first load the screen, here's what you'll see:

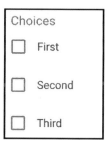

Here's what it looks like when you select the first two choices:

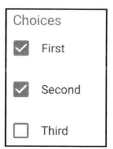

How it works...

Let's take a closer look at the CheckboxGroup component:

```
const CheckboxGroup = ({ values, label, onChange }) => (
  <FormControl component="fieldset">
    <FormLabel component="legend">{label}</FormLabel>
    <FormGroup>
      {values.map((value, index) => (
        <FormControlLabel
```

```
            key={index}
            control={
              <Checkbox
                checked={value.checked}
                onChange={onChange(index)}
              />
            }
            label={value.label}
          />
      ))}
    </FormGroup>
  </FormControl>
);
```

This is the abstraction that allows you to render groups of checkbox options on the various screens throughout your app. There are several Material-UI components involved with rendering a group of checkboxes—CheckboxGroup takes care of this for you so that you just need to worry about passing it an array of values, label, and an onChange handler.

Next, let's look at how CheckboxGroup is rendered by your application component:

```
<CheckboxGroup
  label="Choices"
  values={values}
  onChange={onChange}
/>
```

You only need to worry about structuring the values array and passing it to the CheckboxGroup component whenever your application needs to render a group of related checkbox options. Lastly, let's look at state and the onChange() handler used to toggle the checked state of the value:

```
const [values, setValues] = useState([
  { label: 'First', checked: false },
  { label: 'Second', checked: false },
  { label: 'Third', checked: false }
]);

const onChange = index => ({ target: { checked } }) => {
  const newValues = [...values];
  const value = values[index];

  newValues[index] = { ...value, checked };

  setValues(newValues);
};
```

The `checked` property is changed based on the index argument and the `target.checked` value.

There's more...

Let's add a `List` component to this example so that you can better visualize the state changes that happen when checkboxes are checked/unchecked. Here's the additional Material-UI components that you'll need to import:

```
import List from '@material-ui/core/List';
import ListItem from '@material-ui/core/ListItem';
import ListItemIcon from '@material-ui/core/ListItemIcon';
import ListItemText from '@material-ui/core/ListItemText';
import Typography from '@material-ui/core/Typography';
```

The idea is to have this list render the labels of checked items. Let's render this list right below the `CheckboxGroup` component:

```
<Fragment>
  <CheckboxGroup
    label="Choices"
    values={values}
    onChange={onChange}
  />
  <Typography variant="h6">Selection</Typography>
  <List>
    {values
      .filter(value => value.checked)
      .map((value, index) => (
        <ListItem key={index}>
          <ListItemText>{value.label}</ListItemText>
        </ListItem>
    ))}
  </List>
</Fragment>
```

The `filter()` call on `values` will only include values where the `checked` property is `true`. When the screen first loads, you'll see an empty list because nothing is checked by default:

As you start making selections, you'll see the selection list change as a reflection of the application state changes:

See also

- Selection demos: `https://material-ui.com/demos/selection-controls/`
- `Checkbox` API documentation: `https://material-ui.com/api/checkbox/`
- `FormHelperText` API documentation: `https://material-ui.com/api/form-helper-text/`

- **FormControlLabel API documentation:** https://material-ui.com/api/form-control-label/
- **FormGroup API documentation:** https://material-ui.com/api/form-group/
- **FormControl API documentation:** https://material-ui.com/api/form-control/
- **FormLabel API documentation:** https://material-ui.com/api/form-label/

Customizing checkbox items

The default appearance of Material-UI Checkbox components tries to resemble the native browser checkbox input element. You can change the icon that's used for both the checked and the unchecked state of the component. Even after you change the icons used by Checkbox, any color changes are still honored.

How to do it...

Here's some code that imports several Material-UI icons and uses them to configure the icons used by the Checkbox components:

```
import React, { useState, useEffect } from 'react';

import FormGroup from '@material-ui/core/FormGroup';
import FormControlLabel from '@material-ui/core/FormControlLabel';
import Checkbox from '@material-ui/core/Checkbox';

import AccountBalance from '@material-ui/icons/AccountBalance';
import AccountBalanceOutlined from '@material-ui/icons/AccountBalanceOutlined';
import Backup from '@material-ui/icons/Backup';
import BackupOutlined from '@material-ui/icons/BackupOutlined';
import Build from '@material-ui/icons/Build';
import BuildOutlined from '@material-ui/icons/BuildOutlined';

const initialItems = [
  {
    name: 'AccountBalance',
    Icon: AccountBalanceOutlined,
    CheckedIcon: AccountBalance
  },
  {
    name: 'Backup',
    Icon: BackupOutlined,
```

```
      CheckedIcon: Backup
    },
    {
      name: 'Build',
      Icon: BuildOutlined,
      CheckedIcon: Build
    }
];

export default function CustomizingCheckboxItems() {
  const [items, setItems] = useState({});

  useEffect(() => {
    setItems(
      initialItems.reduce(
        (state, item) => ({ ...state, [item.name]: false }),
        {}
      )
    );
  }, []);

  const onChange = e => {
    setItems({ [e.target.name]: e.target.checked });
  };

  return (
    <FormGroup>
      {initialItems.map(({ name, Icon, CheckedIcon }, index) => (
        <FormControlLabel
          key={index}
          control={
            <Checkbox
              checked={items[name]}
              onChange={onChange}
              inputProps={{ name }}
              icon={<Icon fontSize="small" />}
              checkedIcon={<CheckedIcon fontSize="small" />}
            />
          }
          label={name}
        />
      ))}
    </FormGroup>
  );
}
```

Here's what the checkboxes look like when the screen first loads:

These checkboxes are unchecked. Here's what they look like when they're checked:

How it works...

Let's walk through what's happening here. The `initialItems` array is the starting point for the construction of the checkboxes:

```
const initialItems = [
  {
    name: 'AccountBalance',
    Icon: AccountBalanceOutlined,
    CheckedIcon: AccountBalance
  },
  {
    name: 'Backup',
    Icon: BackupOutlined,
    CheckedIcon: Backup
  },
  {
    name: 'Build',
    Icon: BuildOutlined,
    CheckedIcon: Build
  }
];
```

Each item has a `name` component to identify the checkbox, as well as checked/unchecked `Icon` components. Next, let's take a look at how the state of the `CustomizingCheckboxItems` component is initialized:

```
const [items, setItems] = useState({});

useEffect(() => {
  setItems(
    initialItems.reduce(
      (state, item) => ({ ...state, [item.name]: false }),
      {}
    )
  );
}, []);
```

The state is initialized to an object by reducing the `initialItems` array. For each item in the array, the state of this component will have a property that's initialized to false. The name of the property is based on the `name` property of the item. So, for example, the component state will look something like this after it's reduced:

```
{
  AccountBalance: false,
  Backup: false,
  Build: false
}
```

These properties are used to store the checked state of each checkbox. Next, let's look at how each `Checkbox` component is rendered based on the `initialItems` array:

```
<FormGroup>
  {initialItems.map(({ name, Icon, CheckedIcon }, index) => (
    <FormControlLabel
      key={index}
      control={
        <Checkbox
          checked={items[name]}
          onChange={onChange}
          inputProps={{ name }}
          icon={<Icon fontSize="small" />}
          checkedIcon={<CheckedIcon fontSize="small" />}
        />
      }
      label={name}
    />
  ))}
</FormGroup>
```

The key properties that customize each of the checkboxes are `icon` and `checkedIcon`. These properties use the `Icon` and `CheckIcon` properties from the items array, respectively.

There's more...

Because the icons that you're using to customize the `Checkbox` component are Material-UI components, you can change the color of the checkbox and have it work the same as would without custom icons. For example, you could set the color of the checkboxes in this example to default:

```
<Checkbox
  color="default"
  checked={items[name]}
  onChange={onChange}
  inputProps={{ name }}
  icon={<Icon fontSize="small" />}
  checkedIcon={<CheckedIcon fontSize="small" />}
/>
```

Here's how this would look with every checkbox checked:

With the color set to the default, the color doesn't change when a checkbox goes from unchecked to checked. This doesn't matter much, though, because the icons go from an outline theme to a filled theme. Just the shape change is enough to indicate that the item is checked.

Let's try it out with `primary`, just for fun:

```
<Checkbox
  color="primary"
  checked={items[name]}
  onChange={onChange}
  inputProps={{ name }}
  icon={<Icon fontSize="small" />}
```

```
    checkedIcon={<CheckedIcon fontSize="small" />}
 />
```

Here's how this looks with everything checked:

See also

- `Selection` **demos:** https://material-ui.com/demos/selection-controls/
- `Checkbox` **API documentation:** https://material-ui.com/api/checkbox/
- `FormControlLabel` **API documentation:** https://material-ui.com/api/form-control-label/
- `FormGroup` **API documentation:** https://material-ui.com/api/form-group/

Abstracting radio button groups

Radio button groups are similar to checkbox groups. The key difference is that radios are used when only one value should be selected. Also, like checkbox groups, radio button groups require several Material-UI components that can be encapsulated and reused throughout an application.

How it works...

Here's some code that captures all of the pieces required to put together a radio button group into a single component:

```
import React, { useState } from 'react';

import Radio from '@material-ui/core/Radio';
import { default as MaterialRadioGroup } from '@material-ui/core/RadioGroup';
```

```
import FormControlLabel from '@material-ui/core/FormControlLabel';
import FormControl from '@material-ui/core/FormControl';
import FormLabel from '@material-ui/core/FormLabel';

const options = [
  { label: 'First', value: 'first' },
  { label: 'Second', value: 'second' },
  { label: 'Third', value: 'third' }
];

const RadioGroup = ({ value, options, name, label, onChange }) => (
  <FormControl component="fieldset">
    <FormLabel component="legend">{label}</FormLabel>
    <MaterialRadioGroup
      name={name}
      value={value}
      onChange={onChange}
      disabled
    >
      {options.map((option, index) => (
        <FormControlLabel
          key={index}
          control={<Radio />}
          value={option.value}
          label={option.label}
        />
      ))}
    </MaterialRadioGroup>
  </FormControl>
);

export default function AbstractingRadioButtonGroups() {
  const [value, setValue] = useState('first');

  const onChange = e => {
    setValue(e.target.value);
  };

  return (
    <RadioGroup
      value={value}
      options={options}
      name="radio1"
      label="Pick One"
      onChange={onChange}
    />
  );
}
```

Here's what you'll see when you first load the screen:

Here's what the component looks like if you were to click on the third option:

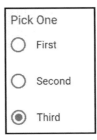

Because these options all belong to the same radio group, only one option can be checked at a time.

How it works...

Let's take a closer look at the RadioGroup component in this example:

```
const RadioGroup = ({ value, options, name, label, onChange }) => (
  <FormControl component="fieldset">
    <FormLabel component="legend">{label}</FormLabel>
    <MaterialRadioGroup name={name} value={value} onChange={onChange}>
      {options.map((option, index) => (
        <FormControlLabel
          key={index}
          control={<Radio />}
          value={option.value}
          label={option.label}
        />
      ))}
    </MaterialRadioGroup>
  </FormControl>
);
```

The `options` property should have an array value, which is then mapped to the `FormControlLabel` components. The `control` property uses the `Radio` component to render each radio control. Unlike checkbox groups, the `onChange` property is on the `MaterialRadioGroup` component instead of on each individual `Radio`. This is because there's only ever a single active value, which is managed by `MaterialRadioGroup`.

 The Material-UI `RadioGroup` component is imported with the `MaterialRadioGroup` alias because we're creating a component of the same name. This is fine, as long as you're clear about which packages own which components.

Next, let's see how the `RadioGroup` component is rendered:

```
<RadioGroup
  value={value}
  options={options}
  name="radio1"
  label="Pick One"
  onChange={onChange}
/>
```

The `name` property is what ties everything together. It's important that radio buttons that are part of the same group have the same name. This abstraction takes care of this for you by only requiring the name in one place. Here's what the `options` array looks like:

```
const options = [
  { label: 'First', value: 'first' },
  { label: 'Second', value: 'second' },
  { label: 'Third', value: 'third' }
];
```

The idea with radio groups is that they only ever have one value. The value properties in the `options` array are the allowed values—but only one is active. The last thing worth looking at with this example is the `onChange` handler and the state structure of the application component:

```
const [value, setValue] = useState('first');

const onChange = e => {
  setValue(e.target.value);
};
```

This is how the initial radio selection is set. When it changes, the value state is updated to the value of the selected radio.

There's more...

You can disable the entire radio button group by setting the `disabled` property on the `FormControl` component:

```
<FormControl component="fieldset" disabled>
  ...
</FormControl>
```

When you disable the control, you can't interact with it at all. Here's what this looks like:

In other scenarios, you will only want to disable one of the options. You can support this in the `RadioGroup` component by checking for a `disabled` property in the `options` array:

```
<FormControlLabel
  key={index}
  control={<Radio disabled={option.disabled} />}
  value={option.value}
  label={option.label}
/>
```

Here is how you would disable an option in the `options` array:

```
const options = [
  { label: 'First', value: 'first' },
  { label: 'Second', value: 'second', disabled: true },
  { label: 'Third', value: 'third' }
];
```

Here's how the radio group looks with the **Second** option disabled:

While the **Second** option is disabled, there's no way to activate it because the user cannot interact with it.

 Be careful about disabling the option that's active by default. There's no way for this to not cause confusion for the user. You can activate another option in the group, but then you can't activate the option that was active to begin with.

See also

- `Selection` demos: https://material-ui.com/demos/selection-controls/
- `Radio` API documentation: https://material-ui.com/api/radio/
- `RadioGroup` API documentation: https://material-ui.com/api/radio-group/
- `FormControlLabel` API documentation: https://material-ui.com/api/form-control-label/
- `FormControl` API documentation: https://material-ui.com/api/form-control/
- `FormLabel` API documentation: https://material-ui.com/api/form-label/

Radio button types

There are a number of radio button aspects that you can customize to create your own type of radio button group. While the underlying principle of selecting a single value from several options doesn't change, you can make the radio button group design fit any application.

How to do it...

Let's say that, based on the layout of your screen, and in order to stay consistent with other screens in your app, you need to create a radio group with the following design traits:

- A single row is used to present options
- There are icons and text for each option
- The primary theme color is used for selected options

Here's some code that does this:

```
import React, { Fragment, useState } from 'react';

import Radio from '@material-ui/core/Radio';
import RadioGroup from '@material-ui/core/RadioGroup';
import FormControlLabel from '@material-ui/core/FormControlLabel';
import FormControl from '@material-ui/core/FormControl';
import FormLabel from '@material-ui/core/FormLabel';

import Car from '@material-ui/icons/DirectionsCar';
import CarOutlined from '@material-ui/icons/DirectionsCarOutlined';
import Bus from '@material-ui/icons/DirectionsBus';
import BusOutlined from '@material-ui/icons/DirectionsBusOutlined';
import Train from '@material-ui/icons/Train';
import TrainOutlined from '@material-ui/icons/TrainOutlined';

export default function RadioButtonTypes() {
  const [value, setValue] = useState('train');

  const onChange = e => {
    setValue(e.target.value);
  };

  return (
    <FormControl component="fieldset">
      <FormLabel component="legend">Travel Mode</FormLabel>
      <RadioGroup name="travel" value={value} onChange={onChange} row>
        <FormControlLabel
          value="car"
          control={
            <Radio
              color="primary"
              icon={<CarOutlined />}
              checkedIcon={<Car />}
            />
          }
          label="Car"
```

```
          labelPlacement="bottom"
        />
        <FormControlLabel
          value="bus"
          control={
            <Radio
              color="primary"
              icon={<BusOutlined />}
              checkedIcon={<Bus />}
            />
          }
          label="Bus"
          labelPlacement="bottom"
        />
        <FormControlLabel
          value="train"
          control={
            <Radio
              color="primary"
              icon={<TrainOutlined />}
              checkedIcon={<Train />}
            />
          }
          label="Train"
          labelPlacement="bottom"
        />
      </RadioGroup>
    </FormControl>
  );
}
```

Here's what the radio group looks like when the screen first loads:

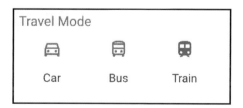

You can change the default selection by clicking on any of the other icons or labels. The icon state is updated to reflect the change:

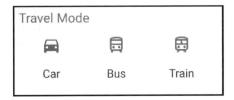

How it works...

It seems that we were able to meet the criteria set forth for the radio button group. Let's walk through the code to see how each requirement was met. First, the group is rendered horizontally with each radio button on the same row. This is done by passing the `row` property to the `RadioGroup` component:

```
<RadioGroup
  name="travel"
  value={value}
  onChange={onChange}
  row
>
```

The label of each radio is displayed underneath each radio button because this works better with the row layout of the group. This is done by setting the `labelPlacement` property value of `FormControlLabel`. The radio color uses the primary color from the Material-UI theme when selected. It's also using custom icons for checked and unchecked states:

```
<Radio
  color="primary"
  icon={<BusOutlined />}
  checkedIcon={<Bus />}
/>
```

Both of these enhancements are handled by the `Radio` component.

See also

- `Selection` **demos:** https://material-ui.com/demos/selection-controls/
- `Radio` **API documentation:** https://material-ui.com/api/radio/
- `RadioGroup` **API documentation:** https://material-ui.com/api/radio-group/
- `FormControlLabel` **API documentation:** https://material-ui.com/api/form-control-label/
- `FormControl` **API documentation:** https://material-ui.com/api/form-control/
- `FormLabel` **API documentation:** https://material-ui.com/api/form-label/

Replacing checkboxes with switches

Material-UI has a control which is very similar to a checkbox, called a switch. The main visual distinction between the two components is that a switch has more emphasis on the toggling on/off action. In a mobile environment, users might feel more accustomed to the `Switch` component. In any other environment, you're probably best sticking with regular `Checkbox` components.

How to do it...

Let's say that, instead of creating a component that abstracts a group of `Checkbox` components, you you want want to do the same thing with the `Switch` components. Here's the code:

```
import React, { Fragment, useState } from 'react';

import FormLabel from '@material-ui/core/FormLabel';
import FormControl from '@material-ui/core/FormControl';
import FormGroup from '@material-ui/core/FormGroup';
import FormControlLabel from '@material-ui/core/FormControlLabel';
import FormHelperText from '@material-ui/core/FormHelperText';
import Switch from '@material-ui/core/Switch';

const SwitchGroup = ({ values, label, onChange }) => (
  <FormControl component="fieldset">
    <FormLabel component="legend">{label}</FormLabel>
    <FormGroup>
      {values.map((value, index) => (
        <FormControlLabel
```

```
              key={index}
              control={
                <Switch
                  checked={value.checked}
                  onChange={onChange(index)}
                />
              }
              label={value.label}
            />
          ))}
        </FormGroup>
      </FormControl>
  );

  export default function ReplacingCheckboxesWithSwitches() {
    const [values, setValues] = useState([
      { label: 'First', checked: false },
      { label: 'Second', checked: false },
      { label: 'Third', checked: false }
    ]);

    const onChange = index => ({ target: { checked } }) => {
      const newValues = [...values];
      const value = values[index];

      newValues[index] = { ...value, checked };
      setValues(newValues);
    };

    return (
      <SwitchGroup
        label="Choices"
        values={values}
        onChange={onChange}
      />
    );
  }
```

Here's what the switch group looks like when the screen first loads:

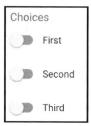

Here's what the switch group looks like with every switch turned on:

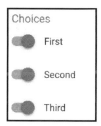

How it works...

Anywhere that you can use a `Checkbox` component, you can also use a `Switch` component. This code was taken from the *Abstracting checkbox groups* section from earlier in this chapter. The `Checkbox` components were replaced with `Switch` components.

There's more...

Rather than having divergent code paths for handling `Checkbox` versus `Switch` components, you could enhance the `SwitchGroup` component to accept a `checkbox` Boolean property that, when `true`, uses `Checkbox` as the control instead of `Switch`. Here's what the new `SwitchGroup` looks like:

```
const SwitchGroup = ({ values, label, onChange }) => (
  <FormControl component="fieldset">
    <FormLabel component="legend">{label}</FormLabel>
    <FormGroup>
      {values.map((value, index) => (
        <FormControlLabel
          key={index}
```

```
            control={
              <Switch
                checked={value.checked}
                onChange={onChange(index)}
              />
            }
            label={value.label}
          />
        ))}
      </FormGroup>
    </FormControl>
  );
```

And here's an example that shows both versions of the control being rendered side by side:

```
<Fragment>
  <SwitchGroup
    label="Switch Choices"
    values={values}
    onChange={this.onChange}
  />
  <SwitchGroup
    label="Switch Choices"
    values={values}
    onChange={onChange}
    checkbox
  />
</Fragment>
```

The second SwitchGroup component uses the checkbox property to render the Checkbox components instead of the Switch components. Here's what the result looks like:

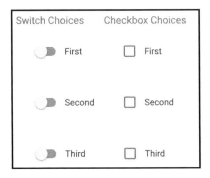

Here's what you'll see if you select the first option in either the switch choices or the checkbox choices group:

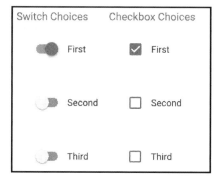

They are both updated because both fields share the same application state.

See also

- `Selection` **demos:** `https://material-ui.com/demos/selection-controls/`

Controlling selects with state

Some forms involve making selections from a list of values. This is kind of like choosing a radio button option from a radio button group. With the Material-UI `Select` component, you get something that looks more like a traditional HTML select element. Often, web application forms have several selects that depend on one another. In React/Material-UI applications, these selects are controlled through the `state` component.

How to do it...

Let's say that your screen has two selects—a category select and a product select. Initially, only the category select is populated and enabled. The product select depends on the category select—once a category is selected, the product select is enabled and populated with the appropriate products. Here's the code to do this:

```
import React, { Fragment, useState } from 'react';

import { makeStyles } from '@material-ui/styles';
```

```
import InputLabel from '@material-ui/core/InputLabel';
import MenuItem from '@material-ui/core/MenuItem';
import FormHelperText from '@material-ui/core/FormHelperText';
import FormControl from '@material-ui/core/FormControl';
import Select from '@material-ui/core/Select';

const useStyles = makeStyles(theme => ({
  control: { margin: theme.spacing(2), minWidth: 200 }
}));

export default function ControllingSelectsWithState() {
  const classes = useStyles();

  const [categories, setCategories] = useState([
    { label: 'Category 1', id: 1 },
    { label: 'Category 2', id: 2 },
    { label: 'Category 3', id: 3 }
  ]);

  const [products, setProducts] = useState([
    { label: 'Product 1', id: 1, category: 1 },
    { label: 'Product 2', id: 2, category: 1 },
    { label: 'Product 3', id: 3, category: 1 },
    { label: 'Product 4', id: 4, category: 2 },
    { label: 'Product 5', id: 5, category: 2 },
    { label: 'Product 6', id: 6, category: 2 },
    { label: 'Product 7', id: 7, category: 3 },
    { label: 'Product 8', id: 8, category: 3 },
    { label: 'Product 9', id: 9, category: 3 }
  ]);

  const setters = {
    categories: setCategories,
    products: setProducts
  };
  const collections = { categories, products };

  const onChange = e => {
    const setCollection = setters[e.target.name];
    const collection = collections[e.target.name].map(item => ({
      ...item,
      selected: false
    }));
    const index = collection.findIndex(
      item => item.id === e.target.value
    );

    collection[index] = { ...collection[index], selected: true };
```

```
    setCollection(collection);
};

const category = categories.find(category => category.selected) || {
  id: ''
};
const product = products.find(product => product.selected) || {
  id: ''
};

return (
  <Fragment>
    <FormControl className={classes.control}>
      <InputLabel htmlFor="categories">Category</InputLabel>
      <Select
        value={category.id}
        onChange={onChange}
        inputProps={{
          name: 'categories',
          id: 'categories'
        }}
      >
        <MenuItem value="">
          <em>None</em>
        </MenuItem>
        {categories.map(category => (
          <MenuItem key={category.id} value={category.id}>
            {category.label}
          </MenuItem>
        ))}
      </Select>
    </FormControl>
    <FormControl
      className={classes.control}
      disabled={category.id === ''}
    >
      <InputLabel htmlFor="Products">Product</InputLabel>
      <Select
        value={product.id}
        onChange={onChange}
        inputProps={{
          name: 'products',
          id: 'values'
        }}
      >
        <MenuItem value="">
          <em>None</em>
        </MenuItem>
```

```
            {products
              .filter(product => product.category === category.id)
              .map(product => (
                <MenuItem key={product.id} value={product.id}>
                  {product.label}
                </MenuItem>
            ))}
        </Select>
      </FormControl>
    </Fragment>
  );
}
```

Here's what you'll see when the screen first loads:

The category select is populated with options for you to choose from. The product select is disabled because no category has been selected. Here's what the category select looks like when it's open:

Once you select a category, you should be able to open the product select and make a product selection:

How it works...

The two `Select` components in this example have state dependencies. That is, the state of the product select depends on the state of the category select. This is because the options displayed in the product select are filtered based on the chosen category. Let's take a closer look at the state:

```
const [categories, setCategories] = useState([
  { label: 'Category 1', id: 1 },
  { label: 'Category 2', id: 2 },
  { label: 'Category 3', id: 3 }
]);

const [products, setProducts] = useState([
  { label: 'Product 1', id: 1, category: 1 },
  { label: 'Product 2', id: 2, category: 1 },
  { label: 'Product 3', id: 3, category: 1 },
  { label: 'Product 4', id: 4, category: 2 },
  { label: 'Product 5', id: 5, category: 2 },
  { label: 'Product 6', id: 6, category: 2 },
  { label: 'Product 7', id: 7, category: 3 },
  { label: 'Product 8', id: 8, category: 3 },
  { label: 'Product 9', id: 9, category: 3 }
]);
```

The `categories` and `products` arrays represent the options of the two selects on the screen. The selected option is marked with a `selected` Boolean property value of `true`. No options are selected by default. Both selects use the same `onChange()` handler:

```
const setters = {
  categories: setCategories,
  products: setProducts
};
const collections = { categories, products };

const onChange = e => {
  const setCollection = setters[e.target.name];
  const collection = collections[e.target.name].map(item => ({
    ...item,
    selected: false
  }));
  const index = collection.findIndex(
    item => item.id === e.target.value
  );

  collection[index] = { ...collection[index], selected: true };
  setCollection(collection);
};
```

The array to use depends on the value of `e.target.name`—which will be either categories or products. Once the collection value is initialized with the appropriate array, the `selected` property is set to `false` for every value. Then, the selected value is looked up based on `e.target.value`, and the `selected` property is set to `true` for this value.

Next, let's break down what's happening in the rest of the `ControllingSelectsWithState` component. First, the `category` and `product` selections are looked up from the component state:

```
const category = categories.find(category => category.selected) || {
  id: ''
};
const product = products.find(product => product.selected) || {
  id: ''
};
```

You have to make sure that an object with an `id` property is always assigned to these constants, because this is expected later on. The empty string will match the empty value option, so that it is selected by default. Next, let's see how the category options are rendered:

```
{categories.map(category => (
  <MenuItem key={category.id} value={category.id}>
    {category.label}
  </MenuItem>
))}
```

This is a straightforward mapping of values in the `categories` array to the `MenuItem` components. The options in the select `category` never change; in other words, the product options change based on the selected category—let's see how this is done:

```
{products
  .filter(product => product.category === category.id)
  .map(product => (
    <MenuItem key={product.id} value={product.id}>
      {product.label}
    </MenuItem>
  ))}
```

Before each product is mapped to a `MenuItem` component, the `products` array is filtered based on the selected category using `filter()`.

See Also

- `Selection` **demos:** https://material-ui.com/demos/selects/
- `InputLabel` **API documentation:** https://material-ui.com/api/input-label/
- `MenuItem` **API documentation:** https://material-ui.com/api/menu-item/
- `FormHelperText` **API documentation:** https://material-ui.com/api/form-helper-text/
- `FormControl` **API documentation:** https://material-ui.com/api/form-control/
- `Select` **API documentation:** https://material-ui.com/api/select/

Selecting multiple items

Users can select multiple values from the `Select` components. This involves using an array as the selected value state.

How to do it...

Here's some code that renders `Select` with several values. You can select as many values as you like:

```
import React, { useState } from 'react';

import { makeStyles } from '@material-ui/styles';
import Select from '@material-ui/core/Select';
import Input from '@material-ui/core/Input';
import InputLabel from '@material-ui/core/InputLabel';
import MenuItem from '@material-ui/core/MenuItem';
import FormControl from '@material-ui/core/FormControl';

const options = [
  { id: 1, label: 'First' },
  { id: 2, label: 'Second' },
  { id: 3, label: 'Third' },
  { id: 4, label: 'Fourth' },
  { id: 5, label: 'Fifth' }
];

const useStyles = makeStyles(theme => ({
  formControl: {
    margin: theme.spacing(1),
    minWidth: 100,
    maxWidth: 280
  }
}));

export default function SelectingMultipleItems() {
  const classes = useStyles();
  const [selected, setSelected] = useState([]);

  const onChange = e => {
    setSelected(e.target.value);
  };

  return (
    <FormControl className={classes.formControl}>
```

```
        <InputLabel htmlFor="multi">Value</InputLabel>
        <Select
          multiple
          value={selected}
          onChange={onChange}
          input={<Input id="multi" />}
        >
          {options.map(option => (
            <MenuItem key={option.id} value={option.id}>
              {option.label}
            </MenuItem>
          ))}
        </Select>
      </FormControl>
    );
  }
```

Here's what the selection looks like when it's first opened:

Here's what the select looks like with the first, third, and fifth options selected:

Now that you've made your selections, you can click somewhere on the screen outside the menu to close it, or you can hit the *Esc* key. You'll be able to see your selections in the text input:

How it works...

Let's start by taking a look at how the `Select` component is rendered:

```
<Select
  multiple
  value={selected}
  onChange={onChange}
  input={<Input id="multi" />}
>
  {options.map(option => (
    <MenuItem key={option.id} value={option.id}>
      {option.label}
    </MenuItem>
  ))}
</Select>
```

The `options` array values are mapped to `MenuItem` components, just like any other `Select`. The `multiple` property tells the component to allow the user to make multiple selections. The `selected` state of the `SelectingMultipleItems` component is an array, which holds the selected values. This array is populated by the `onChange` handler:

```
const onChange = e => {
  setSelected(e.target.value);
};
```

Because the `multiple` property was used, `e.target.value` is an array of selected values—you can just update the selected state using this value as is.

There's more...

Rather than having the selected items show up as a comma-separated list of `test`, you can make the items stand out by mapping the selected values to `Chip` components. Let's make a component that will handle this:

```
function Selected({ selected }) {
  const classes = useStyles();

  return selected.map(value => (
    <Chip
      key={value}
      label={options.find(option => option.id === value).label}
      className={classes.chip}
    />
  ));
}
```

This code block shows how you can use this component in the `renderValue` property of the `Select` component:

```
<Select
  multiple
  value={selected}
  onChange={onChange}
  input={<Input id="multi" />}
  renderValue={selected => <Selected selected={selected} />}
>
  {options.map(option => (
    <MenuItem key={option.id} value={option.id}>
      {option.label}
    </MenuItem>
  ))}
</Select>
```

Now, when you make multiple selections, they'll render as `Chip` components:

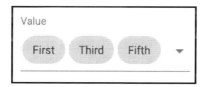

See also

- Selection **demos:** https://material-ui.com/demos/selects/
- Select **API documentation:** https://material-ui.com/api/select/
- Input **API documentation:** https://material-ui.com/api/input/
- InputLabel **API documentation:** https://material-ui.com/api/input-label/
- MenuItem **API documentation:** https://material-ui.com/api/menu-item/
- FormControl **API documentation:** https://material-ui.com/api/form-control/
- Chip **API documentation:** https://material-ui.com/api/chip/

Pickers - Selecting Dates and Times

14

In this chapter, we will cover the following topics:

- Using date pickers
- Using time pickers
- Setting initial date and time values
- Combining date and time components
- Integrating other date and time packages

Introduction

Most applications need to allow the user to select date and time values. For example, if a form includes a scheduling piece, the user needs an intuitive way to select date and time values. With Material-UI applications, you can use the date and time picker components that ship with the library.

Using date pickers

To use a date picker in Material-UI applications, you can leverage the `TextField` component. It accepts a `type` property that you can set to `date`. However, you have to take care of a few other things in addition to changing the text field type.

How to do it...

Here's some code that renders a date picker text field for the user, and another text field that displays the date in another format as the date selection changes:

```
import React, { Fragment, useState } from 'react';

import { makeStyles } from '@material-ui/styles';
import TextField from '@material-ui/core/TextField';

const useStyles = makeStyles(theme => ({
  textField: { margin: theme.spacing(1) }
}));

export default function UsingDatePickers() {
  const classes = useStyles();
  const [date, setDate] = useState('');

  const onChange = e => {
    setDate(e.target.value);
  };

  const dateFormatted = date
    ? new Date(`${date}T00:00:00`).toLocaleDateString()
    : null;

  return (
    <Fragment>
      <TextField
        value={date}
        onChange={onChange}
        label="My Date"
        type="date"
        className={classes.textField}
        InputLabelProps={{
          shrink: true
        }}
      />
      <TextField
        value={dateFormatted}
        label="Updated Date Value"
        className={classes.textField}
        InputLabelProps={{
          shrink: true
        }}
        InputProps={{ readOnly: true }}
      />
    </Fragment>
```

```
    );
  }
```

Here's what you'll see when the page first loads:

The **My Date** field to the left is the date picker. The **Updated Date Value** field to the right shows the selected date in a different format. Here's what the date picker looks like when it receives focus:

The year portion of the date is highlighted. You can type the year, or you can use the up/down arrow button to change the selected value. You change to the month or day portion of the date by hitting the *Tab* key or by using your mouse pointer. The drop-down arrow to the far right will display the following native browser date picker when clicked:

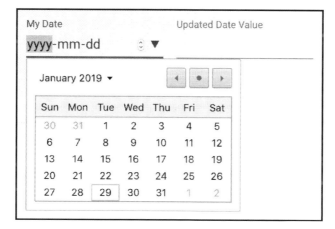

Once you've made a date selection, here's what the **My Date** and **Updated Date Value** fields look like:

My Date	Updated Date Value
2019-01-31	1/31/2019

How it works...

Let's start by taking a look at the date picker `TextField` component:

```
<TextField
  value={date}
  onChange={onChange}
  label="My Date"
  type="date"
  className={classes.textField}
  InputLabelProps={{
    shrink: true
  }}
/>
```

Most of the date picker functionality comes from the `type` property that is set to `date`. This applies the input mask and the native browser date picker control. Because of the input mask value, the `shrink` input property needs to be `true` to avoid overlap. The `value` property comes from the state of the `UsingDatePickers` component. This value defaults to an empty string, but it needs to be in a specific format. The date picker text field will put the date value in the correct format, so the `onChange()` handler doesn't actually have to do anything other than set the `date` state.

The **Updated Date Value** field uses a different format for the date. Let's take a look at how this is done:

```
const dateFormatted = date
  ? new Date(`${date}T00:00:00`).toLocaleDateString()
  : null;
```

First, you have to take the `date` string from the component state and use it to construct a new `Date` instance. To do this, you need to append the time string to the date string. This makes it a valid ISO string, and enables the date to be constructed without any surprises. Now you can use any of the date formatting functions available to `date` instances, such as `toLocaleDateString()`.

Now you can pass `dateFormatted` to the second text field, which is read-only since it's only used to display values:

```
<TextField
  value={dateFormatted}
  label="Updated Date Value"
  className={classes.textField}
  InputLabelProps={{
    shrink: true
  }}
  InputProps={{ readOnly: true }}
/>
```

There's more...

There are a couple of improvements that could be made to the preceding example. For starters, you could have a `DatePicker` component that hides some of the details about turning a `TextField` component into something that picks dates. Further, it would be nice if the new `DatePicker` component supported actual `Date` instances as values.

First, you'll need a utility function that can format `Date` instances into the string format expected by the `TextField` component when it's being used as a date picker:

```
function formatDate(date) {
  const year = date.getFullYear();
  const month = date.getMonth() + 1;
  const day = date.getDate();

  return [
    year,
    month < 10 ? `0${month}` : month,
    day < 10 ? `0${day}` : day
  ].join('-');
}
```

The `formatDate()` function takes a `Date` instance and returns a string in the format of YYYY-MM-dd. Now, you're ready to build the `DatePicker` component:

```
const DatePicker = ({ date, ...props }) => (
  <TextField
    value={date instanceof Date ? formatDate(date) : date}
    type="date"
    InputLabelProps={{
      shrink: true
    }}
```

```
      {...props}
  />
);
```

The `DatePicker` component renders a `TextField` component. It has the `type` property value set to `date` and the `shrink` input property set to `true`. It also sets the `value` – first it checks whether the `date` property is a `Date` instance, and if it is, calls `formatDate()`. Otherwise, the `date` argument is used as is.

Now, let's replace the `TextField` component in the previous example with the `DatePicker` component:

```
<Fragment>
  <DatePicker
    date={date}
    onChange={onChange}
    label="My Date"
    className={classes.textField}
  />
  <TextField
    value={dateFormatted}
    label="Updated Date Value"
    className={classes.textField}
    InputLabelProps={{
      shrink: true
    }}
    InputProps={{ readOnly: true }}
  />
</Fragment>
```

The `onChange`, `label`, and `className` properties are passed to the `TextField` component as they were before. The big difference with the `DatePicker` component is that you don't need to pass `type` or `InputProps`, and that `date` is used instead of `value`.

See also

- Picker demos: `https://material-ui.com/demos/pickers/`
- `TextField` API documentation: `https://material-ui.com/api/text-field/`

Using time pickers

Like date pickers, time pickers help users input time values. Also like date pickers, time pickers in Material-UI applications are derived from the `TextInput` components.

How to do it...

Let's create the same abstraction that's used in the *Using date pickers* section, only this time, it's meant for the `time` pickers:

```
import React, { Fragment, useState } from 'react';

import { makeStyles } from '@material-ui/styles';
import TextField from '@material-ui/core/TextField';

const useStyles = makeStyles(theme => ({
  textField: { margin: theme.spacing(1) }
}));

const TimePicker = ({ time, ...props }) => (
  <TextField
    value={time}
    type="time"
    InputLabelProps={{
      shrink: true
    }}
    inputProps={{
      step: 300
    }}
    {...props}
  />
);

export default function UsingTimePickers() {
  const classes = useStyles();
  const [time, setTime] = useState('');

  const onChange = e => {
    setTime(e.target.value);
  };

  return (
    <Fragment>
      <TimePicker
        time={time}
```

```
        onChange={onChange}
        label="My Time"
        className={classes.textField}
      />
      <TextField
        value={time}
        label="Updated Time Value"
        className={classes.textField}
        InputLabelProps={{
          shrink: true
        }}
        InputProps={{ readOnly: true }}
      />
    </Fragment>
  );
}
```

Here's what you'll see when the page first loads:

Once the **My Time** field receives focus, you can change the individual time pieces using the up/down arrow keys or the up/down arrow buttons that are displayed to the right of the time value:

The **Updated Time Value** field doesn't get updated until the full time is selected in the **My Time** field, because there's no time value until this happens:

How it works...

The structure of the `TimePicker` component is very similar to the `DatePicker` component from the previous recipe. The main difference is that `TimePicker` doesn't support the `Date` instances because it only deals with time. Because there's no date piece, using the `Date` instances to express only time is a lot more difficult than expressing only the date:

```
const TimePicker = ({ time, ...props }) => (
  <TextField
    value={time}
    type="time"
    InputLabelProps={{
      shrink: true
    }}
    inputProps={{
      step: 300
    }}
    {...props}
  />
);
```

The `TimePicker` component sets the same properties on `TextField` as the `DatePicker` component. Additionally, the `step` value of `300` makes the minute portion of the time move by five minutes at a time.

See also

- Picker demos: `https://material-ui.com/demos/pickers/`
- `TextField` API documentation: `https://material-ui.com/api/text-field/`

Setting initial date and time values

Date and time pickers can have default date and time values, respectively. For example, a common scenario is to have these inputs default to the current date and time.

How to do it...

Let's say that you have a date picker and a time picker on a screen in your app. You want the `date` field to default to the current date and the `time` field to default to the current time. To do this, it's best to rely on the `Date` instances to set the initial `Date/Time` value. However, a little work is involved, since you can't natively pass the `Date` instances to the `TextField` components. Here's an example that shows how this can work:

```
import React, { Fragment, useState } from 'react';

import { makeStyles } from '@material-ui/styles';
import TextField from '@material-ui/core/TextField';

const useStyles = makeStyles(theme => ({
  textField: { margin: theme.spacing.unit }
}));

function formatDate(date) {
  const year = date.getFullYear();
  const month = date.getMonth() + 1;
  const day = date.getDate();

  return [
    year,
    month < 10 ? `0${month}` : month,
    day < 10 ? `0${day}` : day
  ].join('-');
}

function formatTime(date) {
  const hours = date.getHours();
  const minutes = date.getMinutes();

  return [
    hours < 10 ? `0${hours}` : hours,
    minutes < 10 ? `0${minutes}` : minutes
  ].join(':');
}

const DatePicker = ({ date, ...props }) => (
  <TextField
    value={date instanceof Date ? formatDate(date) : date}
    type="date"
    InputLabelProps={{
      shrink: true
    }}
    {...props}
```

```
    />
);

const TimePicker = ({ time, ...props }) => (
  <TextField
    value={time instanceof Date ? formatTime(time) : time}
    type="time"
    InputLabelProps={{
      shrink: true
    }}
    inputProps={{
      step: 300
    }}
    {...props}
  />
);

export default function SettingInitialDateAndTimeValues() {
  const classes = useStyles();
  const [datetime, setDatetime] = useState(new Date());

  const onChangeDate = e => {
    if (!e.target.value) {
      return;
    }

    const [year, month, day] = e.target.value
      .split('-')
      .map(n => Number(n));

    const newDatetime = new Date(datetime);
    newDatetime.setYear(year);
    newDatetime.setMonth(month - 1);
    newDatetime.setDate(day);

    setDatetime(newDatetime);
  };

  const onChangeTime = e => {
    const [hours, minutes] = e.target.value
      .split(':')
      .map(n => Number(n));

    const newDatetime = new Date(datetime);
    newDatetime.setHours(hours);
    newDatetime.setMinutes(minutes);

    setDatetime(newDatetime);
```

```
    };

    return (
      <Fragment>
        <DatePicker
          date={datetime}
          onChange={onChangeDate}
          label="My Date"
          className={classes.textField}
        />
        <TimePicker
          time={datetime}
          onChange={onChangeTime}
          label="My Time"
          className={classes.textField}
        />
      </Fragment>
    );
}
```

Here's what you'll see when the screen first loads:

My Date	My Time
2019-02-01	02:22 PM

The date and time that you see will depend on when you load the screen. You can then change the date and time values.

How it works...

What's nice about this approach is that you only have one piece of state to work with, datetime, which is a Date instance. Let's step through the code to see how this is made possible, starting with the initial state of the UsingDatePickers component:

```
const [datetime, setDatetime] = useState(new Date());
```

The current date and time is assigned to the datetime state. Next, let's look at the two formatting functions that enable the Date instances to work with the TextField components:

```
function formatDate(date) {
  const year = date.getFullYear();
```

```
  const month = date.getMonth() + 1;
  const day = date.getDate();

  return [
    year,
    month < 10 ? `0${month}` : month,
    day < 10 ? `0${day}` : day
  ].join('-');
}

function formatTime(date) {
  const hours = date.getHours();
  const minutes = date.getMinutes();

  return [
    hours < 10 ? `0${hours}` : hours,
    minutes < 10 ? `0${minutes}` : minutes
  ].join(':');
}
```

Both of these functions, `formatDate()` and `formatTime()`, take a `Date` instance as an argument, and `return` a string-formatted value that works with the `TextField` component. Next, let's look at the `onChangeDate()` handler:

```
const onChangeDate = e => {
  if (!e.target.value) {
    return;
  }

  const [year, month, day] = e.target.value
    .split('-')
    .map(n => Number(n));

  const newDatetime = new Date(datetime);
  newDatetime.setYear(year);
  newDatetime.setMonth(month - 1);
  newDatetime.setDate(day);

  setDatetime(newDatetime);
};
```

The first check that happens in `onChangeDate()` is for the `value` property. The reason this check needs to happen is so that the date picker can actually allow the user to select an invalid date, such as Feb 31. By not changing the `state` when this invalid date is selected, you're actually preventing invalid dates from being selected.

Next, the `year`, `month`, and `day` values are split and mapped to numbers. Then, the new `newDatetime` value is initialized by creating a new `Date` instance using `datetime` as the value. This is done to preserve the time selection. Finally, `setYear()`, `setMonth()`, and `setDate()` are used to update the `Date` instance without changing the time.

Lastly, let's go over the `onChangeTime()` handler:

```
const onChangeTime = e => {
  const [hours, minutes] = e.target.value
    .split(':')
    .map(n => Number(n));

  const newDatetime = new Date(datetime);
  newDatetime.setHours(hours);
  newDatetime.setMinutes(minutes);

  setDatetime(newDatetime);
};
```

The `onChangeTime()` handler follows the same general pattern as `onChangeDate()`. It's simpler because there are fewer values and no need to check for invalid times – every day has 24 hours.

See also

- Picker demos: `https://material-ui.com/demos/pickers/`
- `TextField` API documentation: `https://material-ui.com/api/text-field/`

Combining date and time components

If your application needs to collect the date and time from the user, you don't necessarily need two `TextField` components. Instead, you can combine them both into a single field.

How to do it...

You can use a single `TextInput` component to collect date and time input from the user by setting the `type` property to `datetime-local`:

```
import React, { Fragment, useState } from 'react';

import { makeStyles } from '@material-ui/styles';
import TextField from '@material-ui/core/TextField';

const useStyles = makeStyles(theme => ({
  textField: { margin: theme.spacing(1) }
}));

const formatDate = date =>
  date
    .toISOString()
    .split(':')
    .slice(0, 2)
    .join(':');

const DateTimePicker = ({ date, ...props }) => (
  <TextField
    value={
      date instanceof Date
        ? date.toISOString().replace('Z', '')
        : date
    }
    type="datetime-local"
    InputLabelProps={{
      shrink: true
    }}
    {...props}
  />
);

export default function CombiningDateAndTimeComponents() {
  const classes = useStyles();
  const [datetime, setDatetime] = useState(new Date());

  const onChangeDate = e => {
    setDatetime(new Date(`${e.target.value}Z`));
  };

  return (
    <DateTimePicker
      date={formatDate(datetime)}
```

```
        onChange={onChangeDate}
        label="My Date/Time"
        className={classes.textField}
      />
    );
  }
```

Here's what you'll see when the screen first loads:

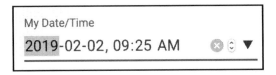

This is how the field looks when the field has focus and the controls for changing the **Date/Time** are shown:

My Date/Time
2019-02-02, 09:25 AM

How it works...

When you use the `datetime-local` type of input, it simplifies working with the `Date` instances. Let's take a look at the `onChangeDate()` handler:

```
const onChangeDate = e => {
  setDatetime(new Date(`${e.target.value}Z`));
};
```

You can pass `e.target.value` as the argument to a new `Date` instance, which then becomes the new `datetime` state value. Finally, let's take a look at the `formatDate()` function that's used to pass the correct value to the `value` property of `TextField`:

```
const formatDate = date =>
  date
    .toISOString()
    .split(':')
    .slice(0, 2)
    .join(':');
```

The reason to use this function is to remove the seconds and milliseconds from the `value` property. Otherwise, these will show up as values in the input field that the user can then select. It's very uncommon to have the user select seconds or milliseconds when choosing a time.

See also

- **Picker demos:** `https://material-ui.com/demos/pickers/`
- `TextField` **API documentation:** `https://material-ui.com/api/text-field/`

Integrating other date and time packages

You aren't stuck with only using `TextField` components for `Date/Time` selection in your Material-UI application. There are packages available that make the `Date/Time` selection experience feel more like traditional Material Design components.

How to do it...

The `material-ui-pickers` package has a `DatePicker` component and a `TimePicker` component. Here's some code that shows you how to use both components:

```
import React, { useState } from 'react';
import 'date-fns';
import DateFnsUtils from '@date-io/date-fns';

import { makeStyles } from '@material-ui/styles';
import Grid from '@material-ui/core/Grid';

import {
  MuiPickersUtilsProvider,
  TimePicker,
  DatePicker
} from 'material-ui-pickers';

const useStyles = makeStyles(theme => ({
  grid: {
    width: '65%'
  }
}));
```

```
export default function IntegratingWithOtherDateAndTimePackages() {
  const classes = useStyles();
  const [datetime, setDatetime] = useState(new Date());

  const onChange = datetime => {
    setDatetime(datetime);
  };

  return (
    <MuiPickersUtilsProvider utils={DateFnsUtils}>
      <Grid container className={classes.grid} justify="space-around">
        <DatePicker
          margin="normal"
          label="Date picker"
          value={datetime}
          onChange={onChange}
        />
        <TimePicker
          margin="normal"
          label="Time picker"
          value={datetime}
          onChange={onChange}
        />
      </Grid>
    </MuiPickersUtilsProvider>
  );
}
```

Here's what you'll see when the screen first loads:

Date picker	Time picker
February 1st	11:35 PM

Here's what you'll see when you click on the **Date picker** field:

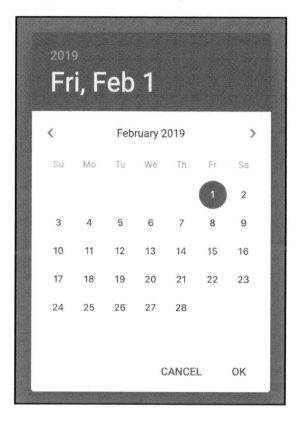

You can use this dialog to make your date selection, then click on **OK** to change it. Here's what you'll see when you click on the **Time picker** field:

How it works...

The `DatePicker` and `TimePicker` components from the `material-ui-pickers` package display dialogs that render other Material-UI components, which makes selecting a date/time easier. Rather than having to interact with text inputs directly, you can show your users dialogs such as these that are themed to look like the rest of your application and provide a visual interaction for selecting dates/times.

See also

- Picker demos: `https://material-ui.com/demos/pickers/`
- Material-UI pickers: `https://github.com/chingyawhao/material-ui-next-pickers`

Dialogs - Modal Screens for User Interactions

15

In this chapter, we will cover the following topics:

- Collecting form input
- Confirming actions
- Displaying alerts
- API integration
- Creating fullscreen dialogs
- Scrolling dialog content

Introduction

At some point during interactions with your application, the user is going to have to supply some information to the application, make a yes/no decision, or acknowledge important information. Material-UI has a dialog component that is ideally suited for these types of scenarios—when you need a modal display that doesn't disrupt the current screen content.

Collecting form input

Dialogs can come in handy when you need to collect input from the user, but you don't want to lose the current screen. For example, the user is looking at a screen that shows a list of items and wants to create a new item. A dialog could display the necessary form fields and, once the new item is created, the dialog closes and the user is right back at their item list.

How to do it...

Let's say that your application allows for the creation of new users. For example, from the screen that shows a list of users, the user clicks on a button that shows a dialog containing the fields for creating a new user. Here's an example of how to do this:

```
import React, { Fragment, useState } from 'react';

import Button from '@material-ui/core/Button';
import TextField from '@material-ui/core/TextField';
import Dialog from '@material-ui/core/Dialog';
import DialogActions from '@material-ui/core/DialogActions';
import DialogContent from '@material-ui/core/DialogContent';
import DialogContentText from '@material-ui/core/DialogContentText';
import DialogTitle from '@material-ui/core/DialogTitle';
import Snackbar from '@material-ui/core/Snackbar';

export default function CollectingFormInput() {
  const [dialogOpen, setDialogOpen] = useState(false);
  const [snackbarOpen, setSnackbarOpen] = useState(false);
  const [snackbarMessage, setSnackbarMessage] = useState('');
  const [first, setFirst] = useState('');
  const [last, setLast] = useState('');
  const [email, setEmail] = useState('');

  const onDialogOpen = () => {
    setDialogOpen(true);
  };

  const onDialogClose = () => {
    setDialogOpen(false);
    setFirst('');
    setLast('');
    setEmail('');
  };

  const onSnackbarClose = (e, reason) => {
    if (reason === 'clickaway') {
      return;
    }

    setSnackbarOpen(false);
    setSnackbarMessage('');
  };

  const onCreate = () => {
    setSnackbarOpen(true);
```

```
      setSnackbarMessage(`${first} ${last} created`);
      onDialogClose();
    };

    return (
      <Fragment>
        <Button color="primary" onClick={onDialogOpen}>
          New User
        </Button>
        <Dialog open={dialogOpen} onClose={onDialogClose}>
          <DialogTitle>New User</DialogTitle>
          <DialogContent>
            <TextField
              autoFocus
              margin="normal"
              label="First Name"
              InputProps={{ name: 'first' }}
              onChange={e => setFirst(e.target.value)}
              value={first}
              fullWidth
            />
            <TextField
              margin="normal"
              label="Last Name"
              InputProps={{ name: 'last' }}
              onChange={e => setLast(e.target.value)}
              value={last}
              fullWidth
            />
            <TextField
              margin="normal"
              label="Email Address"
              type="email"
              InputProps={{ name: 'email' }}
              onChange={e => setEmail(e.target.value)}
              value={email}
              fullWidth
            />
          </DialogContent>
          <DialogActions>
            <Button onClick={onDialogClose} color="primary">
              Cancel
            </Button>
            <Button
              variant="contained"
              onClick={onCreate}
              color="primary"
            >
```

```
                Create
              </Button>
            </DialogActions>
          </Dialog>
          <Snackbar
            open={snackbarOpen}
            message={snackbarMessage}
            onClose={onSnackbarClose}
            autoHideDuration={4000}
          />
        </Fragment>
    );
  }
```

Here's the button you'll see when the screen first loads:

Here's the dialog that you'll see when you click on the **NEW USER** button:

You can then fill out the three fields for creating a new user and click the **CREATE** button. The dialog will close, and you'll see the following `Snackbar` component displayed:

How it works...

The visibility of the dialog and the snackbar are controlled by Boolean state
values, dialogOpen and snackbarOpen, respectively. The values of the fields within the
dialog component are also stored in the state of the CollectingFormInput component.
Let's take a closer look at the dialog markup:

```
<Dialog open={dialogOpen} onClose={onDialogClose}>
  <DialogTitle>New User</DialogTitle>
  <DialogContent>
    <TextField
      autoFocus
      margin="normal"
      label="First Name"
      InputProps={{ name: 'first' }}
      onChange={e => setFirst(e.target.value)}
      value={first}
      fullWidth
    />
    <TextField
      margin="normal"
      label="Last Name"
      InputProps={{ name: 'last' }}
      onChange={e => setLast(e.target.value)}
      value={last}
      fullWidth
    />
    <TextField
      margin="normal"
      label="Email Address"
      type="email"
      InputProps={{ name: 'email' }}
      onChange={e => setEmail(e.target.value)}
      value={email}
      fullWidth
    />
  </DialogContent>
  <DialogActions>
    <Button onClick={onDialogClose} color="primary">
      Cancel
    </Button>
    <Button
      variant="contained"
      onClick={onCreate}
      color="primary"
    >
      Create
```

```
      </Button>
    </DialogActions>
  </Dialog>
```

The `Dialog` component is the parent for several other components that make up the various pieces of `dialog`. The `DialogTitle` component renders the dialog title, while the `DialogActions` component is used to render action buttons at the bottom of the dialog. The `DialogContent` component is used to render the main content of the dialog—the three text fields for creating a new user.

There are two properties for each of these `TextField` components that are relevant for rendering inside of a dialog. First, the `fullWidth` property extends the field horizontally so that it's the same width as the dialog. This generally works well with forms that only have a few fields. Second, the `margin` property is set to `normal`, which provides the appropriate vertical spacing between fields in the dialog.

Next, let's walk through the event handlers of this component, starting with `onDialogOpen()`:

```
const onDialogOpen = () => {
  setDialogOpen(true);
};
```

This will show the dialog by changing the `dialogOpen` state to `true`. Next, let's look at `onDialogClose()`:

```
const onDialogClose = () => {
  setDialogOpen(false);
  setFirst('');
  setLast('');
  setEmail('');
};
```

This will close the dialog by setting the `dialogOpen` state to `false`. It also resets the form field values to empty strings so that they're empty the next time the dialog is displayed. Up next, we have `onSnackbarClose()`:

```
const onSnackbarClose = (e, reason) => {
  if (reason === 'clickaway') {
    return;
  }

  setSnackbarOpen(false);
  setSnackbarMessage('');
};
```

If the `reason` argument is `clickaway`, then there's nothing to do. Otherwise, the `snackbarOpen` state changes to `false`, which will hide the snackbar. The `snackbarMessage` state is set to an empty string so that the message doesn't display again in case the snackbar is opened without setting a new message first. Finally, we have the `onCreate()` handler:

```
const onCreate = () => {
  setSnackbarOpen(true);
  setSnackbarMessage(`${first} ${last} created`);
  onDialogClose();
};
```

This will show the snackbar by setting `snackbarOpen` to `true`. It also sets the `snackbarMessage` value that includes accessing the `first` and `last` state values. Then, `onDialogClose()` is called to hide the dialog and reset the form fields. The snackbar is closed after four seconds because the `autoHideDuration` value was set to `4000`.

See also

- `Dialog` demos: https://material-ui.com/demos/dialogs/
- `Dialog` API documentation: https://material-ui.com/api/dialog/
- `DialogActions` API documentation: https://material-ui.com/api/dialog-actions/
- `DialogContent` API documentation: https://material-ui.com/api/dialog-content/
- `DialogContentText` API documentation: https://material-ui.com/api/dialog-content-text/
- `Snackbar` API documentation: https://material-ui.com/api/snackbar/
- `TextField` API documentation: https://material-ui.com/api/text-field/
- `Button` API documentation: https://material-ui.com/api/button/

Confirming actions

Confirmation dialogs act as a safety net for your users. They're useful when the user is about to perform something that could potentially be dangerous, but not for every conceivable action in the app. An action can be considered dangerous if, once performed, it cannot be reverted. An example of a dangerous action would be deleting an account or processing a payment. In these cases, you should always use a confirmation dialog.

How to do it...

Confirmation dialogs should be straightforward so that the user can easily read what is about to happen and can decide whether to cancel the action or to continue. Here's some code that shows a confirmation dialog before executing an action:

```
import React, { Fragment, useState } from 'react';

import Button from '@material-ui/core/Button';
import DialogTitle from '@material-ui/core/DialogTitle';
import DialogContent from '@material-ui/core/DialogContent';
import DialogContentText from '@material-ui/core/DialogContentText';
import DialogActions from '@material-ui/core/DialogActions';
import Dialog from '@material-ui/core/Dialog';

export default function ConfirmingActions() {
  const [open, setOpen] = useState(false);

  const onShowConfirm = () => {
    setOpen(true);
  };

  const onConfirm = () => {
    setOpen(false);
  };

  return (
    <Fragment>
      <Button color="primary" onClick={onShowConfirm}>
        Confirm Action
      </Button>
      <Dialog
        disableBackdropClick
        disableEscapeKeyDown
        maxWidth="xs"
        open={open}
      >
        <DialogTitle>Confirm Delete Asset</DialogTitle>
        <DialogContent>
          <DialogContentText>
            Are you sure you want to delete the asset? This action
            cannot be undone.
          </DialogContentText>
        </DialogContent>
        <DialogActions>
          <Button onClick={onDialogClose} color="primary">
            Cancel
```

```
        </Button>
        <Button
          variant="contained"
          onClick={onConfirm}
          color="primary"
        >
          Confirm
        </Button>
      </DialogActions>
    </Dialog>
  </Fragment>
);
}
```

Here's what the confirmation dialog looks like when it's displayed by clicking on the
CONFIRM button:

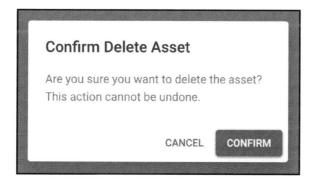

You can either click on the **CANCEL** dialog action to close the dialog without doing
anything, or you can click on the **CONFIRM** dialog action that will actually execute the
action before closing the dialog.

How it works...

The `DialogContentText` component is used to render the confirmation message in the
dialog. It's really just a thin wrapper around a `Typography` component. The two interesting
properties passed to the dialog component are `disableBackdropClick`
and `disableEscapeKeyDown`, which prevent the confirmation dialog from being closed by
clicking somewhere on the screen outside of the dialog or by hitting the *Esc* key,
respectively.

The idea with these two properties is to get the user to explicitly acknowledge that they're performing an action that requires their close attention, or that they're opting out of performing it.

See also

- `Dialog` demos: `https://material-ui.com/demos/dialogs/`
- `Dialog` API documentation: `https://material-ui.com/api/dialog/`
- `DialogActions` API documentation: `https://material-ui.com/api/dialog-actions/`
- `DialogContent` API documentation: `https://material-ui.com/api/dialog-content/`
- `DialogContentText` API documentation: `https://material-ui.com/api/dialog-content-text/`
- `Button` API documentation: `https://material-ui.com/api/button/`

Displaying alerts

Alert dialogs are similar to confirmation dialogs. You can think of alerts as really important snackbars that cannot be ignored. Like confirmations, alerts cause interruption and have to be explicitly acknowledged to get rid of them. Furthermore, alert dialogs might not be displayed as the direct result of an action taken by the user. Alerts can be displayed as the result of changes to the environment the user is interacting with.

How to do it...

Let's say that your application needs to be able to alert users when their allotted disk space is running low. Here's an example that shows what the alert might look like:

```
import React, { Fragment, useState } from 'react';

import Button from '@material-ui/core/Button';
import DialogContent from '@material-ui/core/DialogContent';
import DialogContentText from '@material-ui/core/DialogContentText';
import DialogActions from '@material-ui/core/DialogActions';
import Dialog from '@material-ui/core/Dialog';

export default function ConfirmingActions() {
```

```
const [open, setOpen] = useState(false);

return (
  <Fragment>
    <Button color="primary" onClick={() => setOpen(true)}>
      Show Alert
    </Button>
    <Dialog open={open}>
      <DialogContent>
        <DialogContentText>
          Disk space critically low. You won't be able to perform
          any actions until you free up some space by deleting
          assets.
        </DialogContentText>
      </DialogContent>
      <DialogActions>
        <Button
          variant="contained"
          onClick={() => setOpen(false)}
          color="primary"
        >
          Got It
        </Button>
      </DialogActions>
    </Dialog>
  </Fragment>
);
}
```

And here's what the alert dialog looks like when it's displayed by clicking on the show alert button:

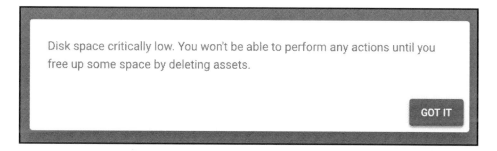

How it works...

Alerts aren't much different from regular dialogs in that you use them to collect input from the user. The principle with alerts is to keep them short and to the point. For example, this alert dialog doesn't have a title. It's able to get the point across without a title – if the user doesn't start deleting stuff, they're not going to be able to do anything.

There's more...

You can make your alerts a little more eye-catching by adding an icon to the alert message and the button that dismisses the alert. Here's the modified example:

```
import React, { Fragment, useState } from 'react';

import { makeStyles } from '@material-ui/styles';
import Button from '@material-ui/core/Button';
import DialogContent from '@material-ui/core/DialogContent';
import DialogContentText from '@material-ui/core/DialogContentText';
import DialogActions from '@material-ui/core/DialogActions';
import Dialog from '@material-ui/core/Dialog';
import Grid from '@material-ui/core/Grid';

import WarningIcon from '@material-ui/icons/Warning';
import CheckIcon from '@material-ui/icons/Check';

const useStyles = makeStyles(theme => ({
  rightIcon: {
    marginLeft: theme.spacing(1)
  }
}));

export default function ConfirmingActions() {
  const classes = useStyles();
  const [open, setOpen] = useState(false);

  return (
    <Fragment>
      <Button color="primary" onClick={() => setOpen(true)}>
        Show Alert
      </Button>
      <Dialog open={open}>
        <DialogContent>
          <Grid container>
            <Grid item xs={2}>
              <WarningIcon fontSize="large" color="secondary" />
```

```
        </Grid>
        <Grid item xs={10}>
          <DialogContentText>
            Disk space critically low. You won't be able to
            perform any actions until you free up some space by
            deleting assets.
          </DialogContentText>
        </Grid>
      </Grid>
    </DialogContent>
    <DialogActions>
      <Button
        variant="contained"
        onClick={() => setOpen(false)}
        color="primary"
      >
        Got It
        <CheckIcon className={classes.rightIcon} />
      </Button>
    </DialogActions>
  </Dialog>
</Fragment>
  );
}
```

Here's what the new alert looks like:

See also

- `Dialog` **demos:** `https://material-ui.com/demos/dialogs/`
- `Dialog` **API documentation:** `https://material-ui.com/api/dialog/`
- `DialogActions` **API documentation:** `https://material-ui.com/api/dialog-actions/`

- `DialogContent` **API documentation:** https://material-ui.com/api/dialog-content/
- `DialogContentText` **API documentation:** https://material-ui.com/api/dialog-content-text/
- `Button` **API documentation:** https://material-ui.com/api/button/

API integration

Dialogs often need data supplied to it from an API endpoint. The challenge is displaying the dialog in a loading state while the user waits for the API data to load behind the scenes.

How to do it...

Let's say that your application needs to display a dialog with a `Select` component for selecting an item. The options for the select are populated from an API endpoint, so you need to handle the latency between the user opening the dialog and the API data arriving. Here's an example that shows one way to do this:

```
import React, { Fragment, useState } from 'react';

import { makeStyles } from '@material-ui/styles';
import Button from '@material-ui/core/Button';
import DialogTitle from '@material-ui/core/DialogTitle';
import DialogContent from '@material-ui/core/DialogContent';
import DialogContentText from '@material-ui/core/DialogContentText';
import DialogActions from '@material-ui/core/DialogActions';
import Dialog from '@material-ui/core/Dialog';
import LinearProgress from '@material-ui/core/LinearProgress';
import MenuItem from '@material-ui/core/MenuItem';
import Select from '@material-ui/core/Select';

const useStyles = makeStyles(theme => ({
  dialog: { minHeight: 200 },
  select: { width: '100%' }
}));

const fetchItems = () =>
  new Promise(resolve => {
    setTimeout(() => {
      resolve([
        { id: 1, name: 'Item 1' },
        { id: 2, name: 'Item 2' },
```

```
        { id: 3, name: 'Item 3' }
      ]);
    }, 3000);
  });

const MaybeLinearProgress = ({ loading, ...props }) =>
  loading ? <LinearProgress {...props} /> : null;

const MaybeSelect = ({ loading, ...props }) =>
  loading ? null : <Select {...props} />;

export default function APIIntegration() {
  const classes = useStyles();
  const [open, setOpen] = useState(false);
  const [loading, setLoading] = useState(false);
  const [items, setItems] = useState([]);
  const [selected, setSelected] = useState('');

  const onShowItems = () => {
    setOpen(true);
    setLoading(true);

    fetchItems().then(items => {
      setLoading(false);
      setItems(items);
    });
  };

  const onClose = () => {
    setOpen(false);
  };

  const onSelect = e => {
    setSelected(e.target.value);
  };

  return (
    <Fragment>
      <Button color="primary" onClick={onShowItems}>
        Select Item
      </Button>
      <Dialog
        open={open}
        classes={{ paper: classes.dialog }}
        maxWidth="xs"
        fullWidth
      >
        <DialogTitle>Select Item</DialogTitle>
```

```
<DialogContent>
  <MaybeLinearProgress loading={loading} />
  <MaybeSelect
    value={selected}
    onChange={onSelect}
    className={classes.select}
    loading={loading}
  >
    <MenuItem value="">
      <em>None</em>
    </MenuItem>
    {items.map(item => (
      <MenuItem key={item.id} index={item.id} value={item.id}>
        {item.name}
      </MenuItem>
    ))}
  </MaybeSelect>
</DialogContent>
<DialogActions>
  <Button
    disabled={loading}
    onClick={onClose}
    color="primary"
  >
    Cancel
  </Button>
  <Button
    disabled={loading}
    variant="contained"
    onClick={onClose}
    color="primary"
  >
    Select
  </Button>
</DialogActions>
      </Dialog>
    </Fragment>
  );
}
```

Here's what the dialog looks like when it's first opened:

The dialog displays a `LinearProgress` component and disables the dialog action buttons while the API data is loading. Once the response arrives, here's what the dialog looks like:

The linear progress bar is gone, the dialog action buttons are enabled, and there's a **Select Item** field visible for the user to select an item. Here's the **Select Item** showing the items that are loading from the API:

How it works...

Let's walk through the major parts of this code, starting with the mock API function:

```
const fetchItems = () =>
  new Promise(resolve => {
    setTimeout(() => {
      resolve([
        { id: 1, name: 'Item 1' },
        { id: 2, name: 'Item 2' },
        { id: 3, name: 'Item 3' }
      ]);
    }, 3000);
  });
```

The `fetchItems()` function simulates an API function by returning a promise that resolves an array of data after three seconds. This allows you to see what users will see while waiting for an actual API endpoint to respond. Next, let's look at the two utility components that help with rendering or hiding the select and the progress indicators:

```
const MaybeLinearProgress = ({ loading, ...props }) =>
  loading ? <LinearProgress {...props} /> : null;

const MaybeSelect = ({ loading, ...props }) =>
  loading ? null : <Select {...props} />;
```

The idea is that you don't want to render the `LinearProgress` component while loading is `false`. Conversely, you don't want to render the `Select` component while loading is `true`. Let's take a look at `onShowItems()` next:

```
const onShowItems = () => {
  setOpen(true);
  setLoading(true);

  fetchItems().then(items => {
    setLoading(false);
    setItems(items);
  });
};
```

First, the dialog is opened by setting open to `true` and the progress indicator is displayed by setting loading to `true`. Then, the API `fetchItems()` function is called, and when the `Promise` it returns is resolved, `loading` is set to `false` and the `items` array is updated. This hides the progress indicator and shows the select that is now populated with items.

See also

- Dialog **demos:** https://material-ui.com/demos/dialogs/
- Dialog **API documentation:** https://material-ui.com/api/dialog/
- DialogActions **API documentation:** https://material-ui.com/api/dialog-actions/
- DialogContent **API documentation:** https://material-ui.com/api/dialog-content/
- DialogContentText **API documentation:** https://material-ui.com/api/dialog-content-text/
- Button **API documentation:** https://material-ui.com/api/button/
- LinearProgress **API documentation:** https://material-ui.com/api/linear-progress/
- MenuItem **API documentation:** https://material-ui.com/api/menu-item/
- Select **API documentation:** https://material-ui.com/api/select/

Creating fullscreen dialogs

With fullscreen dialogs, you have more space to render information. Most of the time, you won't need full screen dialogs. In less common cases, your dialog needs as much space as possible to render information.

How to do it...

Let's say that, from some screen in your application, there's a button that exports data for the user. When clicked, you want to give the user a preview of the data that's about to be exported before they confirm. Here's what the code looks like:

```
import React, { Fragment, useState } from 'react';

import { makeStyles } from '@material-ui/styles';
import Button from '@material-ui/core/Button';
import Dialog from '@material-ui/core/Dialog';
import AppBar from '@material-ui/core/AppBar';
import Toolbar from '@material-ui/core/Toolbar';
import IconButton from '@material-ui/core/IconButton';
import Typography from '@material-ui/core/Typography';
import Slide from '@material-ui/core/Slide';
import Table from '@material-ui/core/Table';
```

```
import TableBody from '@material-ui/core/TableBody';
import TableCell from '@material-ui/core/TableCell';
import TableHead from '@material-ui/core/TableHead';
import TableRow from '@material-ui/core/TableRow';

import CloseIcon from '@material-ui/icons/Close';

const useStyles = makeStyles(theme => ({
  appBar: {
    position: 'relative'
  },
  flex: {
    flex: 1
  }
}));

const Transition = props => <Slide direction="up" {...props} />;

const id = (function*() {
  let id = 0;
  while (true) {
    id += 1;
    yield id;
  }
})();

const rowData = (name, calories, fat, carbs, protein) => ({
  id: id.next().value,
  name,
  calories,
  fat,
  carbs,
  protein
});

const rows = [
  rowData('Frozen yoghurt', 159, 6.0, 24, 4.0),
  rowData('Ice cream sandwich', 237, 9.0, 37, 4.3),
  rowData('Eclair', 262, 16.0, 24, 6.0),
  rowData('Cupcake', 305, 3.7, 67, 4.3),
  rowData('Gingerbread', 356, 16.0, 49, 3.9)
];

export default function FullScreenDialogs() {
  const classes = useStyles();
  const [open, setOpen] = useState(false);

  const onOpen = () => {
```

```
    setOpen(true);
};

const onClose = () => {
  setOpen(false);
};

return (
  <Fragment>
    <Button variant="outlined" color="primary" onClick={onOpen}>
      Export Data
    </Button>
    <Dialog
      fullScreen
      open={open}
      onClose={onClose}
      TransitionComponent={Transition}
    >
      <AppBar className={classes.appBar}>
        <Toolbar>
          <IconButton
            color="inherit"
            onClick={onClose}
            aria-label="Close"
          >
            <CloseIcon />
          </IconButton>
          <Typography
            variant="h6"
            color="inherit"
            className={classes.flex}
          >
            Export Data
          </Typography>
          <Button color="inherit" onClick={onClose}>
            Export
          </Button>
        </Toolbar>
      </AppBar>
      <Table className={classes.table}>
        <TableHead>
          <TableRow>
            <TableCell>Dessert (100g serving)</TableCell>
            <TableCell align="right">Calories</TableCell>
            <TableCell align="right">Fat (g)</TableCell>
            <TableCell align="right">Carbs (g)</TableCell>
            <TableCell align="right">Protein (g)</TableCell>
          </TableRow>
```

```
      </TableHead>
      <TableBody>
        {rows.map(row => (
          <TableRow key={row.id}>
            <TableCell component="th" scope="row">
              {row.name}
            </TableCell>
            <TableCell align="right">{row.calories}</TableCell>
            <TableCell align="right">{row.fat}</TableCell>
            <TableCell align="right">{row.carbs}</TableCell>
            <TableCell align="right">{row.protein}</TableCell>
          </TableRow>
        ))}
      </TableBody>
    </Table>
  </Dialog>
</Fragment>
);
}
```

Here is what the dialog looks like when it's opened:

✕ Export Data				EXPORT
Dessert (100g serving)	Calories	Fat (g)	Carbs (g)	Protein (g)
Frozen yoghurt	159	6	24	4
Ice cream sandwich	237	9	37	4.3
Eclair	262	16	24	6
Cupcake	305	3.7	67	4.3
Gingerbread	356	16	49	3.9

You can click on the **X** button beside the dialog title to close the dialog, or you can click on the **EXPORT** button to the right.

How it works...

Let's look at the properties that are passed to the `Dialog` component:

```
<Dialog
  fullScreen
  open={open}
  onClose={onClose}
  TransitionComponent={Transition}
>
```

The `fullScreen` Boolean property is how the dialog is rendered in fullscreen mode. The `TransitionComponent` property changes the way that dialog is transitioned onto the screen.

Because the dialog is displayed in fullscreen mode, you might want to change the way that the title and actions are displayed to the user, as is shown in this example. Instead of using the `DialogTitle` and `DialogAction` components, you can use the `AppBar` and `Toolbar` components:

```
<AppBar className={classes.appBar}>
  <Toolbar>
    <IconButton
      color="inherit"
      onClick={onClose}
      aria-label="Close"
    >
      <CloseIcon />
    </IconButton>
    <Typography
      variant="h6"
      color="inherit"
      className={classes.flex}
    >
      Export Data
    </Typography>
    <Button color="inherit" onClick={onClose}>
      Export
    </Button>
  </Toolbar>
</AppBar>
```

This makes the title, close action, and main action more visible to the user.

See also

- Dialog **demos:** https://material-ui.com/demos/dialogs/
- Dialog **API documentation:** https://material-ui.com/api/dialog/
- AppBar **API documentation:** https://material-ui.com/api/app-bar/
- Toolbar **API documentation:** https://material-ui.com/api/toolbar/
- Table **API documentation:** https://material-ui.com/api/table/

Scrolling dialog content

It can be hard to find enough vertical space to fit all of your content into a dialog. When the dialog runs out of space, a vertical scrollbar is added.

How to do it...

Let's say that you have a long table of data that you need to display in a dialog for the user before exporting to another format. The user will need the ability to scroll through the table rows. Here's an example:

```
import React, { Fragment, useState } from 'react';

import Button from '@material-ui/core/Button';
import Dialog from '@material-ui/core/Dialog';
import DialogTitle from '@material-ui/core/DialogTitle';
import DialogContent from '@material-ui/core/DialogContent';
import DialogActions from '@material-ui/core/DialogActions';
import Table from '@material-ui/core/Table';
import TableBody from '@material-ui/core/TableBody';
import TableCell from '@material-ui/core/TableCell';
import TableHead from '@material-ui/core/TableHead';
import TableRow from '@material-ui/core/TableRow';

const id = (function*() {
  let id = 0;
  while (true) {
    id += 1;
    yield id;
  }
})();

const rowData = (name, calories, fat, carbs, protein) => ({
```

```
    id: id.next().value,
    name,
    calories,
    fat,
    carbs,
    protein
  });

const rows = new Array(50)
  .fill(null)
  .reduce(
    result =>
      result.concat([
        rowData('Frozen yoghurt', 159, 6.0, 24, 4.0),
        rowData('Ice cream sandwich', 237, 9.0, 37, 4.3),
        rowData('Eclair', 262, 16.0, 24, 6.0),
        rowData('Cupcake', 305, 3.7, 67, 4.3),
        rowData('Gingerbread', 356, 16.0, 49, 3.9)
      ]),
    []
  );

export default function FullScreenDialogs() {
  const [open, setOpen] = useState(false);

  const onOpen = () => {
    setOpen(true);
  };

  const onClose = () => {
    setOpen(false);
  };

  return (
    <Fragment>
      <Button variant="outlined" color="primary" onClick={onOpen}>
        Export Data
      </Button>
      <Dialog open={open} onClose={onClose}>
        <DialogTitle>Desserts</DialogTitle>
        <DialogContent>
          <Table>
            <TableHead>
              <TableRow>
                <TableCell>Dessert (100g serving)</TableCell>
                <TableCell align="right">Calories</TableCell>
                <TableCell align="right">Fat (g)</TableCell>
                <TableCell align="right">Carbs (g)</TableCell>
```

```
                        <TableCell align="right">Protein (g)</TableCell>
                      </TableRow>
                    </TableHead>
                    <TableBody>
                      {rows.map(row => (
                        <TableRow key={row.id}>
                          <TableCell component="th" scope="row">
                            {row.name}
                          </TableCell>
                          <TableCell align="right">{row.calories}</TableCell>
                          <TableCell align="right">{row.fat}</TableCell>
                          <TableCell align="right">{row.carbs}</TableCell>
                          <TableCell align="right">{row.protein}</TableCell>
                        </TableRow>
                      ))}
                    </TableBody>
                  </Table>
                </DialogContent>
                <DialogActions>
                  <Button onClick={onClose} color="primary">
                    Cancel
                  </Button>
                  <Button
                    variant="contained"
                    onClick={onClose}
                    color="primary"
                  >
                    Export
                  </Button>
                </DialogActions>
              </Dialog>
            </Fragment>
          );
        }
```

Here's what the dialog looks like when it's opened:

Desserts

Dessert (100g serving)	Calories	Fat (g)	Carbs (g)	Protein (g)
Frozen yoghurt	159	6	24	4
Ice cream sandwich	237	9	37	4.3
Eclair	262	16	24	6
Cupcake	305	3.7	67	4.3
Gingerbread	356	16	49	3.9
Frozen yoghurt	159	6	24	4
Ice cream sandwich	237	9	37	4.3
Eclair	262	16	24	6
Cupcake	305	3.7	67	4.3
Gingerbread	356	16	49	3.9
Frozen	159	6	24	4

CANCEL **EXPORT**

If you move your mouse pointer over the table rows and start scrolling, the table rows scroll up and down in between the dialog title and the dialog action buttons.

How it works...

By default, dialog content will scroll within the `Paper` component of the dialog (the `DialogContent` component), so there's no need to specify a property. However, you can pass the `body` value to the `scroll` property of the `Dialog` component. This will make the height of the dialog change to accommodate the content.

See also

- `Dialog` **demos:** https://material-ui.com/demos/dialogs/
- `Dialog` **API documentation:** https://material-ui.com/api/dialog/
- `Table` **API documentation:** https://material-ui.com/api/table/

16
Menus - Display Actions That Pop Out

In this chapter, we will cover the following topics:

- Composing menus with state
- Menu scrolling options
- Using menu transitions
- Customizing menu items

Introduction

Menus are used to organize a set of commands that can be executed by the user. Typically, a menu has some context, such as a details screen for some resource in the application. Material-UI comes with a Menu component that enables you to organize commands for a given screen.

Composing menus with state

The Menu components are used to perform some actions. Think of menus as a combination of lists and buttons. Menus are best suited for scenarios when you only want to show the menu items temporarily. The visibility of the menu and the menu items can be controlled via the component state.

How to do it...

Let's say that a component in your application has a menu button that, when clicked, displays a menu with several options in it. The options could change based on other pieces of state in the application, such as permissions, or the state of another resource. Here's the source to build this component:

```
import React, { Fragment, useState } from 'react';

import { makeStyles } from '@material-ui/styles';
import Button from '@material-ui/core/Button';
import Menu from '@material-ui/core/Menu';
import MenuItem from '@material-ui/core/MenuItem';
import MenuIcon from '@material-ui/icons/Menu';

const useStyles = makeStyles(theme => ({
  rightIcon: {
    marginLeft: theme.spacing(1)
  }
}));

export default function ComposingMenusWithState() {
  const onOpen = e => {
    setAnchorEl(e.currentTarget);
  };

  const onClose = () => {
    setAnchorEl(null);
  };

  const classes = useStyles();
  const [anchorEl, setAnchorEl] = useState(null);
  const [items, setItems] = useState([
    { name: 'First', onClick: onClose },
    { name: 'Second', onClick: onClose },
    { name: 'Third', onClick: onClose },
    { name: 'Fourth', onClick: onClose, disabled: true }
  ]);

  return (
    <Fragment>
      <Button onClick={onOpen}>
        Menu
        <MenuIcon className={classes.rightIcon} />
      </Button>
      <Menu
        anchorEl={anchorEl}
```

```
                open={Boolean(anchorEl)}
                onClose={onClose}
            >
                {items.map((item, index) => (
                    <MenuItem
                        key={index}
                        onClick={item.onClick}
                        disabled={item.disabled}
                    >
                        {item.name}
                    </MenuItem>
                ))}
            </Menu>
        </Fragment>
    );
}
```

Here's what you'll see when the screen first loads:

When you click on the **MENU** button, the menu is displayed as follows:

How it works...

Let's start by looking at the state of the `ComposingMenusWithState` component:

```
const [anchorEl, setAnchorEl] = useState(null);
const [items, setItems] = useState([
    { name: 'First', onClick: onClose },
    { name: 'Second', onClick: onClose },
    { name: 'Third', onClick: onClose },
```

```
    { name: 'Fourth', onClick: onClose, disabled: true }
  ]);
```

The `anchorEl` state references the element that the menu is anchored to when the menu is open. When it's null, the menu are closed. The `items` array contains the menu items. The `name` property is rendered as the menu item text. The `onClick` function is called when the menu item is selected. The `disabled` property disables the item when `true`. Next, let's look at the `onOpen()` and `onClose()` handlers:

```
  const onOpen = e => {
    setAnchorEl(e.currentTarget);
  };

  const onClose = () => {
    setAnchorEl(null);
  };
```

When the user clicks on the menu button, the `anchorEl` state is set to `e.currentTarget`—this is the button that was clicked and is how the menu knows where to render itself. When the menu is closed, this is set to `null` and results in the menu being hidden. Finally, let's look at the `Menu` markup:

```
  <Menu
    anchorEl={anchorEl}
    open={Boolean(anchorEl)}
    onClose={onClose}
  >
    {items.map((item, index) => (
      <MenuItem
        key={index}
        onClick={item.onClick}
        disabled={item.disabled}
      >
        {item.name}
      </MenuItem>
    ))}
  </Menu>
```

The `open` property expects a Boolean, which is why changing the `anchorEl` state results in `Boolean(anchorEL)` either opening or closing the menu as the user interacts with it. The `items` state is then mapped to the `MenuItem` components.

There's more...

If your application has several screens you could make your own `Menu` component that takes care of mapping items to the `MenuItem` components. Let's modify this example to build a menu abstraction and to further illustrate how menu items can change state as the application data changes over time. Here's the modified example:

```
import React, { Fragment, useState, useEffect } from 'react';

import { makeStyles } from '@material-ui/styles';
import Button from '@material-ui/core/Button';
import Menu from '@material-ui/core/Menu';
import MenuItem from '@material-ui/core/MenuItem';
import MenuIcon from '@material-ui/icons/Menu';

const useStyles = makeStyles(theme => ({
  rightIcon: {
    marginLeft: theme.spacing.unit
  }
}));

const MyMenu = ({ items, onClose, anchorEl }) => (
  <Menu
    anchorEl={anchorEl}
    open={Boolean(anchorEl)}
    onClose={onClose}
  >
    {items.map((item, index) => (
      <MenuItem
        key={index}
        onClick={item.onClick}
        disabled={item.disabled}
      >
        {item.name}
      </MenuItem>
    ))}
  </Menu>
);

export default function ComposingMenusWithState() {
  const classes = useStyles();
  const [anchorEl, setAnchorEl] = useState(null);
  const [items, setItems] = useState([
    { name: 'Enable Fourth' },
    { name: 'Second', onClick: onClose },
    { name: 'Third', onClick: onClose },
    { name: 'Fourth', onClick: onClose, disabled: true }
```

```
    ]);

  useEffect(() => {
    const toggleFourth = () => {
      let newItems = [...items];

      newItems[3] = { ...items[3], disabled: !items[3].disabled };
      newItems[0] = {
        ...items[0],
        name: newItems[3].disabled
          ? 'Enable Fourth'
          : 'Disable Fourth'
      };

      setItems(newItems);
    };

    const newItems = [...items];
    newItems[0] = { ...items[0], onClick: toggleFourth };
    setItems(newItems);
  });

  const onOpen = e => {
    setAnchorEl(e.currentTarget);
  };

  const onClose = () => {
    setAnchorEl(null);
  };

  return (
    <Fragment>
      <Button onClick={onOpen}>
        Menu
        <MenuIcon className={classes.rightIcon} />
      </Button>
      <MyMenu items={items} onClose={onClose} anchorEl={anchorEl} />
    </Fragment>
  );
}
```

The MyMenu component takes the onClose handler, the anchorEl state, and the items array as properties. To show how you can update the menu item state and have them render (even while the menu is open), there's a new toggleFourth() handler that's applied to the onClick property of the first menu item. It's applied inside of useEffect(), because this is the only way for toggleFourth() to get the new items value; when it changes, we have to redefine the function and then reassign it to onClick. This will toggle the text of the first menu item and the disabled state of the Fourth item. Here's what the menu looks when it's first opened:

Here's what the menu looks like after clicking on the first menu item:

The text of the first item has been toggled, and the fourth item is now enabled. You can keep clicking on the first item to keep toggling the states of these two items.

See also

- Menu demos: https://material-ui.com/demos/menus/
- Menu API documentation: https://material-ui.com/api/menu/
- MenuItem API documentation: https://material-ui.com/api/menu-item/

Menu scrolling options

Sometimes menus have lots of options. This can pose a problem with regard to the height of the menu. Instead of having really long menus displayed, you can place a maximum height on the menu and have it scroll vertically.

How to do it...

Let's say that you need to render a menu with more options than can reasonably be rendered at once on the screen. Also, one of the menu items can be in a selected state. Here's some code that shows how to deal with this situation:

```
import React, { Fragment, useState } from 'react';

import { makeStyles } from '@material-ui/styles';
import IconButton from '@material-ui/core/IconButton';
import Menu from '@material-ui/core/Menu';
import MenuItem from '@material-ui/core/MenuItem';
import MenuIcon from '@material-ui/icons/Menu';

const items = [
  'None',
  'Atria',
  'Callisto',
  'Dione',
  'Ganymede',
  'Hangouts Call',
  'Luna',
  'Oberon',
  'Phobos',
  'Pyxis',
  'Sedna',
  'Titania',
  'Triton',
  'Umbriel'
];

const ITEM_HEIGHT = 48;

const useStyles = makeStyles(theme => ({
  menuPaper: { maxHeight: ITEM_HEIGHT * 4.5, width: 200 }
}));

export default function MenuScrollingOptions() {
  const classes = useStyles();
```

```
  const [anchorEl, setAnchorEl] = useState(null);
  const [selected, setSelected] = useState('');

  const onOpen = e => {
    setAnchorEl(e.currentTarget);
  };

  const onClose = () => {
    setAnchorEl(null);
  };

  const onSelect = selected => () => {
    setSelected(selected);
    setAnchorEl(null);
  };

  return (
    <Fragment>
      <IconButton onClick={onOpen}>
        <MenuIcon />
      </IconButton>
      <Menu
        anchorEl={anchorEl}
        open={Boolean(anchorEl)}
        onClose={onClose}
        PaperProps={{
          classes: { elevation8: classes.menuPaper }
        }}
      >
        {items.map((item, index) => (
          <MenuItem
            key={index}
            selected={index === selected}
            onClick={onSelect(index)}
          >
            {item}
          </MenuItem>
        ))}
      </Menu>
    </Fragment>
  );
}
```

Initially, no item is selected. Here's what the menu looks like when it's opened for the first time:

You can scroll through the menu items. Here's what the bottom of the menu looks like:

You can make a selection that closes the menu. The selection is preserved, so that the next time you open the menu, you'll see the selected item:

When the menu has a selected item, the Menu component will scroll to the selected item automatically. You can test this by scrolling the selected item out of view before closing the menu then reopening it. You'll see the selected item in the middle of the menu.

How it works...

Let's start by looking at the menuPaper style used in this example:

```
const ITEM_HEIGHT = 48;

const useStyles = makeStyles(theme => ({
  menuPaper: { maxHeight: ITEM_HEIGHT * 4.5, width: 200 }
}));
```

The ITEM_HEIGHT value is an approximation of the height of each menu item. The multiplier (4.5) is an approximation of how many menu items should fit on the screen. Now, let's jump into the Menu component markup:

```
<Menu
  anchorEl={anchorEl}
  open={Boolean(anchorEl)}
  onClose={onClose}
  PaperProps={{
    classes: { elevation8: classes.menuPaper }
  }}
>
  {items.map((item, index) => (
    <MenuItem
      key={index}
      selected={index === selected}
      onClick={onSelect(index)}
    >
      {item}
    </MenuItem>
  ))}
</Menu>
```

The selected property of each MenuItem component is set to true if the selected state matches the index of the current item. The menuPaper class is applied via the PaperProps property, but there's an elevation8 property inside where the class is actually applied. This is because if you just assign the class via className, the Menu component will just override the maxHeight style. To get around this, you have to use a more specific CSS API. The Paper component has several elevation points—the higher the number, the more shadow that is applied (giving the element the appearance of being higher).

The default elevation of `Paper` is 2. But the `Menu` component uses a `Popover` component to render `Paper` that changes the elevation to 8. Long story short, the `elevation8` CSS API enabled you to apply styles from a class that override the defaults. This is how you get a scrollable menu.

See also

- `Menu` **demos:** https://material-ui.com/demos/menus/
- `Menu` **API documentation:** https://material-ui.com/api/menu/
- `MenuItem` **API documentation:** https://material-ui.com/api/menu-item/

Using menu transitions

You can change the transition that's used by the `Menu` component. By default, `Menu` uses the `Grow` transition component.

How to do it...

To demonstrate how to apply different transitions to the `Menu` component, we'll add some transition options to Storybook for this example. You can change the transition component that's used, as well as the duration of the transition using the following code:

```
import React, { Fragment, useState } from 'react';

import { makeStyles } from '@material-ui/styles';
import Button from '@material-ui/core/Button';
import Menu from '@material-ui/core/Menu';
import MenuItem from '@material-ui/core/MenuItem';
import Collapse from '@material-ui/core/Collapse';
import Fade from '@material-ui/core/Fade';
import Grow from '@material-ui/core/Grow';
import Slide from '@material-ui/core/Slide';

import MenuIcon from '@material-ui/icons/Menu';

const useStyles = makeStyles(theme => ({
  rightIcon: {
    marginLeft: theme.spacing.unit
  }
}));
```

```
export default function UsingMenuTransitions({
  transition,
  duration
}) {
  const classes = useStyles();
  const [anchorEl, setAnchorEl] = useState(null);

  const onOpen = e => {
    setAnchorEl(e.currentTarget);
  };

  const onClose = () => {
    setAnchorEl(null);
  };

  return (
    <Fragment>
      <Button onClick={onOpen}>
        Menu
        <MenuIcon className={classes.rightIcon} />
      </Button>
      <Menu
        anchorEl={anchorEl}
        open={Boolean(anchorEl)}
        onClose={onClose}
        transitionDuration={duration}
        TransitionComponent={
          {
            collapse: Collapse,
            fade: Fade,
            grow: Grow,
            slide: Slide
          }[transition]
        }
      >
        <MenuItem onClick={onClose}>Profile</MenuItem>
        <MenuItem onClick={onClose}>My account</MenuItem>
        <MenuItem onClick={onClose}>Logout</MenuItem>
      </Menu>
    </Fragment>
  );
}
```

You'll see the different transition options in the Storybook **Knobs** panel. When you change the transition, you'll notice the difference when you open and close the menu. Unfortunately, I can't capture a screenshot of these transitions.

How it works...

The `transition` property passed to the `UsingMenuTransitions` component comes from Storybook and is used to determine the transition used. Let's take a closer look at the `TransitionComponent` property that's used by `Menu` to determine which transition to use:

```
TransitionComponent={
  {
    collapse: Collapse,
    fade: Fade,
    grow: Grow,
    slide: Slide
  }[transition]
}
```

The `transition` string maps to a Material-UI transition component that you can pass to `Menu`.

See also

- `Menu` demos: https://material-ui.com/demos/menus/
- `Menu` API documentation: https://material-ui.com/api/menu/
- `MenuItem` API documentation: https://material-ui.com/api/menu-item/
- `Collapse` API documentation: https://material-ui.com/api/collapse/
- `Fade` API documentation: https://material-ui.com/api/collapse/
- `Grow` API documentation: https://material-ui.com/api/grow/
- `Slide` API documentation: https://material-ui.com/api/slide/

Customizing menu items

You can change regular menu items that have `onClick` handlers into something more elaborate. For example, you might want a menu with links to other screens in your app.

How to do it...

Let's say that you're using `react-router` in your application to control the navigation from one screen to another, and you would like to use a `Menu` component to `render` links. Here's an example that shows how to do this:

```
import React, { Fragment, useState } from 'react';
import { Switch, Route, Link } from 'react-router-dom';

import { makeStyles } from '@material-ui/styles';
import Button from '@material-ui/core/Button';
import Menu from '@material-ui/core/Menu';
import MenuItem from '@material-ui/core/MenuItem';
import Typography from '@material-ui/core/Typography';
import MenuIcon from '@material-ui/icons/Menu';

const NavMenuItem = ({ color, ...props }) => (
  <Switch>
    <Route
      exact
      path={props.to}
      render={() => <MenuItem selected component={Link} {...props} />}
    />
    <Route
      path="/"
      render={() => <MenuItem component={Link} {...props} />}
    />
  </Switch>
);

const useStyles = makeStyles(theme => ({
  rightIcon: {
    marginLeft: theme.spacing(1)
  }
}));

export default function CustomizingMenuItems() {
  const classes = useStyles();
  const [anchorEl, setAnchorEl] = useState(null);

  const onOpen = e => {
    setAnchorEl(e.currentTarget);
  };

  const onClose = () => {
    setAnchorEl(null);
  };
```

```
    return (
      <Fragment>
        <Button onClick={onOpen}>
          Menu
          <MenuIcon className={classes.rightIcon} />
        </Button>
        <Menu
          anchorEl={anchorEl}
          open={Boolean(anchorEl)}
          onClose={onClose}
        >
          <NavMenuItem to="/" onClick={onClose}>
            Home
          </NavMenuItem>
          <NavMenuItem to="/page1" onClick={onClose}>
            Page 1
          </NavMenuItem>
          <NavMenuItem to="/page2" onClick={onClose}>
            Page 2
          </NavMenuItem>
        </Menu>
        <Switch>
          <Route
            exact
            path="/"
            render={() => <Typography>home content</Typography>}
          />
          <Route
            path="/page1"
            render={() => <Typography>page 1 content</Typography>}
          />
          <Route
            path="/page2"
            render={() => <Typography>page 2 content</Typography>}
          />
        </Switch>
      </Fragment>
    );
  }
```

Here's what you'll see when the screen first loads:

MENU ≡

home content

Here's what the **MENU** looks like when it's opened:

Try clicking on **Page 1**. This should close the **MENU** and change the content rendered below the **MENU**, because you just navigated to another screen, as shown in the following screenshot:

The active link is reflected in the menu. Here's what the menu looks like if you open it from **Page 1**:

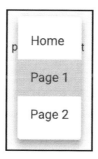

How it works...

Let's start by looking at the `NavMenuItem` component:

```
const NavMenuItem = ({ color, ...props }) => (
  <Switch>
    <Route
      exact
      path={props.to}
      render={() => <MenuItem selected component={Link} {...props} />}
```

```
      />
      <Route
        path="/"
        render={() => <MenuItem component={Link} {...props} />}
      />
    </Switch>
  );
```

This will render a `MenuItem` component based on the current route. If the `to` property value matches the current route, then the `selected` property will be `true`—this is how the menu item appears to be selected when you open the menu. Next, let's look at the `Menu` markup:

```
<Menu
  anchorEl={anchorEl}
  open={Boolean(anchorEl)}
  onClose={onClose}
>
  <NavMenuItem to="/" onClick={onClose}>
    Home
  </NavMenuItem>
  <NavMenuItem to="/page1" onClick={onClose}>
    Page 1
  </NavMenuItem>
  <NavMenuItem to="/page2" onClick={onClose}>
    Page 2
  </NavMenuItem>
</Menu>
```

Instead of rendering the `MenuItem` components, you can render the `NavMenuItem` components. These result in links being rendered with the selected property set to `true` for the current route. Note that the `to` property is required here in order to link to another page, and the `onClick` handler is necessary in order to close the menu as the page transition happens.

See also

- `Menu` **demos:** https://material-ui.com/demos/menus/
- `Menu` **API documentation:** https://material-ui.com/api/menu/
- `MenuItem` **API documentation:** https://material-ui.com/api/menu-item/

Typography - Control Font Look and Feel

17

In this chapter, we will cover the following topics:

- Types of typography
- Using theme colors
- Aligning text
- Wrapping text

Introduction

The `Typography` component is used by Material-UI to render text on the screen. You can use `Typography` on its own, but it is also used internally by other Material-UI components that render text. Instead of using other HTML elements to render your text, using `Typography` components allows Material-UI to handle the application of theme styles using consistent font types, and also handle font behavior in a uniform way.

Types of typography

The `Typography` component is used any time you want to render text in a Material-UI application. The type of text, or variant, is specified as a string value that's passed to the `variant` property.

How to do it...

Here's an example that shows how to render all of the available `Typography` variants:

```
import React, { Fragment } from 'react';

import Typography from '@material-ui/core/Typography';

const MyTypography = ({ variant, ...props }) => (
  <Typography variant={variant || 'inherit'} {...props} />
);

const TypesOfTypography = () => (
  <Fragment>
    <Typography variant="h1">h1 variant</Typography>
    <Typography variant="h2">h2 variant</Typography>
    <Typography variant="h3">h3 variant</Typography>
    <Typography variant="h4">h4 variant</Typography>
    <Typography variant="h5">h5 variant</Typography>
    <Typography variant="h6">h6 variant</Typography>
    <Typography variant="subtitle1">subtitle1 variant</Typography>
    <Typography variant="subtitle2">subtitle2 variant</Typography>
    <Typography variant="body1">body1 variant</Typography>
    <Typography variant="body2">body2 variant</Typography>
    <Typography variant="subtitle1">subtitle1 variant</Typography>
    <Typography variant="caption">caption variant</Typography>
    <Typography variant="button">button variant</Typography>
    <Typography variant="overline">overline variant</Typography>
    <Typography variant="title" component="div">
      <Typography variant="inherit">
        inherited title variant
      </Typography>
      <Typography variant="inherit">
        another inherited title variant
      </Typography>
      <Typography variant="caption">
        overridden caption variant
      </Typography>
    </Typography>
```

```
          <MyTypography variant="title" component="div">
            <MyTypography>inherited title variant</MyTypography>
            <MyTypography>another inherited title variant</MyTypography>
            <MyTypography variant="caption">
              overridden caption variant
            </MyTypography>
          </MyTypography>
        </Fragment>
    );

    export default TypesOfTypography;
```

Here's what the heading variants look like:

Finally, here are what the remaining variants look like:

How it works...

The value that you pass to the `variant` property determines the styles that are applied to the text. The styles for each of these variants are defined by the theme, and can be customized from theme to theme.

It can be tempting to add your own variant names, or to add font styles outside of the typography variants. I would advise against this, because doing so breaks the common font vocabulary based on Material Design. If you stray from the typography variant conventions, you'll end up with variant names that only make sense to you, or worse, variants that don't work because of font styles applied to text from outside of the typography system.

There's more...

If you want your `Typography` component to inherit the variant styles from its parent, you can use the `inherit` variant value, as shown in the following example:

```
<Typography variant="title" component="div">
  <Typography variant="inherit">
    inherited title variant
  </Typography>
  <Typography variant="inherit">
    another inherited title variant
  </Typography>
  <Typography variant="caption">
    overridden caption variant
  </Typography>
</Typography>
```

The parent `Typography` component uses the `title` variant. It also changes its component to be a `div` element, because it's not actually rendering text as direct children—think of it as a container for font styles. Inside, there are three child `Typography` components. The first two have `inherit` as the `variant` property value, so they'll actually get the `title` variant. The third `Typography` child uses `caption` as its variant, so it will not inherit `title`.

Here's what the result looks like:

```
inherited title variant
another inherited title variant
overridden caption variant
```

One adjustment to this approach that you might consider is to have `inherit` as the default variant. This way, you don't have to keep typing `variant="inherit"` if you have lots of child `Typography` components that need to inherit font styles. Here's a component that does this:

```
const MyTypography = ({ variant, ...props }) => (
  <Typography variant={variant || 'inherit'} {...props} />
);
```

The `MyTypography` component will render a `Typography` component with a `variant` value of `inherit`, but only if the `variant` property wasn't passed. Let's change the preceding code to use this new component:

```
<MyTypography variant="title" component="div">
  <MyTypography>inherited title variant</MyTypography>
  <MyTypography>another inherited title variant</MyTypography>
  <MyTypography variant="caption">
    overridden caption variant
  </MyTypography>
</MyTypography>
```

The result is exactly the same. The only difference is that now you don't need to provide the `variant` property for variants that you want to inherit.

See also

- `Typography` demos: https://material-ui.com/style/typography/
- `Typography` API documentation: https://material-ui.com/api/typography/

Using theme colors

Text that is rendered using the `Typography` component can use colors from the Material-UI theme used by the app.

How to do it...

For this example, you'll find a Storybook control that allows you to change the color of the text using predefined **Color** names from the theme, as shown in the following screenshot:

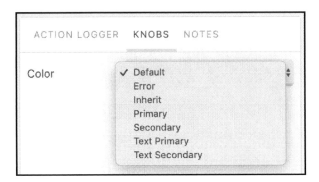

Here's the source for the example that uses the selected color by passing it to the `color` property of each `Typography` component:

```
import React, { Fragment } from 'react';

import Typography from '@material-ui/core/Typography';

const UsingThemeColors = ({ color }) => (
  <Fragment>
    <Typography variant="h1" color={color}>
      h1 variant
    </Typography>
    <Typography variant="h2" color={color}>
      h2 variant
    </Typography>
    <Typography variant="h3" color={color}>
      h3 variant
    </Typography>
    <Typography variant="h4" color={color}>
      h4 variant
    </Typography>
    <Typography variant="h5" color={color}>
      h5 variant
    </Typography>
    <Typography variant="h6" color={color}>
      h6 variant
    </Typography>
    <Typography variant="subtitle1" color={color}>
      subtitle1 variant
```

```
      </Typography>
      <Typography variant="subtitle2" color={color}>
        subtitle2 variant
      </Typography>
      <Typography variant="body1" color={color}>
        body1 variant
      </Typography>
      <Typography variant="body2" color={color}>
        body2 variant
      </Typography>
      <Typography variant="caption" color={color}>
        caption variant
      </Typography>
      <Typography variant="button" color={color}>
        button variant
      </Typography>
      <Typography variant="overline" color={color}>
        overline variant
      </Typography>
    </Fragment>
);

export default UsingThemeColors;
```

How it works...

Let's walk through how each of these colors change the appearance of the different Typography variants:

Default	The default color uses whatever color is defined in the styles for the Typography variant in question	h1 variant h2 variant h3 variant h4 variant h5 variant h6 variant subtitle1 variant subtitle2 variant body1 variant body2 variant headline variant title variant subheading variant caption variant BUTTON VARIANT OVERLINE VARIANT

Error	The `error` color applies the `palette.error.main` theme color to the text	h1 variant h2 variant h3 variant h4 variant h5 variant h6 variant subtitle1 variant subtitle2 variant body1 variant body2 variant headline variant title variant subheading variant caption variant BUTTON VARIANT OVERLINE VARIANT
Inherit	The `Typography` component will inherit the font color of its parent component	h1 variant h2 variant h3 variant h4 variant h5 variant h6 variant subtitle1 variant subtitle2 variant body1 variant body2 variant headline variant title variant subheading variant caption variant BUTTON VARIANT OVERLINE VARIANT

Primary	The `primary` color applies the `palette.primary.main` theme color to the text	h1 variant h2 variant h3 variant h4 variant h5 variant h6 variant subtitle1 variant subtitle2 variant body1 variant body2 variant headline variant title variant subheading variant caption variant BUTTON VARIANT OVERLINE VARIANT
Secondary	The `secondary` color applies the `palette.secondary.main` theme color to the text	h1 variant h2 variant h3 variant h4 variant h5 variant h6 variant subtitle1 variant subtitle2 variant body1 variant body2 variant headline variant title variant subheading variant caption variant BUTTON VARIANT OVERLINE VARIANT

Text Primary	The `textPrimary` color applies the `palette.text.primary` theme color to the text	h1 variant h2 variant h3 variant h4 variant h5 variant h6 variant subtitle1 variant subtitle2 variant body1 variant body2 variant headline variant title variant subheading variant caption variant BUTTON VARIANT OVERLINE VARIANT
Text Secondary	The `textSecondary` color applies the `palette.text.secondary` theme color to the text	h1 variant h2 variant h3 variant h4 variant h5 variant h6 variant subtitle1 variant subtitle2 variant body1 variant body2 variant headline variant title variant subheading variant caption variant BUTTON VARIANT OVERLINE VARIANT

See also

- Typography **demos**: https://material-ui.com/style/typography/
- Typography **API documentation**: https://material-ui.com/api/typography/

Aligning text

Aligning text in user interfaces is common. Unfortunately, it isn't easy. With Material-UI grids and typography, you can create abstractions that make it a little easier to align text.

How to do it...

If you're trying to align your text horizontally to the left, right, or center, then you can use the `align` property of your `Typography` component, as demonstrated in the following code:

```
<Typography align="center">My Centered Text</Typography>
```

This is shorthand for using the `text-align` style, so that you don't have to keep adding CSS to your components for the more common alignment scenarios. However, sometimes you need the ability to align your text both horizontally and vertically.

For example, let's say that you have a 200x200 `Paper` element, and you need the ability to render text in the bottom-right corner. Let's illustrate this example with some code:

```
import React from 'react';

import { withStyles } from '@material-ui/core/styles';
import Typography from '@material-ui/core/Typography';
import Paper from '@material-ui/core/Paper';
import Grid from '@material-ui/core/Grid';

const styles = theme => ({
  paper: {
    width: 200,
    height: 200,
    padding: theme.spacing(1)
  }
});

const MyPaper = withStyles(styles)(
  ({ horizontalAlign, verticalAlign, classes, ...props }) => (
    <Grid
      container
      component={Paper}
      className={classes.paper}
      alignContent={verticalAlign}
      justify={horizontalAlign}
      {...props}
    />
```

```
  )
);

const MyTypography = ({ ...props }) => (
  <Grid item component={Typography} {...props} />
);

const AligningText = ({ ...props }) => (
  <MyPaper {...props}>
    <MyTypography {...props}>Text</MyTypography>
  </MyPaper>
);

export default AligningText;
```

Here's what you'll see when the screen first loads:

How it works...

There are two Storybook controls for aligning the text, as follows:

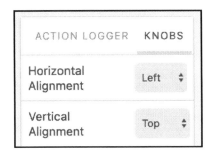

The horizontal alignment control changes the `horizontalAlign` property that is passed to the `MyPaper` component. Likewise, the vertical alignment control changes the `verticalAlign` property value. The `horizontalAlign` value is passed to the `justify` property of the `Grid` component, while the `verticalAlign` property goes to the `alignContent` property.

What's neat about the `Grid` components is that you can pass them a `component` property and this will be rendered instead of the `div` element that's rendered by default. In other words, you can make the `Paper` component a grid container and the `Typography` component that you're trying to align a grid item. You don't have to render the `Grid` components and then your actual content as children. You can make your content the grid.

Here's what the grid looks like when you set `justify="center"` and `alignContent="flex-end"`:

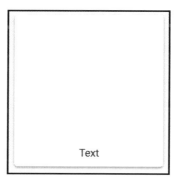

And here's what it looks like what you set `justify="flex-end"` and `alignContent="flex-start"`:

See also

- Typography **demos:** https://material-ui.com/style/typography/
- Typography **API documentation:** https://material-ui.com/api/typography/

Wrapping text

The Typography components that you use to render text in your application need to be aware of scenarios where text wraps. This means that, when there isn't enough horizontal space to render a line of text, it continues onto the next line. This can have undesirable layout consequences if you don't anticipate how text might wrap.

How to do it...

Let's look at an example where you have two Paper components that render text using Typography **components:**

```
import React, { Fragment } from 'react';
import clsx from 'clsx';

import { withStyles } from '@material-ui/core/styles';
import Typography from '@material-ui/core/Typography';
import Paper from '@material-ui/core/Paper';

const styles = theme => ({
  paper: {
    minWidth: 300,
    padding: theme.spacing(2),
    margin: theme.spacing(3)
  },
  fixedHeight: { height: 100 },
  responsive: {
    [theme.breakpoints.down('xs')]: {
      overflow: 'hidden',
      textOverflow: 'ellipsis',
      whiteSpace: 'nowrap'
    }
  }
});

const WrappingText = withStyles(styles)(({ classes }) => (
  <Fragment>
```

```
      <Paper className={classes.paper}>
        <Typography noWrap>
          Lorem ipsum dolor sit amet, consectetur adipiscing elit, sed
          do eiusmod tempor incididunt ut labore
        </Typography>
      </Paper>
      <Paper className={clsx(classes.paper, classes.fixedHeight)}>
        <Typography className={classes.responsive}>
          Sed ut perspiciatis unde omnis iste natus error sit voluptatem
          accusantium doloremque laudantium, totam rem aperiam, eaque
          ipsa quae ab illo inventore veritatis et quasi architecto
          beatae vitae dicta sunt explicabo. Nemo enim ipsam voluptatem
          quia voluptas sit aspernatur aut odit aut fugit, sed quia
          consequuntur magni dolores eos qui ratione voluptatem sequi
          nesciunt.
        </Typography>
      </Paper>
    </Fragment>
));

export default WrappingText;
```

Here's what you'll see when the screen first loads:

Lorem ipsum dolor sit amet, consectetur adipiscing elit, sed do eiusmod tempor incididunt ut labore

Sed ut perspiciatis unde omnis iste natus error sit voluptatem accusantium doloremque laudantium, totam rem aperiam, eaque ipsa quae ab illo inventore veritatis et quasi architecto beatae vitae dicta sunt explicabo. Nemo enim ipsam voluptatem quia voluptas sit aspernatur aut odit aut fugit, sed quia consequuntur magni dolores eos qui ratione voluptatem sequi nesciunt.

The first `Paper` component doesn't have a set the `height` component, and has a single line of text that fits within the current screen width. The second `Paper` component does have a set `height`, and the text in the second `Paper` component is wrapped so that it fits on the screen.

How it works...

Now, let's try changing the screen resolution, making the available width in which to render text smaller. Here's what you'll see:

> Lorem ipsum dolor sit amet, consectetur adipiscing elit, sed do eiusmod tempor incididunt ut labore
>
> Sed ut perspiciatis unde omnis iste natus error sit voluptatem accusantium doloremque laudantium, totam rem aperiam, eaque ipsa quae ab illo inventore veritatis et quasi architecto beatae vitae dicta sunt explicabo. Nemo enim ipsam voluptatem quia voluptas sit aspernatur aut odit aut fugit, sed quia consequuntur magni dolores eos qui ratione voluptatem sequi nesciunt.

There are wrapping issues in both `Paper` components. In the first, the wrapped text causes the the height of the component to change because it doesn't have a fixed height. This has a domino effect with regard to layout that may or may not be problematic, depending on your design. In the second `Paper` component, `height` is fixed, which means that the wrapped text overflows out of the component, which looks terrible.

There's more...

Let's fix the text wrapping in both of the `Paper` components in this example. The following is a modified version:

```
import React, { Fragment } from 'react';
import clsx from 'clsx';

import { withStyles } from '@material-ui/core/styles';
import Typography from '@material-ui/core/Typography';
import Paper from '@material-ui/core/Paper';

const styles = theme => ({
  paper: {
    minWidth: 300,
```

```
      padding: theme.spacing(2),
      margin: theme.spacing(3)
    },
    fixedHeight: { height: 100 },
    responsive: {
      [theme.breakpoints.down('xs')]: {
        overflow: 'hidden',
        textOverflow: 'ellipsis',
        whiteSpace: 'nowrap'
      }
    }
  }
});

const WrappingText = withStyles(styles)(({ classes }) => (
  <Fragment>
    <Paper className={classes.paper}>
      <Typography noWrap>
        Lorem ipsum dolor sit amet, consectetur adipiscing elit, sed
        do eiusmod tempor incididunt ut labore
      </Typography>
    </Paper>
    <Paper className={clsx(classes.paper, classes.fixedHeight)}>
      <Typography className={classes.responsive}>
        Sed ut perspiciatis unde omnis iste natus error sit voluptatem
        accusantium doloremque laudantium, totam rem aperiam, eaque
        ipsa quae ab illo inventore veritatis et quasi architecto
        beatae vitae dicta sunt explicabo. Nemo enim ipsam voluptatem
        quia voluptas sit aspernatur aut odit aut fugit, sed quia
        consequuntur magni dolores eos qui ratione voluptatem sequi
        nesciunt.
      </Typography>
    </Paper>
  </Fragment>
));

export default WrappingText;
```

Now, when you shrink the width of the screen, this is what the two components look like:

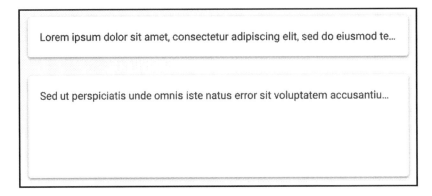

The first `Paper` component was fixed by adding the `noWrap` property to the `Typography` component. This will ensure that the `height` component of the component never changes, by hiding text overflow and adding an ellipsis to indicate that the text has been truncated. This works because you know ahead of time that this is just a single line of text that will never need to wrap when shown on wider displays. The second `Paper` component, on the other hand, needs a different approach, because it does need the ability to wrap.

The solution was to use the Material-UI media query functionality. The call to `theme.breakpoints.down('xs')` results in a class name that's prefixed by a media query for the specified breakpoint, in this case, `xs`. Now, when the screen width shrinks to the `xs` breakpoint, the same styles used for the `noWrap` property are applied to the component.

See also

- `Typography` **demos**: https://material-ui.com/style/typography/
- `Typography` **API documentation**: https://material-ui.com/api/typography/

18
Icons - Enhance Icons to Match Your Look and Feel

In this chapter, you'll learn about the following:

- Coloring icons
- Scaling icons
- Dynamically loading icons
- Themed icons
- Installing more icons

Introduction

Icons play a big part in any Material-UI application. Even if you don't set out to explicitly use them, icons are used by many components by default. If a Material-UI component doesn't use icons by default, you can often find direct support for integrating Material-UI icons. Icons play an important role in the usability of your application—they provide a means to quickly scan the screen for meaning, instead of having to parse text all of the time.

Coloring icons

Material-UI icon components accept a `color` property that takes a named theme color and applies it to the icon.

How to do it...

This example uses a Storybook control to change the `color` property of the icons that are rendered:

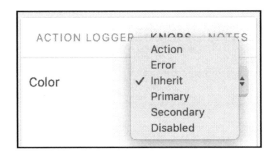

Here's some code that renders several icons that use the selected `color` value:

```
import React, { Fragment } from 'react';

import { withStyles } from '@material-ui/core/styles';

import Cast from '@material-ui/icons/Cast';
import CastConnected from '@material-ui/icons/CastConnected';
import CastForEducation from '@material-ui/icons/CastForEducation';
import Computer from '@material-ui/icons/Computer';
import DesktopMac from '@material-ui/icons/DesktopMac';
import DesktopWindows from '@material-ui/icons/DesktopWindows';
import DeveloperBoard from '@material-ui/icons/DeveloperBoard';
import DeviceHub from '@material-ui/icons/DeviceHub';
import DeviceUnknown from '@material-ui/icons/DeviceUnknown';
import DevicesOther from '@material-ui/icons/DevicesOther';
import Dock from '@material-ui/icons/Dock';
import Gamepad from '@material-ui/icons/Gamepad';

const styles = theme => ({
  icon: { margin: theme.spacing(3) }
});

const IconColorAndState = withStyles(styles)(({ color, classes }) => (
  <Fragment>
    <Cast className={classes.icon} color={color} />
    <CastConnected className={classes.icon} color={color} />
    <CastForEducation className={classes.icon} color={color} />
    <Computer className={classes.icon} color={color} />
    <DesktopMac className={classes.icon} color={color} />
    <DesktopWindows className={classes.icon} color={color} />
```

```
        <DeveloperBoard className={classes.icon} color={color} />
        <DeviceHub className={classes.icon} color={color} />
        <DeviceUnknown className={classes.icon} color={color} />
        <DevicesOther className={classes.icon} color={color} />
        <Dock className={classes.icon} color={color} />
        <Gamepad className={classes.icon} color={color} />
      </Fragment>
  ));

  export default IconColorAndState;
```

How it works...

The color property defaults to inherit, which means that icons will be the same color as their parent components. Let's walk through the different color values and see what these icons from the example look like:

Inherit	The inherit color value will use the color value from the parent component style:	
Primary	The primary color applies the palette.primary.main theme color to the icon:	

Secondary	The `secondary` color applies the `palette.secondary.main` theme color to the icon:	
Action	The `action` color applies the `palette.action.active` theme color to the icon:	
Error	The `error` color applies the `palette.error.main` theme color to the icon:	
Disabled	The `disabled` color applies the `palette.action.disabled` theme color to the icon:	

See also

- Icon demos: `https://material-ui.com/style/icons/`
- Icon API documentation: `https://material-ui.com/api/icon/`

Scaling icons

The `fontSize` property of the Material-UI icon components accepts a string value that represents a predetermined icon size. The reason the property is called `fontSize` instead of `size` is because the `fontSize` CSS property is what determines the size of an icon. The default is `24px`.

How to do it...

This example uses a Storybook control to change the `fontSize` property of the icons that are rendered:

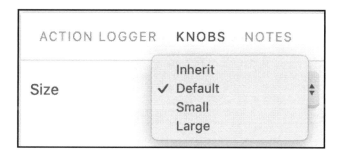

Here's some code that renders several icons that use the selected `fontSize` value:

```
import React, { Fragment } from 'react';

import { withStyles } from '@material-ui/core/styles';

import Cast from '@material-ui/icons/Cast';
import CastConnected from '@material-ui/icons/CastConnected';
import CastForEducation from '@material-ui/icons/CastForEducation';
import Computer from '@material-ui/icons/Computer';
import DesktopMac from '@material-ui/icons/DesktopMac';
import DesktopWindows from '@material-ui/icons/DesktopWindows';
import DeveloperBoard from '@material-ui/icons/DeveloperBoard';
import DeviceHub from '@material-ui/icons/DeviceHub';
```

```
import DeviceUnknown from '@material-ui/icons/DeviceUnknown';
import DevicesOther from '@material-ui/icons/DevicesOther';
import Dock from '@material-ui/icons/Dock';
import Gamepad from '@material-ui/icons/Gamepad';

const styles = theme => ({
  icon: { margin: theme.spacing(3) }
});

const ScalingIcons = withStyles(styles)(({ fontSize, classes }) => (
  <Fragment>
    <Cast className={classes.icon} fontSize={fontSize} />
    <CastConnected className={classes.icon} fontSize={fontSize} />
    <CastForEducation className={classes.icon} fontSize={fontSize} />
    <Computer className={classes.icon} fontSize={fontSize} />
    <DesktopMac className={classes.icon} fontSize={fontSize} />
    <DesktopWindows className={classes.icon} fontSize={fontSize} />
    <DeveloperBoard className={classes.icon} fontSize={fontSize} />
    <DeviceHub className={classes.icon} fontSize={fontSize} />
    <DeviceUnknown className={classes.icon} fontSize={fontSize} />
    <DevicesOther className={classes.icon} fontSize={fontSize} />
    <Dock className={classes.icon} fontSize={fontSize} />
    <Gamepad className={classes.icon} fontSize={fontSize} />
  </Fragment>
));

export default ScalingIcons;
```

How it works...

The default value of fontSize is default. Let's walk through the different size options of
Material-UI icons and see how they look.

Default

The default value sets the icon size to 24 pixels:

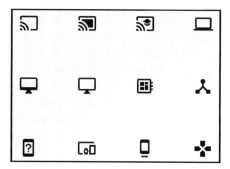

Inherit

The inherit value sets the icon to whatever fontSize its parent component is set to. In this example, the icons inherit 16 pixels as the fontSize:

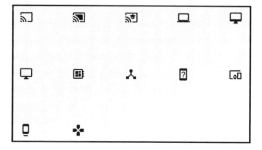

Small

The small value sets the icon size to 20 pixels:

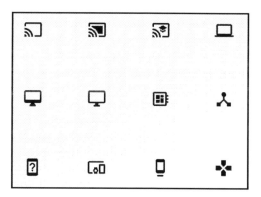

Large

The `large` value sets the icon size to 36 pixels:

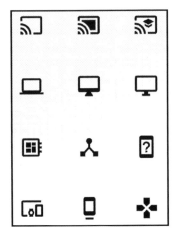

See also

- Icon demos: `https://material-ui.com/style/icons/`
- Icon API documentation: `https://material-ui.com/api/icon/`

Dynamically loading icons

On screens that only have a handful of icons on them, you can directly import them as components without any issues. This can be challenging if you have a screen with many icons or if your application as a whole uses lots of icons (the latter case increases the bundle size). The answer, in both cases, is to load Material-UI icons lazily/dynamically.

How to do it...

You can leverage the `lazy()` higher-order component from React. Also from React, the `Suspense` component provides placeholders in your UI while your `lazy` components are fetched and rendered. This overall approach is how code-splitting is handled in React—Material-UI icons happen to be a good use case.

This example uses a Storybook control to select the icon category to load:

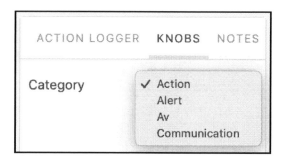

Here's the code to create `lazy icon` components that load dynamically:

```
import React, { lazy, Suspense, Fragment } from 'react';

import { withStyles } from '@material-ui/core/styles';
import CircularProgress from '@material-ui/core/CircularProgress';

const categories = {
  Action: [
    lazy(() => import('@material-ui/icons/ThreeDRotation')),
    lazy(() => import('@material-ui/icons/Accessibility')),
    lazy(() => import('@material-ui/icons/AccessibilityNew')),
    lazy(() => import('@material-ui/icons/Accessible')),
    lazy(() => import('@material-ui/icons/AccessibleForward')),
    lazy(() => import('@material-ui/icons/AccountBalance')),
    lazy(() => import('@material-ui/icons/AccountBalanceWallet')),
    lazy(() => import('@material-ui/icons/AccountBox')),
    lazy(() => import('@material-ui/icons/AccountCircle'))
  ],
  Alert: [
    lazy(() => import('@material-ui/icons/AddAlert')),
    lazy(() => import('@material-ui/icons/Error')),
    lazy(() => import('@material-ui/icons/ErrorOutline')),
    lazy(() => import('@material-ui/icons/NotificationImportant')),
    lazy(() => import('@material-ui/icons/Warning'))
  ],
  Av: [
    lazy(() => import('@material-ui/icons/FourK')),
    lazy(() => import('@material-ui/icons/AddToQueue')),
    lazy(() => import('@material-ui/icons/Airplay')),
    lazy(() => import('@material-ui/icons/Album')),
    lazy(() => import('@material-ui/icons/ArtTrack')),
    lazy(() => import('@material-ui/icons/AvTimer')),
    lazy(() => import('@material-ui/icons/BrandingWatermark')),
    lazy(() => import('@material-ui/icons/CallToAction')),
```

```
      lazy(() => import('@material-ui/icons/ClosedCaption'))
  ],
  Communication: [
    lazy(() => import('@material-ui/icons/AlternateEmail')),
    lazy(() => import('@material-ui/icons/Business')),
    lazy(() => import('@material-ui/icons/Call')),
    lazy(() => import('@material-ui/icons/CallEnd')),
    lazy(() => import('@material-ui/icons/CallMade')),
    lazy(() => import('@material-ui/icons/CallMerge')),
    lazy(() => import('@material-ui/icons/CallMissed')),
    lazy(() => import('@material-ui/icons/CallMissedOutgoing')),
    lazy(() => import('@material-ui/icons/CallReceived'))
  ]
};

const styles = theme => ({
  icon: { margin: theme.spacing(3) }
});

const DynamicallyLoadingIcons = withStyles(styles)(
  ({ category, classes }) => (
    <Suspense fallback={<CircularProgress />}>
      {categories[category].map((Icon, index) => (
        <Icon key={index} className={classes.icon} />
      ))}
    </Suspense>
  )
);

export default DynamicallyLoadingIcons;
```

Here's what you'll see when the screen first loads:

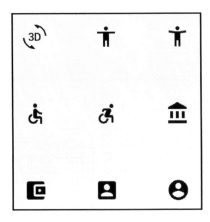

Here's what you'll see if you select the `Av` category:

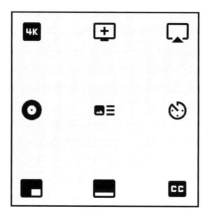

How it works...

The `lazy()` function takes a function that returns a call to `import()`. It returns a `lazy` component:

```
const LazyIcon = lazy(() => import('@material-ui/icons/ThreeDRotation'))
```

This code doesn't actually `import` the `ThreeDRotation` icon. It builds a new component that imports the icon when it's rendered. For example, the following will cause the icon to be imported:

```
<LazyIcon />
```

You can actually see this for yourself if you look at the **Network** tab in `dev` tools while running this example. The `Action` category is selected by default, so you can see the network requests to load the `lazy` components that are being rendered:

0.c45950ddb51a01b0ae52.bun...	GET	200	script	bootstrap...	1.6 KB		2 ms
1.c45950ddb51a01b0ae52.bun...	GET	200	script	bootstrap...	1.7 KB		2 ms
2.c45950ddb51a01b0ae52.bun...	GET	200	script	bootstrap...	1.9 KB		7 ms
3.c45950ddb51a01b0ae52.bun...	GET	200	script	bootstrap...	1.9 KB		4 ms
6.c45950ddb51a01b0ae52.bun...	GET	200	script	bootstrap...	1.7 KB		5 ms
7.c45950ddb51a01b0ae52.bun...	GET	200	script	bootstrap...	1.7 KB		4 ms

Then, if you change the selected category to `Communication`, you'll see several more network requests to load the lazy icons in this category that are now being rendered:

18.c45950ddb51a01b0ae52.bu...	GET	200	script	bootstrap...	1.9 KB		2 ms
19.c45950ddb51a01b0ae52.bu...	GET	200	script	bootstrap...	1.7 KB		2 ms
20.c45950ddb51a01b0ae52.bu...	GET	200	script	bootstrap...	1.7 KB		2 ms
21.c45950ddb51a01b0ae52.bu...	GET	200	script	bootstrap...	1.9 KB		2 ms
22.c45950ddb51a01b0ae52.bu...	GET	200	script	bootstrap...	1.5 KB		3 ms
23.c45950ddb51a01b0ae52.bu...	GET	200	script	bootstrap...	1.6 KB		3 ms
24.c45950ddb51a01b0ae52.bu...	GET	200	script	bootstrap...	1.5 KB		5 ms
25.c45950ddb51a01b0ae52.bu...	GET	200	script	bootstrap...	1.6 KB		5 ms
26.c45950ddb51a01b0ae52.bu...	GET	200	script	bootstrap...	1.5 KB		5 ms

See also

- Icon demos: `https://material-ui.com/style/icons/`
- Icon API documentation: `https://material-ui.com/api/icon/`

Themed icons

Material-UI icons have themes that can be applied to them. They are not to be confused with Material-UI themes that apply styles to every Material-UI component that you use; icon themes are specifically for icons. To use a themed icon, you have to import a different version of it.

How to do it...

To help explore the different icon themes, this example uses a Storybook control that allows you to change the icon theme:

Here's the source:

```
import React, { lazy, Suspense, Fragment } from 'react';

import { withStyles } from '@material-ui/core/styles';
import CircularProgress from '@material-ui/core/CircularProgress';

const themes = {
  Filled: [
    lazy(() => import('@material-ui/icons/Attachment')),
    lazy(() => import('@material-ui/icons/Cloud')),
    lazy(() => import('@material-ui/icons/CloudCircle')),
    lazy(() => import('@material-ui/icons/CloudDone')),
    lazy(() => import('@material-ui/icons/CloudDownload')),
    lazy(() => import('@material-ui/icons/CloudOff')),
    lazy(() => import('@material-ui/icons/CloudQueue')),
    lazy(() => import('@material-ui/icons/CloudUpload')),
    lazy(() => import('@material-ui/icons/CreateNewFolder')),
    lazy(() => import('@material-ui/icons/Folder')),
    lazy(() => import('@material-ui/icons/FolderOpen')),
    lazy(() => import('@material-ui/icons/FolderShared'))
  ],
  Outlined: [
    lazy(() => import('@material-ui/icons/AttachmentOutlined')),
    lazy(() => import('@material-ui/icons/CloudOutlined')),
    lazy(() => import('@material-ui/icons/CloudCircleOutlined')),
    lazy(() => import('@material-ui/icons/CloudDoneOutlined')),
    lazy(() => import('@material-ui/icons/CloudDownloadOutlined')),
    lazy(() => import('@material-ui/icons/CloudOffOutlined')),
    lazy(() => import('@material-ui/icons/CloudQueueOutlined')),
```

```
      lazy(() => import('@material-ui/icons/CloudUploadOutlined')),
      lazy(() => import('@material-ui/icons/CreateNewFolderOutlined')),
      lazy(() => import('@material-ui/icons/FolderOutlined')),
      lazy(() => import('@material-ui/icons/FolderOpenOutlined')),
      lazy(() => import('@material-ui/icons/FolderSharedOutlined'))
    ],
    Rounded: [
      lazy(() => import('@material-ui/icons/AttachmentRounded')),
      lazy(() => import('@material-ui/icons/CloudRounded')),
      lazy(() => import('@material-ui/icons/CloudCircleRounded')),
      lazy(() => import('@material-ui/icons/CloudDoneRounded')),
      lazy(() => import('@material-ui/icons/CloudDownloadRounded')),
      lazy(() => import('@material-ui/icons/CloudOffRounded')),
      lazy(() => import('@material-ui/icons/CloudQueueRounded')),
      lazy(() => import('@material-ui/icons/CloudUploadRounded')),
      lazy(() => import('@material-ui/icons/CreateNewFolderRounded')),
      lazy(() => import('@material-ui/icons/FolderRounded')),
      lazy(() => import('@material-ui/icons/FolderOpenRounded')),
      lazy(() => import('@material-ui/icons/FolderSharedRounded'))
    ],
    TwoTone: [
      lazy(() => import('@material-ui/icons/AttachmentTwoTone')),
      lazy(() => import('@material-ui/icons/CloudTwoTone')),
      lazy(() => import('@material-ui/icons/CloudCircleTwoTone')),
      lazy(() => import('@material-ui/icons/CloudDoneTwoTone')),
      lazy(() => import('@material-ui/icons/CloudDownloadTwoTone')),
      lazy(() => import('@material-ui/icons/CloudOffTwoTone')),
      lazy(() => import('@material-ui/icons/CloudQueueTwoTone')),
      lazy(() => import('@material-ui/icons/CloudUploadTwoTone')),
      lazy(() => import('@material-ui/icons/CreateNewFolderTwoTone')),
      lazy(() => import('@material-ui/icons/FolderTwoTone')),
      lazy(() => import('@material-ui/icons/FolderOpenTwoTone')),
      lazy(() => import('@material-ui/icons/FolderSharedTwoTone'))
    ],
    Sharp: [
      lazy(() => import('@material-ui/icons/AttachmentSharp')),
      lazy(() => import('@material-ui/icons/CloudSharp')),
      lazy(() => import('@material-ui/icons/CloudCircleSharp')),
      lazy(() => import('@material-ui/icons/CloudDoneSharp')),
      lazy(() => import('@material-ui/icons/CloudDownloadSharp')),
      lazy(() => import('@material-ui/icons/CloudOffSharp')),
      lazy(() => import('@material-ui/icons/CloudQueueSharp')),
      lazy(() => import('@material-ui/icons/CloudUploadSharp')),
      lazy(() => import('@material-ui/icons/CreateNewFolderSharp')),
      lazy(() => import('@material-ui/icons/FolderSharp')),
      lazy(() => import('@material-ui/icons/FolderOpenSharp')),
      lazy(() => import('@material-ui/icons/FolderSharedSharp'))
    ]
```

```
};

const styles = theme => ({
  icon: { margin: theme.spacing(3) }
});

const ThemedIcons = withStyles(styles)(({ theme, classes }) => (
  <Suspense fallback={<CircularProgress />}>
    {themes[theme].map((Icon, index) => (
      <Icon fontSize="large" key={index} className={classes.icon} />
    ))}
  </Suspense>
));

export default ThemedIcons;
```

How it works...

If you take a look at the themes object, you can see that each theme has the same icons in it, but their import paths are slightly different. For example, the Attachment icon is imported by the Filled theme, as follows:

```
import('@material-ui/icons/Attachment')
```

In the Rounded theme, here's how the same icon is imported:

```
import('@material-ui/icons/AttachmentOutlined')
```

You append the theme name to the icon name to change the theme of the icon. The same pattern follows for each of them.

 Not every icon changes when the theme changes. It really just depends on the icon shape and whether it makes sense to, with the given theme. The import will still work, but there isn't always a visual change.

Let's explore them now:

Filled	The `Filled` theme is the default. Here's what it looks like when applied to the example:	
Outlined	Take a look at the preceding `Filled` theme—notice that some icons are actually outlined by default. Here's what the `Outlined` theme looks like when applied to the example:	

Rounded	Here's what the `Rounded` theme looks like when applied to the example:	
Two tone	Here's what the `TwoTone` theme looks like when applied to the example:	
Sharp	Here's what the `Sharp` theme looks like when applied to the example:	

See also

- Icon demos: `https://material-ui.com/style/icons/`
- Icon API documentation: `https://material-ui.com/api/icon/`

Installing more icons

The `mdi-material-ui` package provides a staggering number of icons, available for you to use in your Material-UI applications in the same way as you would use the built-in icons.

How to do it...

The first step is to install the package and make it available in your project:

```
npm install --save mdi-material-ui
```

Now you're ready to `import` icons from this package and use them:

```
import React, { Fragment } from 'react';

import { withStyles } from '@material-ui/core/styles';

import Apple from 'mdi-material-ui/Apple';
import Facebook from 'mdi-material-ui/Facebook';
import Google from 'mdi-material-ui/Google';
import Hulu from 'mdi-material-ui/Hulu';
import Linkedin from 'mdi-material-ui/Linkedin';
import Lyft from 'mdi-material-ui/Lyft';
import Microsoft from 'mdi-material-ui/Microsoft';
import Netflix from 'mdi-material-ui/Netflix';
import Npm from 'mdi-material-ui/Npm';
import Reddit from 'mdi-material-ui/Reddit';
import Twitter from 'mdi-material-ui/Twitter';
import Uber from 'mdi-material-ui/Uber';

const styles = theme => ({
  icon: { margin: theme.spacing(3) }
});

const InstallingMoreIcons = withStyles(styles)(({ classes }) => (
  <Fragment>
    <Apple className={classes.icon} />
    <Facebook className={classes.icon} />
```

```
      <Google className={classes.icon} />
      <Hulu className={classes.icon} />
      <Linkedin className={classes.icon} />
      <Lyft className={classes.icon} />
      <Microsoft className={classes.icon} />
      <Netflix className={classes.icon} />
      <Npm className={classes.icon} />
      <Reddit className={classes.icon} />
      <Twitter className={classes.icon} />
      <Uber className={classes.icon} />
   </Fragment>
));

export default InstallingMoreIcons;
```

Here's what the icons look like when you load the screen:

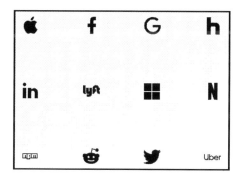

How it works...

The icons from `mdi-material-design` are just like the icons from `@material-ui/icons`.
They're imported and rendered as React components. You find the name of the icon that
you need by looking it up on `https://materialdesignicons.com/`. Anywhere you can use
the official Material-UI icons, such as in buttons, you can also use icons from `mdi-material-ui`.

See also

- The Material Design icons package: `https://materialdesignicons.com/`
- Icon demos: `https://material-ui.com/style/icons/`
- Icon API documentation: `https://material-ui.com/api/icon/`

19
Themes - Centralize the Look and Feel of Your App

Here's what you'll learn in this chapter:

- Understanding the palette
- Comparing light and dark themes
- Customizing typography
- Nesting themes
- Understanding component theme settings

Introduction

Material-UI applications all share a common look and feel—to an extent. This doesn't mean that your banking application is going to look and feel the same as my music library application just because we're both using the same library. The common aspect is that both apps follow Material Design principles. I'm not going to go into depth on Material Design here, because there are ample resources out there that do a much better job than I could ever hope to do. Instead, I want to focus on the fact that Material-UI applications can be themed with a high degree of flexibility, and without the need to sacrifice the principles of Material Design.

Understanding the palette

The first place most people start when building a new Material-UI theme is with the color palette. Color palettes can be very complex with a lot of moving parts: Material-UI themes are no exception, but Material-UI hides a lot of the complexity. Your focus is on the color intentions of the theme while Material-UI uses these color intentions to compute other colors where necessary. Taken straight from the Material-UI theme documentation, the intentions are as follows:

- **Primary**: Used to represent primary interface elements
- **Secondary**: Used to represent secondary interface elements
- **Error**: Used to represent interface elements that the user should be made aware of

How to do it...

Let's build a new theme that sets color intentions using the built-in color objects of Material-UI. To help tweak your theme, this example uses **Hue** and **Shade** Storybook controls:

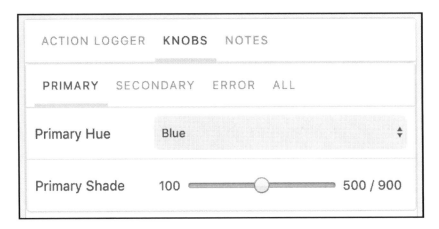

The three color intentions are represented as tabs across the top. The **PRIMARY** intention is currently selected and it has a **Hue** selector and a **Shade** number range. Each intention has the same controls. The **Hue** selector is populated with the same colors available to import from Material-UI:

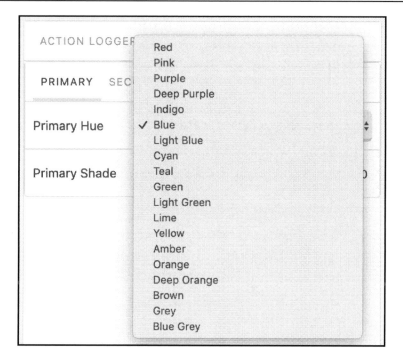

Here's the source that uses these Storybook controls to build a new theme and render some Button and Typography components:

```
import React, { Fragment } from 'react';

import {
  withStyles,
  createMuiTheme,
  MuiThemeProvider
} from '@material-ui/core/styles';
import Button from '@material-ui/core/Button';
import Typography from '@material-ui/core/Typography';

import red from '@material-ui/core/colors/red';
import pink from '@material-ui/core/colors/pink';
import purple from '@material-ui/core/colors/purple';
import deepPurple from '@material-ui/core/colors/deepPurple';
import indigo from '@material-ui/core/colors/indigo';
import blue from '@material-ui/core/colors/blue';
import lightBlue from '@material-ui/core/colors/lightBlue';
import cyan from '@material-ui/core/colors/cyan';
import teal from '@material-ui/core/colors/teal';
import green from '@material-ui/core/colors/green';
import lightGreen from '@material-ui/core/colors/lightGreen';
```

```
import lime from '@material-ui/core/colors/lime';
import yellow from '@material-ui/core/colors/yellow';
import amber from '@material-ui/core/colors/amber';
import orange from '@material-ui/core/colors/orange';
import deepOrange from '@material-ui/core/colors/deepOrange';
import brown from '@material-ui/core/colors/brown';
import grey from '@material-ui/core/colors/grey';
import blueGrey from '@material-ui/core/colors/blueGrey';

const styles = theme => ({
  button: { margin: theme.spacing(2) }
});

const hues = {
  red,
  pink,
  purple,
  deepPurple,
  indigo,
  blue,
  lightBlue,
  cyan,
  teal,
  green,
  lightGreen,
  lime,
  yellow,
  amber,
  orange,
  deepOrange,
  brown,
  grey,
  blueGrey
};

const UnderstandingThePallette = withStyles(styles)(
  ({
    primaryHue,
    primaryShade,
    secondaryHue,
    secondaryShade,
    errorHue,
    errorShade,
    classes
  }) => {
    const theme = createMuiTheme({
      palette: {
        primary: { main: hues[primaryHue][primaryShade] },
```

```
        secondary: { main: hues[secondaryHue][secondaryShade] },
        error: { main: hues[errorHue][errorShade] }
      }
    });

    return (
      <MuiThemeProvider theme={theme}>
        <Button className={classes.button} variant="contained">
          Default
        </Button>
        <Button
          className={classes.button}
          variant="contained"
          color="primary"
        >
          Primary
        </Button>
        <Button
          className={classes.button}
          variant="contained"
          color="secondary"
        >
          Secondary
        </Button>
        <Typography className={classes.button} color="error">
          Error
        </Typography>
      </MuiThemeProvider>
    );
  }
);

export default UnderstandingThePallette;
```

Here's what you'll see when you first load the screen with the **DEFAULT** theme values selected:

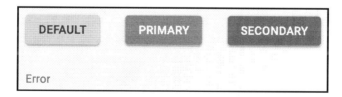

Now, let's change the **DEFAULT** theme color intentions, starting with **PRIMARY**:

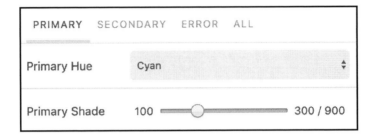

The **Primary Hue** is now **Cyan** with a shade value of **300**. Next, we'll change the **SECONDARY** intention:

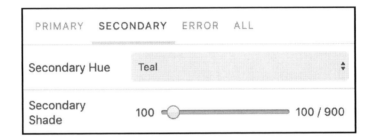

The **Secondary Hue** is now **Teal** with a shade value of **100**. Lastly, we'll change the **ERROR** intention:

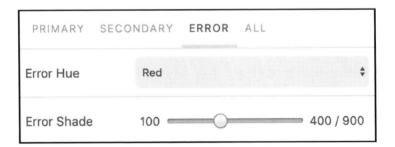

The **Error Hue** is still **Red** for this theme, but slightly lighter with a shade value of **400**. Here's what the end result looks like:

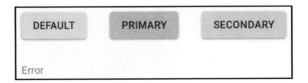

How it works...

Material-UI has core `hues` that can be imported and can help you with building your theme:

```
import red from '@material-ui/core/colors/red';
import pink from '@material-ui/core/colors/pink';
import purple from '@material-ui/core/colors/purple';
import deepPurple from '@material-ui/core/colors/deepPurple';
import indigo from '@material-ui/core/colors/indigo';
import blue from '@material-ui/core/colors/blue';
import lightBlue from '@material-ui/core/colors/lightBlue';
import cyan from '@material-ui/core/colors/cyan';
import teal from '@material-ui/core/colors/teal';
import green from '@material-ui/core/colors/green';
import lightGreen from '@material-ui/core/colors/lightGreen';
import lime from '@material-ui/core/colors/lime';
import yellow from '@material-ui/core/colors/yellow';
import amber from '@material-ui/core/colors/amber';
import orange from '@material-ui/core/colors/orange';
import deepOrange from '@material-ui/core/colors/deepOrange';
import brown from '@material-ui/core/colors/brown';
import grey from '@material-ui/core/colors/grey';
import blueGrey from '@material-ui/core/colors/blueGrey';
```

You don't have to `import` every hue—this is done here because of the Storybook controls that dynamically change the color palette values. Each color value that is imported is an object indexed by the shade value, such as 500, for example. The values are colors expressed in hex, such as `#ffffff`, for example. When using a color expressed in hex, you have to pass it to the `main` property when creating your `theme`:

```
const theme = createMuiTheme({
  palette: {
    primary: { main: hues[primaryHue][primaryShade] },
    secondary: { main: hues[secondaryHue][secondaryShade] },
    error: { main: hues[errorHue][errorShade] }
  }
});
```

The properties `primaryHue`, `primaryShade`, and so on, are the values set by the Storybook controls. The `MuiThemeProvider` component is how the `theme` is actually applied to your Material-UI components. It doesn't have to be the root component of your app, but any Material-UI components that depend on theme styles (`Button`, `Typography`, and so on) need to be children of this component.

The `createMuiTheme()` function is called every time the `main` application component in this example is rendered. In practice, this shouldn't happen. Instead, the theme is created once and passed to the `MuiThemeProvider` component. The reason this is happening here, is so that the theme updates when you change the color values using the Storybook controls.

See also

- Material-UI `theme` documentation: `https://material-ui.com/customization/themes/`
- Material-UI `color` documentation: `https://material-ui.com/style/color/`

Comparing light and dark themes

The color palette of a theme takes a `type` property value that can be either light or dark. By default, themes are light. Changing the theme to dark does not change the other palette values of your theme (`primary`, `secondary`, `error`).

How to do it...

Let's create a dark theme and a light theme. Both themes will use the same color values for the intentions (`primary`, `secondary`, `error`). The example will use a Storybook control to change themes:

Here's the source that uses this value to choose between a `light` and `dark` theme and apply it to the Material-UI components:

```
import React, { Fragment } from 'react';

import {
  withStyles,
  createMuiTheme,
  MuiThemeProvider
} from '@material-ui/core/styles';
import Button from '@material-ui/core/Button';
import Dialog from '@material-ui/core/Dialog';
import DialogActions from '@material-ui/core/DialogActions';
import DialogContent from '@material-ui/core/DialogContent';
import DialogContentText from '@material-ui/core/DialogContentText';
import DialogTitle from '@material-ui/core/DialogTitle';

import red from '@material-ui/core/colors/red';
import pink from '@material-ui/core/colors/pink';
import blue from '@material-ui/core/colors/blue';

const styles = theme => ({
  button: { margin: theme.spacing(2) }
});

const light = createMuiTheme({
  palette: {
    type: 'light',
    primary: blue,
    secondary: pink,
    error: { main: red[600] }
  }
});

const dark = createMuiTheme({
  palette: {
    type: 'dark',
    primary: blue,
    secondary: pink,
    error: { main: red[600] }
  }
});

const LightVersusDarkThemes = withStyles(styles)(
  ({ themeType, classes }) => {
    return (
      <MuiThemeProvider theme={{ dark, light }[themeType]}>
        <Dialog open={true}>
```

```
            <DialogTitle>Use Google's location service?</DialogTitle>
            <DialogContent>
              <DialogContentText id="alert-dialog-description">
                Let Google help apps determine location. This means
                sending anonymous location data to Google, even when no
                apps are running.
              </DialogContentText>
            </DialogContent>
            <DialogActions>
              <Button color="secondary">Disagree</Button>
              <Button variant="contained" color="primary" autoFocus>
                Agree
              </Button>
            </DialogActions>
          </Dialog>
        </MuiThemeProvider>
      );
    }
  );

  export default LightVersusDarkThemes;
```

Here's the dialog that you'll see when the screen first loads:

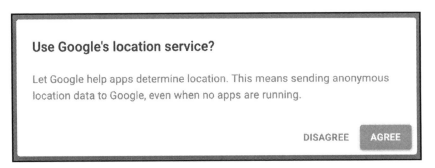

Here's the same dialog with the theme type changed to dark:

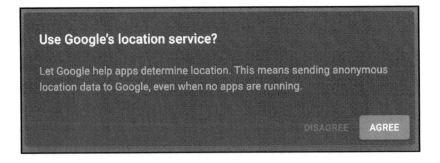

How it works...

When the `palette.type` theme value changes from `light` to `dark`, the following palette values change:

- `palette.text`
- `palette.divider`
- `palette.background`
- `palette.action`

Let's take a look at the two themes used in this example:

```
const light = createMuiTheme({
  palette: {
    type: 'light',
    primary: blue,
    secondary: pink,
    error: { main: red[600] }
  }
});

const dark = createMuiTheme({
  palette: {
    type: 'dark',
    primary: blue,
    secondary: pink,
    error: { main: red[600] }
  }
});
```

These two themes are the same except for the `palette.type` value. Whenever you change this value, new color values are computed for the theme. For example, the new text color that you see in the dialog isn't static—it's a color that's computed by Material-UI in order to provide the optimal contrast between the text color and the background color.

See also

- Material-UI `theme` documentation: `https://material-ui.com/customization/themes/`

Customizing typography

The preferred `typeface` for Material-UI themes is **Roboto**. This is by no means the only option, and, indeed, you can install new typefaces and use them in your custom Material-UI theme.

How to do it...

Let's install a couple of new `typeface` packages so that they're available for use in your application:

```
npm install --save typeface-exo typeface-ubuntu
```

Next, you can add a Storybook control for the example that allows you to switch themes, and, as a result, switch fonts:

Here's what the `Dialog` component looks like when you first load the screen:

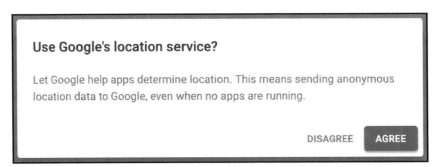

Here's what the `Dialog` component looks like when you change the font type to **Exo**:

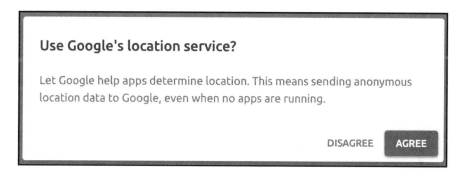

Lastly, here's what the `Dialog` component looks like when you change the font type to **Ubuntu**:

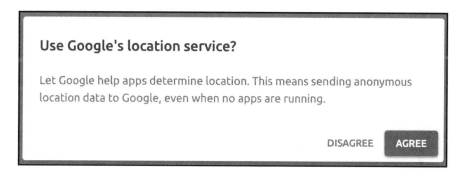

How it works...

The two typefaces that are used in this example are imported:

```
import 'typeface-exo';
import 'typeface-ubuntu';
```

In practice, you'll only `import` the font that your active theme uses, to reduce the size of your build. The `roboto` font that's used all throughout the examples in this book is imported by the Storybook `index` file, since this font is the default theme font and used in every example in this book.

Now that you've imported the typefaces, you've made the font family names available to the theme:

```
const roboto = createMuiTheme({
  typography: {
    fontFamily: '"Roboto", "Helvetica", "Arial", sans-serif'
```

```
    }
  });

  const exo = createMuiTheme({
    typography: {
      fontFamily: '"Exo", "Roboto", "Helvetica", "Arial", sans-serif'
    }
  });

  const ubuntu = createMuiTheme({
    typography: {
      fontFamily: '"Ubuntu", "Roboto", "Helvetica", "Arial", sans-serif'
    }
  });
```

Note that, in the `exo` and `ubuntu` themes, `roboto` is still used as part of the font family, since it's the preferred font for Material-UI; it makes a good fallback.

See also

- Material-UI `theme` documentation: `https://material-ui.com/customization/themes/`

Nesting themes

By nesting `MuiThemeProvider` components, you can compose multiple themes that handle different aspects of a theme into a single theme that's suitable for use in your application.

How to do it...

Let's say that you have a theme that sets the color palette and another theme that changes the border radius. You can merge both themes by nesting the `MuiThemeProvider` components. Here's an example:

```
import React from 'react';

import {
  createMuiTheme,
  MuiThemeProvider
} from '@material-ui/core/styles';
import Button from '@material-ui/core/Button';
```

```
import Dialog from '@material-ui/core/Dialog';
import DialogActions from '@material-ui/core/DialogActions';
import DialogContent from '@material-ui/core/DialogContent';
import DialogContentText from '@material-ui/core/DialogContentText';
import DialogTitle from '@material-ui/core/DialogTitle';

import red from '@material-ui/core/colors/red';
import pink from '@material-ui/core/colors/pink';
import blue from '@material-ui/core/colors/blue';

const Blue = createMuiTheme({
  palette: {
    type: 'light',
    primary: blue,
    secondary: pink,
    error: { main: red[600] }
  }
});

const Rounded = theme =>
  createMuiTheme({
    ...theme,
    shape: {
      borderRadius: 8
    }
  });

const NestingThemes = () => (
  <MuiThemeProvider theme={Blue}>
    <MuiThemeProvider theme={Rounded}>
      <Dialog open={true}>
        <DialogTitle>Use Google's location service?</DialogTitle>
        <DialogContent>
          <DialogContentText>
            Let Google help apps determine location. This means
            sending anonymous location data to Google, even when no
            apps are running.
          </DialogContentText>
        </DialogContent>
        <DialogActions>
          <Button color="secondary">Disagree</Button>
          <Button variant="contained" color="primary" autoFocus>
            Agree
          </Button>
        </DialogActions>
      </Dialog>
    </MuiThemeProvider>
  </MuiThemeProvider>
```

```
);

export default NestingThemes;
```

Here's what you'll see when the screen loads:

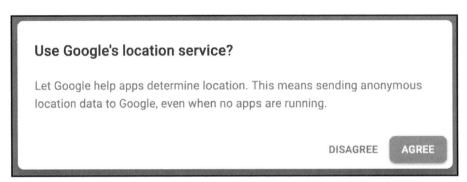

How it works...

The `Blue` theme applies the color palette `theme` settings, while the `Rounded` theme changes the `borderRadius` settings. Both themes are applied to the `Dialog` component—you can see the blue primary button, and the round corners are even more round. Let's take a closer look at the `Rounded` theme:

```
const Rounded = theme =>
  createMuiTheme({
    ...theme,
    shape: {
      borderRadius: 8
    }
  });
```

Instead of being an object, `Rounded` is a function that returns a `theme` object. When you pass a function to the `theme` property of `MuiThemeProvider`, a `theme` argument is passed. This is the outer `theme`, or, in this example, the `Blue` theme. The `theme` is extended by applying the `spread` operator to the `theme` argument, and then passing additional `theme` values to `createMuiTheme()`.

See also

- Material-UI theme documentation: https://material-ui.com/customization/themes/

Understanding component theme settings

Themes can override styles that are specific to component types, such as buttons or drawers. This is useful when you need to apply a style change to every instance of the component in the app. In other words, the style is part of the overall theme, but it applies to just one type of component instead of the color palette for example, which applies to almost every Material-UI component.

How to do it

Let's say that you want the title and the actions of Dialog components centered. Since you want the same style applied for every Dialog component in your app, the theme is the right place to override this setting. Here's how to do it:

```
import React from 'react';

import {
  createMuiTheme,
  MuiThemeProvider
} from '@material-ui/core/styles';
import Button from '@material-ui/core/Button';
import Dialog from '@material-ui/core/Dialog';
import DialogActions from '@material-ui/core/DialogActions';
import DialogContent from '@material-ui/core/DialogContent';
import DialogContentText from '@material-ui/core/DialogContentText';
import DialogTitle from '@material-ui/core/DialogTitle';

const theme = createMuiTheme({
  overrides: {
    MuiDialogTitle: { root: { textAlign: 'center' } },
    MuiDialogActions: { root: { justifyContent: 'center' } }
  }
});

const ComponentThemeSettings = () => (
  <MuiThemeProvider theme={theme}>
    <Dialog open={true}>
```

```
        <DialogTitle>Use Google's location service?</DialogTitle>
        <DialogContent>
          <DialogContentText>
            Let Google help apps determine location. This means sending
            anonymous location data to Google, even when no apps are
            running.
          </DialogContentText>
        </DialogContent>
        <DialogActions>
          <Button color="secondary">Disagree</Button>
          <Button color="primary" autoFocus>
            Agree
          </Button>
        </DialogActions>
      </Dialog>
    </MuiThemeProvider>
  );

  export default ComponentThemeSettings;
```

Here's what the custom dialog looks like:

How it works...

Let's take a closer look at the `overrides` section of the theme:

```
overrides: {
  MuiDialogTitle: { root: { textAlign: 'center' } },
  MuiDialogActions: { root: { justifyContent: 'center' } }
},
```

The `MuiDialogTitle` key corresponds to the `DialogTitle` component, while the `MuiDialogActions` key corresponds to the `DialogActions` component. The `root` key used in both objects is the name of the rule. In more complex components, you can use these keys to target specific parts of the component. The API documentation for each component spells out each of these style rule names that you can target. Then, it's a matter of overriding or providing new styles. The `textAlign` property isn't set by default on the `DialogTitle` component, so you're adding it. The `justifyContent` is set to the right of the `DialogActions` component, which means that you're overriding an existing value.

See also

- Theme override documentation: `https://material-ui.com/customization/overrides/`

20
Styles - Applying Styles to Components

In this chapter, you'll learn about the following topics:

- Basic component styles
- Scoped component styles
- Extending component styles
- Moving styles to themes
- Other styling options

Introduction

The majority of styles that are applied to **Material-UI** components are part of the theme styles. In some cases, you need the ability to style individual components without changing the theme. For example, a button in one feature might need a specific style applied to it that shouldn't change every other button in the app. Material-UI provides several ways to apply custom styles to components as a whole, or to specific parts of components.

Basic component styles

Material uses **JavaScript Style Sheets** (**JSS**) to style its components. You can apply your own JSS using the utilities provided by Material-UI.

How to do it...

The `withStyles()` function is a higher-order function that takes a style object as an argument. The function that it returns takes the component to style as an argument. Here's an example:

```
import React, { useState } from 'react';

import { withStyles } from '@material-ui/core/styles';
import Card from '@material-ui/core/Card';
import CardActions from '@material-ui/core/CardActions';
import CardContent from '@material-ui/core/CardContent';
import Button from '@material-ui/core/Button';
import Typography from '@material-ui/core/Typography';

const styles = theme => ({
 card: {
    width: 135,
    height: 135,
    textAlign: 'center'
  },
  cardActions: {
    justifyContent: 'center'
  }
});

const BasicComponentStyles = withStyles(styles)(({ classes }) => {
  const [count, setCount] = useState(0);

  const onIncrement = () => {
    setCount(count + 1);
  };

  return (
    <Card className={classes.card}>
      <CardContent>
        <Typography variant="h2">{count}</Typography>
      </CardContent>
      <CardActions className={classes.cardActions}>
        <Button size="small" onClick={onIncrement}>
```

```
         Increment
        </Button>
      </CardActions>
    </Card>
  );
});
```

```
export default BasicComponentStyles;
```

Here's what this component looks like:

How it works...

Let's take a closer look at the `styles` defined by this example:

```
const styles = theme => ({
  card: {
    width: 135,
    height: 135,
    textAlign: 'center'
  },
  cardActions: {
    justifyContent: 'center'
  }
});
```

The `styles` that you pass to `withStyles()` can be either a plain object or a function that returns a plain object, as is the case with this example. The benefit of using a function is that the `theme` values are passed to the function as an argument, in case your `styles` need access to the `theme` values. There are two styles defined in this example: `card` and `cardActions`. You can think of these as **Cascading Style Sheets** (CSS) classes. Here's what these two styles would look like as CSS:

```
.card {
  width: 135
  height: 135
```

```
  text-align: center
}

.cardActions {
  justify-content: center
}
```

By calling `withStyles(styles)(MyComponent)`, you're returning a new component that has a `classes` property. This object has all of the classes that you can apply to components now. You can't just do something such as this:

```
<Card className="card" />
```

When you define your `styles`, they have their own build process and every class ends up getting its own generated name. This generated name is what you'll find in the classes object, so this is why you would want to use it.

There's more...

Instead of working with higher-order functions that return new components, you can leverage Material-UI style hooks. This example already relies on the `useState()` hook from React, so using another hook in the component feels like a natural extension of the same pattern that is already in place. Here's what the example looks like when refactored to take advantage of the `makeStyles()` function:

```
import React, { useState } from 'react';

import { makeStyles } from '@material-ui/styles';
import Card from '@material-ui/core/Card';
import CardActions from '@material-ui/core/CardActions';
import CardContent from '@material-ui/core/CardContent';
import Button from '@material-ui/core/Button';
import Typography from '@material-ui/core/Typography';

const useStyles = makeStyles(theme => ({
  card: {
    width: 135,
    height: 135,
    textAlign: 'center'
  },
  cardActions: {
    justifyContent: 'center'
  }
}));
```

```
export default function BasicComponentStyles() {
  const classes = useStyles();
  const [count, setCount] = useState(0);

  const onIncrement = () => {
    setCount(count + 1);
  };

  return (
    <Card className={classes.card}>
      <CardContent>
        <Typography variant="h2">{count}</Typography>
      </CardContent>
      <CardActions className={classes.cardActions}>
        <Button size="small" onClick={onIncrement}>
          Increment
        </Button>
      </CardActions>
    </Card>
  );
}
```

The `useStyles()` hook is built using the `makeStyles()` function—which takes the exact same `styles` argument as `withStyles()`. By calling `useStyles()` within the component, you have your classes object. Another important thing to point out is that `makeStyles` is imported from `@material-ui/styles`, not `@material-ui/core/styles`.

See also

- Material-UI CSS in JS documentation: `https://material-ui.com/css-in-js/basics/`.

Scoped component styles

Most Material-UI components have a CSS API that is specific to the component. This means that instead of having to assign a class name to the `className` property for every component that you need to customize, you can target specific aspects of the component that you want to change. Material-UI has laid the foundation for scoping component styles; you just need to leverage the APIs.

How to do it...

Let's say that you have the following style customizations that you want to apply to the `Button` components used throughout your application:

- Every button needs a margin by default.
- Every button that uses the `contained` variant should have additional top and bottom padding.
- Every button that uses the `contained` variant and the primary color should have additional top and bottom padding, as well as additional left and right padding.

Here's an example that shows how to use the `Button` CSS API to target these three different `Button` types with `styles`:

```
import React, { Fragment } from 'react';

import { withStyles } from '@material-ui/core/styles';
import Button from '@material-ui/core/Button';

const styles = theme => ({
  root: {
    margin: theme.spacing(2)
  },
  contained: {
    paddingTop: theme.spacing(2),
    paddingBottom: theme.spacing(2)
  },
  containedPrimary: {
    paddingLeft: theme.spacing(4),
    paddingRight: theme.spacing(4)
  }
});

const ScopedComponentStyles = withStyles(styles)(
  ({ classes: { root, contained, containedPrimary } }) => (
    <Fragment>
      <Button classes={{ root }}>My Default Button</Button>
      <Button classes={{ root, contained }} variant="contained">
        My Contained Button
      </Button>
      <Button
        classes={{ root, contained, containedPrimary }}
        variant="contained"
        color="primary"
      >
        My Contained Primary Button
```

```
        </Button>
      </Fragment>
  )
);

export default ScopedComponentStyles;
```

Here's what the three rendered buttons look like:

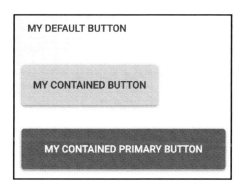

How it works...

The Button CSS API takes named styles and applies them to the component. These same names are used in the styles in this code. For example, root applies to every Button component, whereas contained only applies the styles to the Button components that use the contained variant and the containedPrimary style only applies to Button components that use the contained variant and the primary color.

There's more...

Each style is destructured from the classes property, then applied to the appropriate Button component. However, you don't actually need to do all of this work. Since the Material-UI CSS API takes care of applying styles to components in a way that matches what you're actually targeting, you can just pass the classes directly to the buttons and get the same result. Here's a simplified version of this example:

```
import React, { Fragment } from 'react';

import { withStyles } from '@material-ui/core/styles';
import Button from '@material-ui/core/Button';
```

```
const styles = theme => ({
  root: {
    margin: theme.spacing(2)
  },
  contained: {
    paddingTop: theme.spacing(2),
    paddingBottom: theme.spacing(2)
  },
  containedPrimary: {
    paddingLeft: theme.spacing(4),
    paddingRight: theme.spacing(4)
  }
});

const ScopedComponentStyles = withStyles(styles)(({ classes }) => (
  <Fragment>
    <Button classes={classes}>My Default Button</Button>
    <Button classes={classes} variant="contained">
      My Contained Button
    </Button>
    <Button classes={classes} variant="contained" color="primary">
      My Contained Primary Button
    </Button>
  </Fragment>
));

export default ScopedComponentStyles;
```

The output looks the same because only buttons that match the constraints of the CSS API
get the styles applied to them. For example, the first Button has the root, contained, and
containedPrimary styles passed to the classes property, but only root is applied because
it isn't using the contained variant of the primary color. The second Button also has all
three styles passed to it, but only root and contained are applied. The third Button has
all three styles applied to it because it meets the criteria of each style.

See also

- Material-UI style override documentation: https://material-ui.com/
  customization/overrides/.

Extending component styles

You can extend styles that you apply to one component with styles that you apply to another component. Since your styles are JavaScript objects, one option is to extend one style object with another. The only problem with this approach is that you end up with a lot of duplicate styles properties in the CSS output. A better alternative is to use the jss extend plugin.

How to do it...

Let's say that you want to render three buttons and share some of the styles among them. One approach is to extend generic styles with more specific styles using the jss extend plugin. Here's how to do it:

```
import React, { Fragment } from 'react';
import { JssProvider, jss } from 'react-jss';

import {
  withStyles,
  createGenerateClassName
} from '@material-ui/styles';
import {
  createMuiTheme,
  MuiThemeProvider
} from '@material-ui/core/styles';
import Button from '@material-ui/core/Button';

const styles = theme => ({
  root: {
    margin: theme.spacing(2)
  },
  contained: {
    extend: 'root',
    paddingTop: theme.spacing(2),
    paddingBottom: theme.spacing(2)
  },
  containedPrimary: {
    extend: 'contained',
    paddingLeft: theme.spacing(4),
    paddingRight: theme.spacing(4)
  }
});

const App = ({ children }) => (
  <JssProvider
```

```
      jss={jss}
      generateClassName={createGenerateClassName()}
    >
      <MuiThemeProvider theme={createMuiTheme()}>
        {children}
      </MuiThemeProvider>
    </JssProvider>
);

const Buttons = withStyles(styles)(({ classes }) => (
  <Fragment>
    <Button className={classes.root}>My Default Button</Button>
    <Button className={classes.contained} variant="contained">
      My Contained Button
    </Button>
    <Button
      className={classes.containedPrimary}
      variant="contained"
      color="primary"
    >
      My Contained Primary Button
    </Button>
  </Fragment>
));

const ExtendingComponentStyles = () => (
  <App>
    <Buttons />
  </App>
);

export default ExtendingComponentStyles;
```

Here's what the rendered buttons look like:

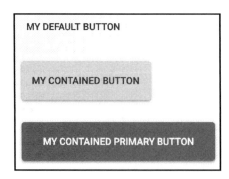

How it works...

The easiest way to use the `jss` extend plugin in your Material-UI application is to use the
default JSS plugin presets, which includes `jss` extend. Material-UI has several JSS plugins
installed by default, but `jss` extend isn't one of them. Let's take a look at the `App`
component in this example to see how this JSS plugin is made available:

```
const App = ({ children }) => (
  <JssProvider
    jss={jss}
    generateClassName={createGenerateClassName()}
  >
    <MuiThemeProvider theme={createMuiTheme()}>
      {children}
    </MuiThemeProvider>
  </JssProvider>
);
```

The `JssProvider` component is how JSS is enabled in Material-UI applications. Normally,
you wouldn't have to interface with it directly, but this is necessary when adding a new JSS
plugin. The `jss` property takes the JSS preset object that includes the `jss extend` plugin.
The `generateClassName` property takes a function from Material-UI that helps generate
class names that are specific to Material-UI.

Next, let's take a closer look at some `styles`:

```
const styles = theme => ({
  root: {
    margin: theme.spacing(2)
  },
  contained: {
    extend: 'root',
    paddingTop: theme.spacing(2),
    paddingBottom: theme.spacing(2)
  },
  containedPrimary: {
    extend: 'contained',
    paddingLeft: theme.spacing(4),
    paddingRight: theme.spacing(4)
  }
});
```

The `extend` property takes the name of a style that you want to extend. In this case, the `contained` style extends `root`. The `containedPrimary` extends `contained` and `root`. Now let's take a look at how this translates into CSS. Here's what the `root` style looks like:

```
.Component-root-1 {
  margin: 16px;
}
```

Next, here's the `contained` style:

```
.Component-contained-2 {
  margin: 16px;
  padding-top: 16px;
  padding-bottom: 16px;
}
```

Finally, here's the `containedPrimary` style:

```
.Component-containedPrimary-3 {
  margin: 16px;
  padding-top: 16px;
  padding-left: 32px;
  padding-right: 32px;
  padding-bottom: 16px;
}
```

Note that the properties from the more-generic properties are included in the more-specific styles. There are some properties duplicated, but this is in CSS, instead of having to duplicate JavaScript object properties. Furthermore, you could put these extended `styles` in a more central location in your code base, so that multiple components could use them.

See also

- Material-UI JSS documentation: `https://material-ui.com/customization/css-in-js/`.

Moving styles to themes

As you develop your Material-UI application, you'll start to notice style patterns that repeat themselves. In particular, styles that apply to one type of component, such as buttons, evolve into a theme.

How to do it...

Let's revisit the example from the *Scoped component styles* section:

```
import React, { Fragment } from 'react';

import { withStyles } from '@material-ui/core/styles';
import Button from '@material-ui/core/Button';

const styles = theme => ({
  root: {
    margin: theme.spacing(2)
  },
  contained: {
    paddingTop: theme.spacing(2),
    paddingBottom: theme.spacing(2)
  },
  containedPrimary: {
    paddingLeft: theme.spacing(4),
    paddingRight: theme.spacing(4)
  }
});

const ScopedComponentStyles = withStyles(styles)(({ classes }) => (
  <Fragment>
    <Button classes={classes}>My Default Button</Button>
    <Button classes={classes} variant="contained">
      My Contained Button
    </Button>
    <Button classes={classes} variant="contained" color="primary">
      My Contained Primary Button
    </Button>
  </Fragment>
));

export default ScopedComponentStyles;
```

Here's what these buttons look like after they have these styles applied to them:

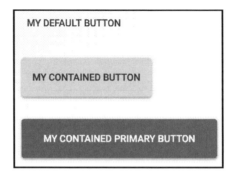

Now, let's say you've implemented these same styles in several places throughout your app because this is how you want your buttons to look. At this point, you've evolved a simple component customization into a theme. When this happens, you shouldn't have to keep implementing the same styles over and over again. Instead, the styles should be applied automatically by using the correct component and the correct property values. Let's move these styles into theme:

```
import React from 'react';

import {
  createMuiTheme,
  MuiThemeProvider
} from '@material-ui/core/styles';
import Button from '@material-ui/core/Button';

const defaultTheme = createMuiTheme();

const theme = createMuiTheme({
  overrides: {
    MuiButton: {
      root: {
        margin: 16
      },
      contained: {
        paddingTop: defaultTheme.spacing(2),
        paddingBottom: defaultTheme.spacing(2)
      },
      containedPrimary: {
        paddingLeft: defaultTheme.spacing(4),
        paddingRight: defaultTheme.spacing(4)
      }
    }
  }
```

```
});

const MovingStylesToThemes = ({ classes }) => (
  <MuiThemeProvider theme={theme}>
    <Button>My Default Button</Button>
    <Button variant="contained">My Contained Button</Button>
    <Button variant="contained" color="primary">
      My Contained Primary Button
    </Button>
  </MuiThemeProvider>
);

export default MovingStylesToThemes;
```

Now, you can use `Button` components without having to apply the same styles every time.

How it works...

Let's take a closer look at how your styles fit into a Material-UI theme:

```
overrides: {
  MuiButton: {
    root: {
      margin: 16
    },
    contained: {
      paddingTop: defaultTheme.spacing(2),
      paddingBottom: defaultTheme.spacing(2)
    },
    containedPrimary: {
      paddingLeft: defaultTheme.spacing(4),
      paddingRight: defaultTheme.spacing(4)
    }
  }
}
```

The `overrides` property is an object that allows you to override component-specific properties of the theme. In this case, it's the `MuiButton` component styles that you want to override. Within `MuiButton`, you have the same CSS API that is used to target specific aspects of components. This makes moving your `styles` into the `theme` straightforward, because there isn't much to change.

One thing that did have to change in this example is the way spacing works. In normal `styles` that are applied via `withStyles()`, you have access to the current theme because it's passed in as an argument. You still need access to the spacing data, but there's no `theme` argument because you're not in a function. Since you're just extending the default `theme`, you can access it by calling `createMuiTheme()` without any arguments, as this example shows.

See also

- Material-UI style overrides documentation: `https://material-ui.com/customization/overrides/`.

Other styling options

There are other styling options available to your Material-UI app beyond `withStyles()`. There's the `styled()` higher-order component function that emulates styled components. You can also jump outside the Material-UI style system and use inline CSS styles or import CSS modules and apply those styles.

How to do it...

Here's a modified version of the *Scoped component styles* example that showcases a few of the alternative style mechanisms available to you in your Material-UI applications:

```
import React, { Fragment } from 'react';

import { styled } from '@material-ui/styles';
import Button from '@material-ui/core/Button';

import styles from './OtherStylingOptions.module.css';

const MyStyledButton = styled(Button)({
  margin: 16,
  paddingTop: 16,
  paddingBottom: 16
});

const OtherStylingOptions = () => (
  <Fragment>
    <Button style={{ margin: 16 }}>My Default Button</Button>
```

```
      <MyStyledButton variant="contained">
        My Contained Button
      </MyStyledButton>
      <Button
        className={styles.primaryContained}
        variant="contained"
        color="primary"
      >
        My Contained Primary Button
      </Button>
    </Fragment>
  );

  export default OtherStylingOptions;
```

How it works...

The first button uses inline CSS properties, expressed as a plain JavaScript object and passed to the `style` property of the `Button` component. The second `Button` uses the `styled()` function to build a `MyStyledButton` component. This function works in much the same way as `withStyles`, the main difference being that its signature is geared toward people used to the styled-component's approach to styling components.

The third `button` uses a style from an imported CSS module. Here's what the module looks like:

```
button.primaryContained {
  margin: 16px;
  padding: 16px 32px;
}
```

Be careful with CSS modules and inline styles. These approaches work fine, but since they're not tightly integrated with the Material-UI styling and theming mechanisms, they require more work to ensure that your styles fit with the rest of the Material-UI components.

See also

- Material-UI style overrides documentation: `https://material-ui.com/customization/overrides/`.
- Material-UI JSS documentation: `https://material-ui.com/css-in-js/api/`.

Other Books You May Enjoy

If you enjoyed this book, you may be interested in these other books by Packt:

React Cookbook
Carlos Santana Roldan

ISBN: 9781783980727

- Gain the ability to wield complex topics such as Webpack and server-side rendering
- Implement an API using Node.js, Firebase, and GraphQL
- Learn to maximize the performance of React applications
- Create a mobile application using React Native
- Deploy a React application on Digital Ocean
- Get to know the best practices when organizing and testing a large React application

React and React Native
Adam Boduch

ISBN: 9781786465658

- Craft reusable React components
- Control navigation using the React Router to help keep your UI in sync with URLs
- Build isomorphic web applications using Node.js
- Use the Flexbox layout model to create responsive mobile designs
- Leverage the native APIs of Android and iOS to build engaging applications with React Native
- Respond to gestures in a way that's intuitive for the user
- Use Relay to build a unified data architecture for your React UIs

Leave a review - let other readers know what you think

Please share your thoughts on this book with others by leaving a review on the site that you bought it from. If you purchased the book from Amazon, please leave us an honest review on this book's Amazon page. This is vital so that other potential readers can see and use your unbiased opinion to make purchasing decisions, we can understand what our customers think about our products, and our authors can see your feedback on the title that they have worked with Packt to create. It will only take a few minutes of your time, but is valuable to other potential customers, our authors, and Packt. Thank you!

Index